PLANNING·ENVIRONMENT·

Series Editors: Yvonne Rydin and Andrew Thornley

The context in which planning operates has changed dramatically in recent years. Economic processes have become increasingly globalized and new spatial patterns of economic activity have emerged. There have been major changes across the globe, not just changing administrations in various countries but also the sweeping away of old ideologies and the tentative emergence of new ones. A new environmental agenda emerged from the Brundtland Report and the Rio Earth Summit prioritizing the goal of sustainable development. The momentum for this has been maintained by continued action at international, national and local levels.

Cities are today faced with new pressures for economic competitiveness, greater accountability and participation, improved quality of life for citizens and global environmental responsibilities. These pressures are often contradictory and create difficult dilemmas for policy-makers, especially in the context of fiscal austerity. New relationships are developing between the levels of state activity and between public and private sectors as different interests respond to the new conditions.

In these changing circumstances, planners, from many backgrounds, in many different organizations, have come to re-evaluate their work. They have had to engage with actors in government, the private sector and non-governmental organizations in discussions over the role of planning in relation to the environment and cities. The intention of the Planning, Environment, Cities series is to explore the changing nature of planning and contribute to the debate about its future.

The series is primarily aimed at students and practitioners of planning and such related professions as estate management, housing and architecture as well as those in politics, public and social administration, geography and urban studies. It comprises both general texts and books designed to make a more particular contribution, in both cases characterized by: an international approach; extensive use of case studies; and emphasis on contemporary relevance and the application of theory to advance planning practice.

Planning · Environment · Cities

Series Editors: Yvonne Rydin and Andrew Thornley

Published

Philip Allmendinger
Planning Theory (2nd edn)

Ruth Fincher and Kurt Iveson
**Planning and Diversity in the City: Redistribution,
Recognition and Encounter**

Patsy Healey
Collaborative Planning (2nd edn)

Patsy Healey
Making Better Places: The Planning Project in the 21st Century

Ted Kitchen
Skills for Planning Practice

Peter Newman and Andrew Thornley
Planning World Cities

Michael Oxley
Economics, Planning and Housing

Yvonne Rydin
Urban and Environmental Planning in the UK (2nd edn)

Geoff Vigar, Patsy Healey and Angela Hull with Simin Davoudi
Planning, Governance and Spatial Strategy in Britain

Forthcoming

Cliff Hague, Euan Hague and Carrie Breitenbach
Regional and Local Economic Development

Other titles planned include

**Introduction to Planning
Urban Design**

Planning, Environment, Cities
Series Standing Order
ISBN 0–333–71703–1 hardback
ISBN 0–333–69346–9 paperback
(outside North America only)

You can receive future titles in this series as they are published. To place a
standing order please contact your bookseller or, in the case of difficulty,
write to us at the address below with your name and address, the title of
the series and the ISBN quoted above.

Customer Services Department, Macmillan Distribution Ltd
Houndmills, Basingstoke, Hampshire RG21 6XS, England

Making Better Places:

The Planning Project in the Twenty-First Century

Patsy Healey

First published 2010 by
PALGRAVE MACMILLAN

Palgrave Macmillan in the UK is an imprint of Macmillan Publishers Limited, registered in England, company number 785998, of Houndmills, Basingstoke, Hampshire RG21 6XS.

Palgrave Macmillan in the US is a division of St Martin's Press LLC, 175 Fifth Avenue, New York, NY 10010.

Palgrave Macmillan is the global academic imprint of the above companies and has companies and representatives throughout the world.

Palgrave® and Macmillan® are registered trademarks in the United States, the United Kingdom, Europe and other countries

ISBN 978–0–230–20056–2 hardback
ISBN 978–0–230–20057–9 paperback

This book is printed on paper suitable for recycling and made from fully managed and sustained forest sources. Logging, pulping and manufacturing processes are expected to conform to the environmental regulations of the country of origin.

A catalogue record for this book is available from the British Library.

A catalog record for this book is available from the Library of Congress.

10 9 8 7 6 5 4 3 2 1
19 18 17 16 15 14 13 12 11 10

Printed in China

Contents

List of Figures, Tables and Boxes

Figures

Tables

Boxes

Tables

Boxes

Preface

This book is about the idea and practice of planning. The planning referred to focuses on developing and improving the places where we live and work. This 'planning', sometimes qualified with the terms 'city', 'urban and regional' or 'spatial', has become widespread around the world, as more and more people live in urban environments and as pressures on other landscapes have become more intense. It responds to people's concerns about improving the conditions of life and about reducing the environmental stress that human activity generates, especially in the crowded conditions of urban living.

Planning activity is often popularly presented as the procedures and practices of 'planning systems', which provide for the making of spatial development plans and make provision for the regulation of private property rights in order to safeguard and promote wider public objectives. Such activity is often criticised for bureaucratic failures and over-ambitious projects. In many parts of the world, planning activity has been drowned out by administrative and political practices that have washed away the motivating purposes for creating such systems.

The purposes of the planning project have always been a subject of critical debate. Most people would agree that the ambition of those promoting planning as an activity is to bring improvements to the qualities of places, with an eye to future opportunities and challenges. Disagreements then arise about what the critical place qualities are, what constitutes an improvement, whose improvement gets to count and how to move from ideas about future possibilities to programmes of action. Such disagreements are not just to be found among specialists in the planning field. They infuse the practice of planning, as all kinds of people get to demand improvements to their localities and dispute proposals put forward. What results then seems to be a matter of politics and legal judgement; that is, of governance. The motivating idea promoted through planning activity sometimes seems to be merely facilitating and mediating such disputation.

One aim of this book is to contribute to extracting the planning project from the narrowing, reductive perspectives with which its many practices have become associated in the later twentieth century. Grand ideas of city building have become tarnished by a reputation for over-ambition, social injustice and financial disaster. Conceptions of territorial development based on outdated models of how urban settlements are formed and sustained have foundered when outcomes have not been as predicted. Land-use ordering practices intended to safeguard amenities and environmental qualities have instead become a tangle of rules and judgements that have long ago lost any relation to the ends they were meant to serve. A focus on conflict mediation lacks a concern with promoting ideas about how to achieve more liveable and sustainable places.

In this book, I argue that the planning project, as a contribution to the development of places and their qualities, has had and should have a wider focus. I suggest that the motivating idea of planning activity, as it has evolved in recent years, centres on a social project for shaping the development of places and their futures, to promote better and more sustainable conditions for the many and not just the few. The primary focus of the book is on how ideas about liveability and sustainability get transformed into programmes of action, which then have material effects on living conditions and local environments. I explore this interaction through three broad areas of practice: the ongoing management of neighbourhood change, the promotion of major development projects and spatial strategy making. In this way, I present the planning field not merely as an enterprise in imagining futures but as a practice of bringing imagined futures into being. I focus on the achievement of particular kinds of futures: not the monumental landscapes that some kings and dictators have valued, but places that provide opportunity, stimulation and convenience for the everyday life of people who live in, visit and do business in them, and that do so in ways that do not undermine the options for future generations.

My second aim is to provide an introduction to the planning field, from the above perspective. The book is not a review of all the many ideas in circulation about ways of life, technologies, physical designs and specific management systems that could make a difference to the way we live now. Instead, I focus on how to arrive at which ideas to pursue and how to realise these ideas in ways that make a difference to place qualities and people's experience of them.

I write this book as an 'insider' in the planning field. But my reason for promoting the 'project' of planning is not primarily because I have a background as a planner. Throughout the world in the twenty-first century, political communities will be challenged to improve the liveability and sustainability of urban environments where more than half the world's population now live. This places considerable demands on the organisation and priorities of governments and governance activities more widely. Despite often deep commitments to improving the quality of life and well-being of citizens, it has not been easy for governments to give adequate policy attention to the quality of the environments in which we live our daily lives. Government activity tended in the twentieth century to 'split up' aspects of ourselves (educating, keeping healthy, getting around, finding work, finding social care and support, and so on) and neglected the challenges we face as we go about all these activities in particular places. Many people are concerned about the qualities of the places where they live. Those concerned with health and well-being are giving increasing attention to the way in which local environments are organised. It is these concerns that provide the ground for greater political attention to place qualities in the coming years. Furthermore, struggles over which qualities and whose concerns about them will be given priority have broader political effects. The capacity of societies to respond to these concerns about place qualities is therefore an important challenge. In the twentieth century, the institutional arenas in which policy systems known as 'town planning', 'urban planning', 'environmental planning' and 'spatial planning' were undertaken provided significant sites for such a politics of place. But as concerns for place qualities widen, such arenas and their practices need to be reconfigured and refreshed within the context of diverse societies, which yet share a commitment to promoting human flourishing in sustainable ways.

I have written this book with several different kinds of reader in mind. One group, naturally, consists of my fellow planners, who have been working in the planning field for some years but would appreciate some refreshment of their understanding of it and the motivations behind it. It is also for students starting out on a career in planning, to provide an idea of the scope, content and values of the field. For both these groups I have tried to take an international perspective, drawing on experiences from many parts of the world. This helps, I believe, to understand our own particular contexts better and to encourage us to be less introverted about our national and local planning systems and cultures. But this book is also for readers in other fields interested in the planning project and prepared to challenge some of the caricatures of the 'planner' and 'planning' to be found in popular discourse and some academic work.

The book conveys a positive attitude and a normative stance. I maintain the positive tone[1] because I believe that promoting more liveable and sustainable places is an important project for the twenty-first century world of highly urbanised societies. It is a project worth struggling for. While well-grounded critique of planning endeavours is always valuable, it is also important to provide examples of experiences where careful planning work has produced substantial benefits for sustainable everyday life. My challenge has been to present these experiences in a way that helps others learn from them, without treating them as easily transferable 'best-practice' recipes. A normative stance – that is, the promotion of a particular set of values – is in my view inherent in the planning project as it has evolved from the mid-twentieth century into the twenty-first. In any case, no study, however 'objective' or 'critical', can avoid some kind of normative stance towards what is being discussed. I believe it is better to be transparent about this, rather than hiding behind some kind of analytical theory or 'external' position. We are all, in one way or another, 'inside' the worlds we are talking about. I therefore write as an advocate for the 'best intentions' of the planning project, and explore what it takes to realise these in different kinds of situations, while recognising the limitations of what is possible and desirable.

Because of the enormous variety of places and institutional contexts in which attempts to manage futures are undertaken, there has been a movement away from the portrayal of principles, protocols and procedures for doing planning work, except at a very general level. Similarly, attempts at capturing and systematising such variety in typologies, while useful for particular purposes, also prove flawed, because so many dimensions of variation produce the dynamics of particular practices. Typologies that select only a few dimensions may easily miss critical reasons for a practice evolving as it does. It is for this reason that the planning field has made much use of the method of 'thick description' of actual cases.[2] I do the same in this book. Using the division into three broad areas of practice (the on-going management of neighbourhood change, the promotion of major projects and spatial strategy making), I present specific examples to illustrate each area. Each case is drawn from several sources and has been checked with those more directly involved than I. These are not offered as a representative sample of planning experience. We rarely know what the 'universe' of planning practices adds up to from which a sample could be taken, and it is not clear what purpose would be served by attempting this.

Instead, the cases are intended as exemplars, to show what work is required to make a significant and sustainable contribution to the quality of daily life for the many. Although the examples are primarily from urban contexts, given that the majority of us now live in urban areas or in places that make use of the facilities and cultural ideas associated with urbanisation, many of the issues raised will have relevance in less urbanised contexts and in the management of complex non-urban environments. Hopefully, the book will prompt readers to draw out such connections.

This raises another tricky problem for any academic writing about the planning field. In organising material, structuring arguments and presenting examples, writers cannot avoid making assumptions and drawing connections among ideas, and between ideas and evidence. The academic disciplines of the social sciences, and of philosophy, encourage reflexivity and debate about alternative perspectives and 'theories' through which assumptions and connections are made. There is a rich tradition of such theory within the planning field (Hillier and Healey 2008). In this book, however, such theory lies in the background, not the foreground, of the text. Where I feel it is helpful, I have provided a brief comment on conceptual debates. Otherwise, I have used a few references or chapter notes to highlight issues where there is particular controversy or emphasis in the realm of conceptual debate, so that interested readers can follow these up or find out more about the positions I take.

The first chapter outlines what I understand as the 'planning project' and its current orientation. I then develop this in relation to understanding how places develop their qualities and meanings for people (Chapter 2), and what is involved in collective action to improve place management and development (Chapter 3). The following chapters present the three broad areas of planning practice identified above. I have divided the first area into two groups. Chapter 4 looks at the activity of shaping changes within neighbourhoods, and Chapter 5 examines the routine work of land-use regulation and of settlement upgrading in a developing-country context. Chapter 6 then focuses on the promotion of major physical development projects aimed at transforming a locale within an urban area. Chapter 7 considers the contribution of place-development strategies. Chapter 8 then turns to what it takes to 'do' planning work, and in particular the contribution of planning expertise. The final chapter reviews the arguments I develop in the book about how place-governance with a planning orientation is achieved, and the relative significance of context and agency in realising the potential of the project to enhance the liveability and sustainability of places for the many, not just the few. At the end of each chapter, I provide suggestions for further reading. Boxes are used in the text to provide more detail on cases or to summarise particular arguments or approaches to issues.

Acknowledgements

Very many people have helped me as I have put this book together. I should like to thank those who have read and commented on individual chapters, and especially those who read the whole text before my final revision. This made me realise the many different ways in which a book like this can be read.

Those who read and commented on individual chapters and in some instances helped me a great deal with the cases were: Carl Abbott, Sy Adler, Antonio Font, Stan Majoor, Tim Marshall, Eric Morgan, Maki Ryu, Willem Salet, Andre Sorensen, Huw Thomas, David Webb and Geoff Wright. Those who read the whole book were Hilary Briggs, Ruth le Guen, Jon Ingold, Ted Kitchen and Bill Solesbury, as well as two anonymous readers chosen by the publishers. I am very grateful to Louis Albrechts, Ted Kitchen, Erik van Rijn and Geoff Wright for allowing me to use their reflections on what it takes to do planning work in Chapter 8. Some others helped me a great deal with particular cases, particularly Carolyn Funck, Kayo Murakami, Maki Ryu and Shun-ichi Watanabe with respect to the Kobe case in Chapter 4; Dirk Schuiling, of the University of Amsterdam, who acted as my guide around Amsterdam neighbourhoods (see Box 2.2); Kath Lawless and Ian Cansfield, for help with the South Tyneside MBC in Chapter 5; Carolyn Kerr, Theresa Subban, Mike Byerley, Phil Martin, Adrian Masson, Alison Todes, Nancy Odendaal and Ken Breetzke for help with the Besters Camp/INK case in Chapter 5. Thanks also to: Luke Holland for Figure 1.1; the Canadian Tourist Board for Figure 1.2; Yosef Jabareen for taking photos for me (Figure 1.3 and 1.4); Alain Motte and Michel Chiappero for Figure 2.3c; the City of Kobe for permission to use the image in Figure 4.2; Mr Miyanashi from Mano Kobe and Associate Professor Aiba from Tokyo Metropolitan University for permission to use the images in Figure 4.3; Ali Madanipour for allowing me to use his photo in Figure 6.4; Stephen Ward for permission to use his version of Abecrombie's Greater London Plan 1944 for Figure 7.1a; the Greater London Authority and Mike Newitt for Figure 7.1b; the City of Amsterdam for Figures 7.2a and 7.2b and for the figures in Box 7.3; Figure 4.1 is courtesy of i-stock and Figure 6.1 is courtesy of the National Archives in Washington,

DC. Where not otherwise attributed, all photographs are by the author.

I must also express my great appreciation to Steven Kennedy, of Palgrave Macmillan, for getting me started on the idea that became this book, though maybe not quite what he had in mind! Also to Stephen Wenham, for his support and enthusiasm for the book as it developed, and to Yvonne Rydin and Andy Thornley, advisers on the planning book series, for their help and encouragement, as well as two anonymous readers selected by the publishers, who gave very useful comments and encouraged me to try to write better! Thanks also to Linda Auld and Sally Osborn for preparing the text for publication.

Chapter 1

The Planning Project

Places in our lives

We care about the places where we live our lives. We get used to their pathways and pleasures, and learn to navigate their tensions and dark corners. We want freedom to find our own ways, but often agitate for collective action to define some rules, some general constraints to protect what we value and to reduce the tensions that arise as we co-exist with others in shared spaces. There are stories from across the world of people mobilising to improve and protect the qualities of the places they live in, work in and care about. Such struggles are especially intense where many different groups, often with different cultures, values and modes of living, share common resources or, as in urban areas, inhabit the same physical space. In these struggles, we form and re-form our ideas of ourselves and our social worlds, of identity and solidarity, of individual freedoms and social responsibilities.

Three cameos illustrate such stories and struggles. They range from routine conflicts over neighbourhood development in England to struggles over knowledge about environmental pollution in New York and well-meaning initiatives in Nazareth, Israel, which ended tragically.

The first case comes from affluent southern England.[1] Ditchling is a small village of around 2000 people on the Sussex Downs, near the motorway from London to Brighton. Here people who have lived in the village for generations mingle with all kinds of people who have moved there, attracted by the image of village life and the reality of a beautiful downland landscape close to the amenities and social worlds of both London and Brighton (see Figure 1.1). In this respect, it is like very many villages across South East England. All kinds of people co-exist here. There are farmers worried about the future of their activity, followers of hunting defending their sport, and a group of artists and craftspeople, linked to a co-operative craft guild set up by engraver Eric Gill in the early twentieth century.

1

Figure 1.1   *Ditchling village*

Source: Luke Holland www.sussex-southdowns-guide.com/films

There are retired managers of multinational companies, retired actresses and singers, including Dame Vera Lynn,[2] and people who have refused promotions if this meant they had to leave their village. There are 44 societies of one kind or another, and a local museum that attracts people from all over the world. Local residents put on shows and get involved in fêtes, festivals and morris dancing. There is some overlapping of the networks of all these different people, but also some carefully maintained distances. Not everyone is happy about the hunting and there are considerable reservations about the lifestyle of the engraver, whose work still attracts so much attention.

Some villagers are prepared to mobilise to defend village quali-ties. The heart of the village has for many years been a formally declared 'conservation area' under English planning legislation. Until recently the village had four pubs. Each had its own clientele and ambience, though some people moved around from pub to pub. However, the owner of one of these, a rather ordinary building with a large garden, saw better prospects in developing the site for hous-ing. Regular drinkers were naturally upset at the prospect of losing their pub, as were the football players, the darts team and the bell ringers, whose regular meeting place it was. Others in the village felt that the loss of one of the pubs meant that the overall assets of the village would be reduced. Some were ideologically troubled and disliked the idea that village assets could be 'stripped' so that private

developers could make money. A few people thought that it
be better to have houses nearby rather than a noisy pub, b
balance, the village 'majority', orchestrated by an action group, ...as
against the development. This view prevailed in the Parish Council.

However, Parish Councils in the English government structure
have very limited powers. The key decision-making body is the
District Council, which covers a much larger area. And District
Councils have only limited powers too. In issues to do with planning
they have to follow national guidelines, which have influenced the
policies in the local plans that they are required to prepare. These
are approved after complex inquiry processes. A planning authority
in England has no powers to demand that an enterprise such as a
pub be kept open. Its powers relate to whether proposed new development can go ahead. In this case, the Ditchling parish councillor
was also the representative of the village on the District Council.
The district councillors realised how much opposition there was in
the village to the housing proposal, but were unsure how to respond
to this, as the local plan had indicated that it would be appropriate
to have a housing development on the site in question. And if the
developer appealed against the council decision and won, costs
would be awarded against the Council, so the Council did not have
very much power either. The district planning officers negotiated a
reduction in the scale of the scheme, but recommended to the councillors that they should approve it. Neither the local plan nor
national planning policy gave them grounds for refusal, and refusal
would not only potentially incur costs, but also could undermine the
Council's reputation as a capable planning authority.

In this context, the application was approved and the housing
development has now been completed. The residents enjoy their
new homes. But many villagers remain deeply upset, not just about
the loss of their pub but about their inability to make their voice
heard. They were horrified that their parish councillor, who had
supported the action group's position, actually supported the decision in favour of the housing development at the Planning
Committee meeting. How, they asked, can a local council override
what a village has voted for? Why are there no rights for villagers to
appeal against a planning decision?[3] How can their local councillor
be so two-faced? Doesn't this show that the national planning laws
are just a 'developer's charter'? Through such everyday encounters
with the English planning system, local residents and their equiva-
lents across the country get a real and uncomfortable experience of
what democracy means in England today.

The second case is about how local knowledge confronted government specialists. It takes us to New York and a neighbourhood in Brooklyn, opposite the downtown on Manhattan Island (see Figure 1.2). The Greenpoint/Williamsburg neighbourhood, as described by Jason Coburn, 'is one of the most polluted communities in New York City' (Corburn 2005:12). Around 160,000 people, from a variety of backgrounds, live in an area that is less than 1300 hectares (5 square miles) in extent. In 2000, it was calculated that over a third of the population lived in poverty.[4] It was also an area with a concentration of industrial plants and many polluting facilities. Studies in recent years showed that the area had a very high concentration of facilities dealing in hazardous substances. In addition, the area suffered pollution from heavy traffic crossing from Manhattan to Brooklyn. The US Environmental Protection Agency and the New York City Department of Environmental Protection had undertaken studies to identify the health consequences of these hazards. Under pressure from the US environmental justice movement, which campaigned for more attention to the environmental hazards suffered by poorer communities, these public agencies set out to study in more depth the relationship between the hazards and health experiences in the area.

Figure 1.2   *Panorama over Brooklyn*

© Jo St Mart.

However, local people were suspicious of this kind of approach. They felt that the 'scientific knowledge' with which such agencies worked might miss their own experience of life 'on the street'. They struggled to get their knowledge recognised by the environmental health scientists. In various ways, they organised community knowledge around different issues. Corburn explores their work in relation to water pollution and local fishing to supplement family diets, the high rates of asthma experienced in the area, the high incidence of lead poisoning among children, and the risks arising from local air pollution. He highlights the way in which local knowledge could indicate cultural practices and fine-grained variations from street to street, which scientists dealing in abstracted data sets could easily miss. Yet, although there were many struggles and suspicions between the trained environmental scientists and community members, in the end what was achieved was a way of joining 'local insights with professional techniques' (Corburn 2005:3). Corburn calls this 'street science' and shows how such a science can both inform decision making about improving health conditions in the area and focus scientific enquiry in new ways. He argues that communities are full of 'experts' in knowledge about the flow of daily life in their areas. What they often lack, especially in poor, ethnically mixed communities, is 'voice', the capacity to make their concerns heard in the wider world that controls the location and regulation of the activities and facilities that cause their problems. Corburn argues that, in the Greenpoint/Williamsburg case, getting heard was the result of several factors: building coalitions among different groups within the neighbourhood who were worried about different aspects of the environment; linking community activism with the wider environmental justice movement; the presence of 'intermediaries' who acted as 'boundary spanners'; connecting community knowledge with professionals in various agencies; and attention to short-term actions that could really make a difference and that residents could recognise.

The third case, from the town of Nazareth in Israel, illustrates how a well-meaning planning initiative can generate disturbing conflicts. It is told by Yosef Jabareen (2006). At the end of the twentieth century around 70,000 people lived there, all of Palestinian background, of whom 67 per cent were Muslim Arabs and 33 per cent Christian Arabs. They had suffered in the mid-twentieth century as a result of the displacement and resettlement produced as the State of Israel was formed. Both groups lost land in this process. Since then, the town's conditions and development had been largely neglected by the Israeli national government. It was left to local initiatives to mobilise improvement activity, but in a situation of limited resources. Living conditions were difficult, but the different groups lived peaceably together and the town was a major international tourist destination.

In the early 1990s, the national government adopted a more positive attitude to the town's development needs. The Mayor of Nazareth was at this time a government member. The ambition of the government, and the Mayor, was to enhance the peace process generally between Israelis and Palestinians, then full of promise, and to improve conditions in the neglected city of Nazareth. This led to an initiative that became the Nazareth 2000 Plan. Nazareth was to be a key location for the 2000 millennium celebrations. The focus was on tourism as a generator of economic benefits – 'a unique cultural-tourist destination for international tourism' (Jabareen 2006:309). The plan included several valuable development projects across the city, with a significant budget allocation. One of these projects was for a new plaza, designed by an Israeli government architect, to create a good view of the town's main monument, the Church of the Annunciation. However, Muslim groups argued that the land had been dedicated to the nearby mosque (see Figure 1.3). It therefore belonged to the Muslim religious community and could not be developed for other purposes.

> On the eve of Easter Sunday, the night between 3 and 4 April 1999, unexpected clashes erupted ... between thousands of (the town's) Christian and Muslim residents. These clashes, which shocked the Palestinian minority in Israel, were the first in modern history between these religious groups who had lived together peacefully in the city for hundreds of years. (Jabareen 2006:305)

The source of the tension was the plan for the new plaza. The promoters of the plan had hoped to host a visit from the Pope as part of the millennium celebrations. But Muslims in the city wanted to build a mosque next to the Church of the Annunciation.

> As a response to the city plan, hundreds of Muslims constructed a large tent at the site of the planned plaza, built the foundations for a new mosque, and initiated a sit-in protest that lasted for four years. Following intensive international interventions (by such leaders as President Bush, the Pope, and President Putin) asking

Figure 1.3 *Nazareth: plaza, mosque and church, with the mosque in the foreground and Church of the Annunciation in the background*

Source: Yosef Jabareen

for the destruction of the tent and the foundations of the mosque, the Government of Israel, deploying thousands of soldiers, destroyed the tent and the beginnings of the mosque in April 2003 ... This event, which began as a plaza plan for a small site in Nazareth, mushroomed beyond that, causing political, social, and cultural urban crises in the city. Above all, it triggered religious conflict in Nazareth ... Astonishingly, the Central Plaza Plan, which simply designates a small piece of land for public use ... succeeded in tearing [a] long-sustained social fabric and creating new social and political risks in Nazareth. (Jabareen 2006:305–6)

By January 2006 the plaza was complete, but was not opened until a few years later (see Figure 1.4). There are many different views in Nazareth about who was responsible for this sad outcome, but all agree that the security of their place of dwelling is worse than it was and they feel divided and fearful in a way that was not present before. 'Today, Nazareth is a city of veils and crucifixes,' said an

Figure 1.4   *Nazareth's new plaza in 2009*

Source: Yosef Jabareen

interviewee. 'Planning served as a conflict producer' (Jabareen 2006:317).

It is from cases such as these that the ideas and practices associated with planning activity get their justifications and meanings. The focus of this broad field of ideas and practices is on deliberate, collective attempts to improve place qualities, as a contribution to the management and development of places. In this respect, it is part of the governance infrastructure that contributes to the physical shaping of locales within an urban area (see Chapter 3). However, it is about much more than this physical shaping and ordering. Planning ideas and planning activity both express, and contribute to, the way people understand and feel about places. They may come to affect and express people's sense of identity as well as their material conditions.

The politics of place

Stories such as those recounted above, which can be repeated from across the globe, have often been treated as somehow 'local' phenomena, below the radar of the great themes of national and international politics and the power play of ideologies and political movements. Yet these apparently local experiences do not only have local effects, and small conflicts can grow into bigger struggles. Even small encounters with planning activity can provide important experiences of the governance institutions in a society, of their strengths and, especially, their failings. When a place-related issue confronts them – a proposed new building, or the expansion of a traffic-generating hospital or school, or a proposal for a new motorway route or airport expansion – people recall and revise their views of what they think about the political arrangements in their society as well as about the particular issue in hand. They learn about what they value, who has the same views as them and who seems to have a different view. They are reminded that they have to co-exist with others. They discover how all kinds of issues interrelate, clash and get tangled up when they come together in particular places. The institutional sites or arenas where 'planning' and local development issues are discussed and where conflicts are arbitrated may then become places where citizens learn about politics. People become aware of how their concerns inter-relate not only with those of their neighbours, but with those of people elsewhere whose concerns are raised in the discussion.

In Europe in the twentieth century, formal governments were not well equipped to deal with this place-centred politics. Some countries were very centralised, making it difficult to grasp citizens' concerns about their living environments. The dominant focus, as politics shifted into more democratic forms, was to provide for people's needs. But the way these needs were thought about was shaped by the class struggles of industrialisation, especially the demand for better conditions for the working classes. These important struggles set the masses in opposition to elites in the search for a more just distribution of resources and less exploitative working conditions. The aim of the welfare states that developed in Western Europe and North America in the second part of the twentieth century was to create welfare by an economic project of full employment through industrial expansion and a social project of better housing, health and education for all. As more and more people came to live in urban environments, the challenge of managing the collective daily life of both people and firms became ever more significant. It is in this context that the ideas and actions associated with the planning field commanded the attention of political leaders. During the twentieth century, the project of improving place qualities moved from the advocacy and experimentation of activists into a significant activity of formal governments. 'Planning systems' were created to regulate how land was used and developed, and how space and place qualities could be provided to serve economic and sociocultural purposes (Sutcliffe 1981, Ward 2002).

This planning project, as it developed in the first part of that century, was advocated both as a means of achieving wider access to economic opportunities and as a way of developing places in which work opportunities, housing provision and social welfare facilities for all could be situated. In the post-World War II period in Europe, planning as city building and rebuilding was a major element in the effort to revive social and economic conditions after the 1930s economic depression and the damage done by wartime bombing. In the US, the planning project was given a different emphasis, focusing on regional development and the promotion of more rational, scientifically informed public administration, both more democratic and more efficient than the patronage politics that grew up in a governance context in which local administrations had considerable autonomy (Friedmann 1973, 1987). However, in both contexts, experts and elite politicians articulated policies on behalf of citizens, who tended to be considered as largely undifferentiated masses with similar wants and needs. As the American sociologist Herbert Gans remarked, planners tended to plan for people like themselves (Gans 1969). Planning systems and development projects were thus rolled out across national territories with little attention to local variety. How such systems then worked out depended on the wider political and administrative context. In decentralised government systems, such as the US, the institutions and instruments made available by planning legislation might release local energies to pursue citizens' concerns about place qualities in inclusive ways, sensitive to different conditions and experiences. But equally, these same institutions and instruments could also be captured by particular interests. Commentators in the later twentieth century argued that governance elites dominated by business coalitions ruled most urban areas in the US (Fainstein and Fainstein 1986, Logan and Molotch 1987). In highly centralised systems, the development of local place management capacity might be ignored in the drive for wider goals such as economic growth (as in Japan, see Chapter 4). Or local management might be shaped to conform to national perceptions of what the planning project should achieve (as in England, see the South Tyneside case in Chapter 5).

However, the general idea of planning as a welfare project

articulated by technical experts faced other challenges when translated into government institutions and procedures. People increasingly questioned the capacity of elites and experts to articulate their concerns. Pressure groups, social movements and lobby groups demanded a greater say in policy-making processes. The diversity of people's experiences, aspirations and social worlds became increasingly evident, as civil rights movements in the 1960s and 1970s challenged systemic injustices, not only of class, but gender, race, ethnic and religious background, and physical ability. From the 1960s, the environmental costs of economic growth and resource exploitation became ever more obvious, leading to fundamental shifts in thinking about the relations and responsibilities of humans to the natural environment. While scientific knowledge was a key resource in this environmental movement, it also opened up such knowledge in ways that allowed people to see that science itself was full of contested concepts and uncertain conclusions, as residents in Greenpoint/Williamsburg argued. So neither scientific knowledge nor political representatives could be trusted to know enough, and especially to know enough about particular conditions in specific places. A wider approach to the intelligence needed to inform place-governance practices was needed.

In any case, the behaviour of those involved in politics and public administration, as reported in the media, seemed to suggest that politicians, their advisers and their officials were as likely to be corruptly pursuing their own interests or those of their favoured cronies as to be committed to the concerns of the citizens they were supposed to represent. Instead of responsible representatives of citizens' concerns, politicians were increasingly perceived as a discrete class, buttressed by self-interested officials and lobby groups, distanced from people's everyday lives. These shifts in thinking about government, politicians and governance capacity, now widely spread across the globe, have reduced citizens' interest in engaging with nation-state politics. Nevertheless, this does not mean that citizens and businesses are not interested in place qualities. Concerns about pollution and congestion, about rights to define which place qualities to promote, about the quality of streets and public spaces, and about access to physical and social facilities and infrastructures, become increasingly important once minimum basic needs for food and shelter are met. And people do not merely want a certain quantity of these place qualities. They want them arranged in such a way that they are accessible to them – physically, socially and in economic terms. Struggles over the quality of place management and development may lead to previously disenfranchised or disaffected citizens re-engaging with political life. In doing so, they may help to transform the qualities of the governance culture of their political community.

In such a context, the nature of planning institutions and practices, and their relation to all kinds of other arenas where place politics are acted out, become more than merely local matters. They begin to shape the overall way in which government and politics are done. They become institutional sites where national priorities, such as promoting economic development or providing more housing, bump up against other concerns about place qualities, such as infrastructure provision, environmental quality and sustainable development principles. They create arenas where international companies and global pressure groups may confront local residents in clashes over development proposals. As the weekly journal *The Economist* has remarked, 'Britain's inefficient planning rules ... [are] a subject that raises passions like few others' (*Economist*, 9 Dec 2006:36). This recognises the intensity of the conflicts that can arise among the

Figure 1.5   *The ambiguous position of planners*

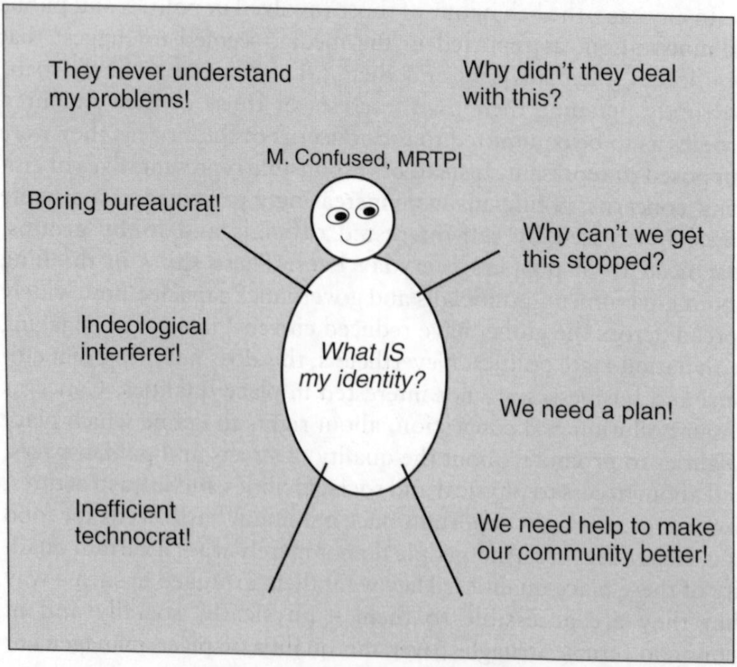

many different people who have a stake in what happens in a place, the 'stakeholders' in place qualities. In such situations, the arenas and institutions created by governments to undertake 'planning' activity are judged both as a hope and a problem. If only we had good planning, some people think, conflicts would become less intense. If only we could get rid of 'planning constraints', these conflicts could be bypassed. Planning activity and those who do planning work are caught in the centre of this ambiguous attitude (see Figure 1.5).

I argue in this book that the politics of place cannot be bypassed. More than half of us now live in urban areas of one kind of another, and have a stake in working out how to combine our own opportunities for flourishing[5] with those of others with whom we co-exist. As thinking creatures always interacting with the rest of the natural world, and with pasts and futures, we also cannot avoid being concerned about how the way we live now may compromise future conditions for life, for ourselves and for others. It therefore matters in the twenty-first century how we, as social beings in political communities, approach the challenges of place management and development.

The evolving planning project

What does it mean to approach place-governance with a planning orientation? Answers to this question evolved significantly through the twentieth century. An enduring concept embedded in the idea of planning is the belief that it is worth acting now to try to bring into being some aspiration for the future. A planning way of approaching place-governance therefore emphasises some aspirations about future place qualities. But what qualities and whose aspirations get to count?

A century ago, as urbanisation proceeded apace in rapidly industrialising countries, the planning project was promoted for several reasons (UN-Habitat 2009). For some, the ambition was to display the power of leaders and their commitment to 'modernising' their cities. There are still leaders today whose ambitions have created the skyscraper displays of Pudong in Shanghai or Dubai in the Gulf States. Such 'grand projects' have been as much about display and beautification as about providing space for urban activities. Another motivation for taking up the planning project was to manage the process of urban expansion. In developed countries in the early to mid-twentieth century, and increasingly now in the urban mega-lopolises of the developing world, national and municipal governments have sought to control urban expansion by regulating how land is used and developed. Major concerns in attempts to regulate urban expansion centred throughout the twentieth century on relating land development to infrastructure provision, and protecting areas where people live from polluting industries. The mechanism of 'zoning' land for particular uses arose from these concerns. Such concerns remain an important idea in the planning project today, emphasising the value of the convenience and operating efficiency of urban areas. A third motivation for the planning project was to make a contribution to redressing the social inequalities that have been a persistent feature of urban life. While the emphasis on beautification seemed to pander to the aspirations of affluent elites, efficiency and convenience were valued by the expanding urban middle classes. But poorer citizens and marginalised minority groups have faced hard struggles to get a foothold from which to satisfy basic needs and access to urban opportunities. Many of those promoting the planning project a century ago were motivated by finding ways to improve housing and living conditions for the poorest. Concern for justice in the way in which urban opportunities are distributed remains an important idea within the planning project.

A century ago, the planning project was conceived primarily in terms of its role in improving the physical fabric of cities. It was closely linked to concepts of the progressive 'modernising' of cities, though there were struggles over whether this modernisation should reflect the ambitions of elites or the aspirations of ordinary city dwellers. However, as the century wore on, much more attention was given to the social and economic dimensions of the way in which places change and develop. Advocates of the planning project became concerned with how local economies developed and how places experiencing economic hardship could be helped by development initiatives. This in turn encouraged more attention to understanding social and economic dynamics, especially through systematic social scientific analysis. Understood in this way, the planning project could be associated with bringing knowledge to bear on public policy choices (Friedmann 1987). But this still left open the question of what and whose knowledge got to count, the issue that preoccupied the residents in Greenpoint/Williamsburg. For many, it seemed once again that it was the knowledge of elites that counted, a distant 'them', far from the worlds of 'us'. This perception came to exist even in states formally committed to promoting the welfare of their citizens, as that welfare often seemed to be articulated in paternalist, top-down ways.

In the second part of the twentieth century these critical voices grew in volume. As projects informed by planning ideas rolled out across city cores, neighbourhoods and peripheries, protest movements and lobby groups began to articulate some serious failings of the planning project. Some of these protests helped to build the positive planning experiences presented in this book. One critique charged the planning project with being little more than a creature of business elites driven by capitalist profit making rather than any concern for the wider collective interest. Others argued that the institutions and practices of formal government planning systems were being used systematically to oppress minorities or, in some post-colonial situations, to allow urban political elites to cream off the benefits of urban development for themselves. Manuel Castells showed in a study of a French city how the machinery of the planning system was used systematically to advance the interests of business and property owners, while limiting the possibilities of working-class residents (Castells 1977).[6] Oren Yiftachel (1994, 1998) later highlighted how planning mechanisms were used in ways that discriminated against Palestinians in Israeli towns. Sub-Saharan African countries provide several examples of political elites using planning systems to maximise personal or tribal benefits.[7] Such experiences and accounts encouraged a critical view of the planning project, as too close to the values of modernising elites and/or potentially corruptible by forms of politics with little concern for the collective interest of a political community.

These criticisms, however, were only in part about the planning project as such. They were just as much about the way in which the institutions and practices set up to advance deliberate place management and development could be subverted by powerful groups. How can governance practices and cultures develop with the capacity to prevent such subversion? How is it possible to undertake place-governance work that gives more attention to people's varied experiences and aspirations about living in urban areas? It is here that the planning project during the later part of the twentieth century came to draw on wider debates about the nature of political community and democratic life. It is not enough to leave the governance of places to elites and their advisers, nor to leave it merely to the mechanisms of formal representative democracy. Citizens and other stakeholders have knowledge to contribute and values to assert. This increases the conflict and argument over what place qualities to privilege and what the priorities for place management and development in any urban area should be. Yet conflict and argument reflect the real diversity of experiences, imaginations and aspirations. This diversity is not only about conflicts between the interests of different groups. Political communities may value, at a general level, the promotion of better living conditions for all, greater efficiency in relating development to infrastructure, better-quality design of the physical fabric of urban areas and more attention to the longer-term environmental consequences of the way we live today. But how do these values get prioritised and translated when specific place management and development actions are taken up? How can one value be balanced against another?

This became a particularly important issue by the end of the twentieth century. By this time, concern for the condition of the natural environment and the relation between humans and nature had become a major concern, as evidence of the damage that human action has caused to our planetary life was difficult to avoid. At the same time, economic activity had become more crisis prone and more globally inter-related, with some places being hubs of dynamic growth and others faced with economic collapse. Reviving business to make 'places' more competitive became a major preoccupation of many countries and cities in the 1980s and 1990s. These economic and environmental concerns co-existed with concerns about social justice, often transformed into an emphasis on how to make political communities more 'cohesive' and less prone to major inequalities and the resentment this generates. In this context, the search for a way of moving into the future in sustainable ways became an orienting goal for many governments, both national and local. Figure 1.6 presents an influential expression of this idea developed within a European context.

Thus, at the beginning of the twenty-first century, a number of concepts have become central to the planning project. The concept of sustainability gives an important slant to thinking about future possibilities. The concept of balancing and integrating diverse values recognises the reality of conflict, but also the necessity of moving beyond disagreement to enable action to be taken where this is considered necessary or appropriate for the political community as a whole. The concept of participation recognises that elites and experts cannot be trusted alone to deliver 'what is best' for communities. The planning project has thus become associated with promoting conceptions of urban life that recognise human diversity, acknowledging that humans need to give respect to the environmental conditions

Figure 1.6   *Balanced and sustainable development:*
A European perspective[8]

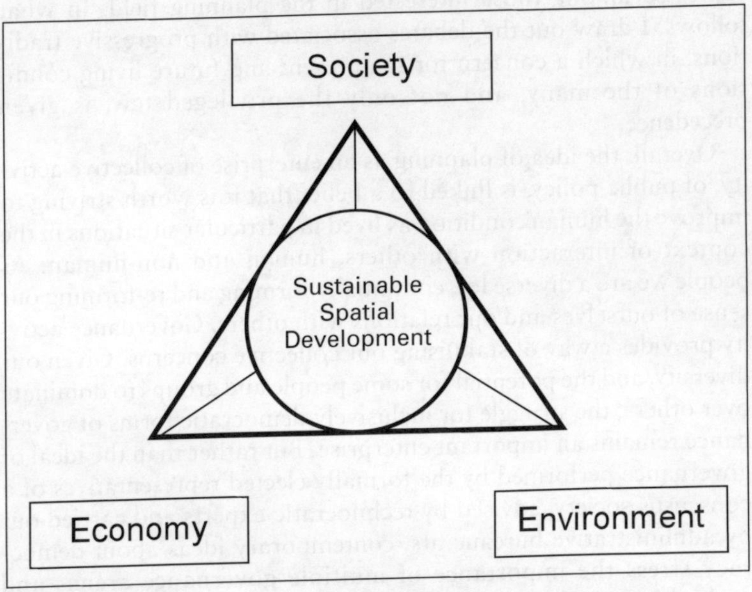

Note: This figure has been redrawn from the *European Spatial Development Perspective* (Committee for Spatial Development 1999:10), a European initiative to promote a spatial planning approach across Europe.

that sustain them and understanding that human flourishing depends on giving attention to multiple dimensions of human existence, as realised in particular places. Within this conception, the planning project partly centres on providing understanding and expertise and making a contribution to public debate about place management and development possibilities. But it also has a practical focus on what is required to realise programmes, policies and projects in specific conditions. It gives attention to practical action, to doing place-governance work. This book provides a journey through examples of such work inspired by a planning orientation.

A focus for the planning project

The planning project is therefore an approach to deliberate place management and development that is infused with a specific orientation or philosophy. It carries with it conceptions of place qualities and of a way of doing governance work. What these conceptions and approaches are and should be is vigorously debated and contested among those interested in the planning field. In what follows, I draw out the debates associated with progressive traditions, in which a concern for the present and future living conditions of the many, and not only the privileged few, is given precedence.

Overall, the idea of planning as an enterprise of collective activity, of public policy, is linked to a belief that it is worth striving to improve the human condition as lived in particular situations in the context of interaction with others, human and non-human. As people we are a diverse lot, continually forming and re-forming our sense of ourselves and our relations with others. Governance activity provides a way of stabilising our collective concerns. Given our diversity, and the potential for some people and groups to dominate over others, the struggle for inclusively democratic forms of governance remains an important enterprise. But rather than the ideal of governance performed by the formally elected representatives of a consensus society, advised by technocratic experts and carried out by administrative bureaucrats, contemporary ideas about democracy stress the importance of multiple governance arenas and multiple ways of establishing legitimacy for collective action. They emphasise the significance of argumentation, discord, lively debate and conflict in generating a rich, inclusive governance culture, which is continually revising itself (see Cunningham 2002, Connolly 2005, Briggs 2008, Callon et al. 2009). The importance of these qualities emerges clearly in the cases discussed in Chapters 4 to 7.

Not only are we diverse, with many different ideas about and needs for collective action, we are highly mobile, as we explore the material world and the worlds of ideas and imagination. We dwell in multiple dimensions of existence, in all kinds of relations with others. In our webs of relations, we are also socially and culturally 'placed', in relation to others and in places of dwelling and encounter. We value these places, as they give shape to our daily life flow, and as they collect meanings through the encounters of daily life and of special occasions and incidents, as the examples of Ditchling and Nazareth illustrate. Nevertheless, my meanings may not be the same as my neighbour's. My social networks are likely to be different, though transecting and interacting with those of my neighbours in various ways. It is the potentials and tensions within these transactions and interactions that arise as we co-exist

> ## Box 1.1 Attributes of a twenty-first century 'planning project'
>
> - An orientation to the future and a belief that action now can shape future potentialities
> - An emphasis on liveability and sustainability for the many, not the few
> - An emphasis on interdependences and interconnectivities between one phenomenon and another, across time and space
> - An emphasis on expanding the knowledgeability of public action, expanding the 'intelligence' of a polity
> - A commitment to open, transparent government processes, to open processes of reasoning in and about the public realm

in places that create the demand for collective action – to promote the opportunities and potentials of place qualities, but also to make the inevitable frictions and tensions more tolerable (see Chapter 2).

With these general points as a context, Box 1.1 lists five distinctive attributes that are central to a progressive interpretation of the planning project in the contemporary period. First, the idea of planning emphasises that it is worth thinking forward into the future with some hope in the ability of collective action to produce better conditions and some belief that it is possible, by setting out on a collective trajectory, to resist pressures that might reduce potentialities and possibilities for some and all, and to open up opportunities that could enhance the future chances of human flourishing. This idea was expressed nicely by the philosopher William James a century ago:

> that which proposes to us, through an act of belief, an end which cannot be attained except by our own efforts, and that which carries us courageously into action in cases where success is not assured to us in advance. (James 1920:82, trans. from original French by author)

This implies a rich and sensitive understanding of the complex ways in which people live in, move around and care about particular places, but it also emphasises that the future does not just happen. It is also in part 'willed' into existence by collective effort.

Secondly, a major strand of thought within the planning field centres on promoting ways to advance the liveability and sustainability of daily life environments, not just for the few but for the many. What is different now from earlier, twentieth century conceptions is that the 'many' are conceived not as a mass with common values and concerns, but as a plurality of individuals and groups, with potentially diverse values and ways of living. In such a conception, economic issues are not neglected. Instead, they are subsumed into a broader conception of human flourishing in a sustainable planetary context.

Thirdly, the planning idea pays attention to the complex ways in which phenomena relate to one another, their 'connectivities'. It encourages people to look for chains of impact, which particular projects and activities create, and how these weave across time and space. It calls for consideration of relations between the various dimensions of our lives – home, work, leisure, etc. – and how we move around to reach them all. It cultivates attention not merely to our individual interests, but to the complex interdependences and obligations we have with other people, other places and other times, in the past and in the future.

Fourthly, the planning idea stresses the importance of knowing about the issues, experiences, potentialities and conflicting pressures that arise in any context of collective action. However, this 'knowing about' does not necessarily imply scientific or systematic knowledge, or technical expertise, though these may be very valuable resources to inform collective action. It also includes all kinds of experiential knowledge and cultural appreciations. Translated into the field of place-governance, this implies drawing on people's experiences of dwelling and moving around in time and space, but also on cultural expressions in all kinds of media, as well as the systematic sciences of urban and regional dynamics.

Fifthly, the planning idea values forms of government that do not hide their processes inside the procedures of bureaucracy or the cloaks and daggers of political gamesmanship. Instead, the ambition is to seek open and transparent ways of arriving at an understanding of what issues are at stake, how they could be addressed and what difference it might make, to what and to whom, if they were to be addressed in one way or another. The idea thus stresses carrying out policy argumentation in the open, in transparent ways. It is this element of the planning idea that has helped to create the paraphernalia of plans, policy statements, visions and strategies that, paradoxically, often then seem to clutter up the practice of planning in many situations. Nevertheless, it is not the idea of open argumentation that is at fault here. The clutter arises partly from a failure to think through carefully what it means to argue in the open, but also because the planning idea itself has been drowned by other ways of doing governance work.

The planning project, then, understood as an orienting and mobilising set of ideas, centres on deliberate collective action; that is, on governance activity, to improve place qualities, infused with a particular orientation. Such an orientation is not necessarily lodged in organisations and government systems that carry the name 'planning'. Because the idea of planning has often been subverted in the practices that invoke the name of planning, I refer to practices that are infused with the project's values by the longer phrase 'place-governance with a planning orientation'. Both as a set of ideas and as practices seeking to realise them, the planning project has arisen in the particular context of complex, urbanised societies. In such situations, we humans, with our diverse experiences and aspirations, are 'throwntogether' (Massey 2005), in political communities and in places, and then have to sort out how to live with each other and with non-humans. When institutionalised, the idea will always be challenged and struggled over. If a stable strategy is arrived at in one period, however inclusive its intentions and however much it has liberated potentialities among most members of the relevant political community, it will also be experienced as a constraining piece of government infrastructure. And the danger of capture by a narrow group of interests or a narrow definition of the project is ever present. The planning idea is always liable to lose its meanings if it settles unreflexively into an organisational niche, discarding elements that do not seem to fit. So practices of place-governance need to be subject to continual evaluation and critique to assess whether they still have any connection to a planning orientation. The general attributes of the planning idea that I have articulated here provide one way to evaluate place-governance practices, and to challenge the subversion of planning-oriented governance practices by narrower, regressive interests.

In the next two chapters, I focus on these attributes more specifically, in relation to the challenges of place-governance. Chapter 2 expands on the relation between people and places, and discusses how attention to place qualities contributes to human flourishing. In Chapter 3, I elaborate on what is involved in undertaking deliberate action with respect to place management and development, and on the dimensions of governance capacity that affect the contribution of the planning project.

Suggested further reading

Much of the literature on planning ideas and practices is based on experiences within particular countries. For wider reviews of the history of planning ideas with respect to improving conditions in towns, cities and urban regions, see:

Boyer, C. (1983) *Dreaming the Rational City*, MIT Press, Cambridge, MA.

Hall, P. (1988) *Cities of Tomorrow*, Blackwell, Oxford.

For a more recent account of urban design ideas within the field, see:

Madanipour, A. (2003) *Public and Private Spaces in the City*, Routledge, London.

For an accessible overview of 'planning theory' discussion of planning ideas, see:

Allmendinger, P. (2009) *Planning Theory* (2nd edn), Palgrave Macmillan, London.

For my own contribution to planning theory discussion, see:

Healey, P. (1997/2006) *Collaborative Planning: Shaping Places in Fragmented Societies*, Macmillan, London.

Chapter 2

Understanding Places

Experiencing places

Planning activity is often associated in the popular mind with disruptions and eyesores: the motorway that leaps across the urban landscape, dividing neighbourhoods and disrupting perspectives; the housing estate given prizes for design that is a nightmare to live in. Yet the planning project of the twentieth century grew in response to the challenge of rapid urban development occurring in a piecemeal fashion in the industrialising nineteenth century. This created burgeoning urban complexes, where dynamism co-existed with extreme pollution, congestion, poverty and health hazards, the 'city of dreadful night' (see Hall 1988). Today, urban megalopolises with multiple centres where many millions of people live, work and do business have emerged in many parts of the world. The challenge is to make urban places liveable, sustainable and accessible, both in their centres and in other places where people congregate and live.

Those advocating improved urban conditions during the twentieth century have made a significant contribution to shaping the physical fabric of urban areas. This is partly the result of major projects that have aimed to improve urban conditions. It is also the product of the adoption of regulations governing how urban land is used and developed. Two examples serve to illustrate this. The first comes from the city centre of an urban area once associated with congestion, pollution and poverty. Newcastle upon Tyne in northern England was a leading city of Britain's industrial revolution in the nineteenth century, but in the twentieth century it was badly affected by global shifts in the location of engineering, shipbuilding, armaments and chemical industries. A short walk through the city centre, very distinctive in its ambience and design, also travels through three generations of planning ideas about what a regional capital city should be like (see Box 2.1).

City centres have always attracted the attention of civic leaders.

Box 2.1   Ambitious plans and city life in Newcastle upon Tyne, England

We start in the 1960s, beside a fine, award-winning City Hall building, with a small park in front full of flowers and fountains. Clustered around the City Hall are two universities, one originating in the nineteenth century. From here it is a short distance to the major hospital. The other university was built here in the 1960s, located deliberately as part of an idea for a 'higher education precinct'. Today, these education, health and administrative centres provide the most important employment sources in the city area. In front, a soot-blackened church is a reminder of the great days

The nineteenth-century Theatre Royal with 1990s repaving

of the nineteenth century, when this was a major entry point for the industrial areas beyond. Now it is where the shopping streets begin, served by an underground metro line, next to a bus station, nicely refurbished as a result of negotiations over the development of the adjacent Marks & Spencer store. The buildings here are a jumble of older structures, interspersed with many more dating from the 1960s and 1970s, with some replacement and refurbishment since. The street is now pedestrianised and a constant tide of people flows

Shop front anticipating a higher street level

past the recently introduced buskers and street stalls. Those who have not been to this area since the 1950s will find it hard to recognise. In those days the main shopping area was further south, in the older nineteenth-century city centre. The present major street, with its intense activity, is the

→

→

product of an ambitious but only partly realised 1960s city centre redevelopment plan, vigorously promoted by the city council. The idea was to create a street level above the present one, with traffic flowing underneath and people at the higher level.

Major waterfront projects on the Tyne river quayside (see also Chapter 6)

Glancing down, the pavement is uneven and cracked, but very soon you arrive at a different perspective as you turn towards a tall monument to the nineteenth-century social reformer Earl Grey, and a splay of grand streets leading down towards the western and southern parts of the city. This large area was all built in the nineteenth century according to a planning scheme promoted by a public–private partnership between the local council, an important local architect and a property developer. The scheme specified layouts and designs in the expectation that shops and offices would be on the ground floor, with apartments above. But the affluent middle classes of the nineteenth century never took up the idea of city centre living, preferring the suburbs located to the north. Many of these upper floors were never occupied and, as the heart of the city centre moved north with the shopping schemes of the 1960s and south with redevelopment along the waterfront in the 1980s, its nineteenth-century fabric slipped into steady decline.

Now it has come alive again with restaurants and cafés spilling out onto the streets, frontages refurbished, offices attracted back and apartments remodelled for students and young professionals who enjoy city centre living. All this has been encouraged by a national government-funded regeneration project that helped to build confidence among property owners and investors, and spent considerable resources on increasing the space for pedestrians, providing high-quality Caithness stone paving and custom-made street furniture.

Box 2.2   Buitenveldert, a 'modernist', yet 'sustainable', planned neighbourhood

Buitenveldert is bordered to the east and west by two large parks (Amstelpark and the Amsterdamse Bos). Fifteen-storey tower blocks and four-storey slab blocks line the main access roads. Within the neighbourhood, the layout of streets, buildings, waterways and parks consists of neat squares and rectangles, with a mixture of slab blocks, three-storey row houses, and three- or four-storey open courtyards. In the centre is a shopping complex, and scattered through the neighbourhood are primary and secondary schools, health services and other public buildings, such as churches, with four sports complexes positioned on the edges of the neighbourhood.

Four-storey slab block

→

They combine concentrations of economic activity, the locations of important cultural activities and public administrations. For both political leaders and wider political communities, the city centre is also an important expression of the 'place' of a city, so local elites have sought to maintain and enhance the physical fabric and social ambience of centres.

In the past, many urban dwellers lived in or adjacent to city centres. But as cities grew larger and citizens more affluent, most people have come to live in the urban conglomerations that spread out from old centres, absorbing surrounding villages and smaller towns as they do so. Some of these areas originated as projects by land developers of one kind or another. Many of them have been more concerned with realising short-term profits out of increasing demand for urban space, though there have often been some private initiatives to create projects for better living conditions. Planning ideas, about the design and management of better neighbourhoods,

Terrace slabs facing interior gardens

While the availability and distribution of services would be welcomed in most urban neighbourhoods, the built form of the housing – the towers, slabs and rows – has since been castigated by design professionals throughout the world. In many cities, it is just such designs that have had to be demolished, because no one wants to live there or because those who do are unable to maintain them, and or are in such conflict with their neighbours that social conditions become tense and dangerous. Such a fate has afflicted other neighbourhoods in Amsterdam. However, Buitenveldert is merely considered a rather 'dull' place, where, 50 years after it was built, mainly elderly residents are being replaced by a new generation of younger families and other types of household. This neighbourhood has become, over the years, just another ordinary suburb in the urban social and physical fabric of the Amsterdam area. According to the City Council's regular surveys of resident satisfaction with their neighbourhoods, the area measures well on criteria of 'liveability'.[1]

about how towns should be designed and, in recent years, about more sustainable ways to produce development, have influenced the design of residential neighbourhoods, through their impact on land use and development regulations, and through their impact on those producing settlement designs.

There are also many examples where a government has acted as the developer of residential neighbourhoods. My second example is of a planned suburb in south west Amsterdam in the Netherlands. The western Netherlands is one of the most densely populated areas in the world. The landscape is created from the vast delta of the Rhine/Maas river system. Urban agglomerations are interspersed with green areas of intensive pastoral farming and horticulture, drained by intricate webs of lakes and canals. Within urban cores in cities such as the capital, Amsterdam, the waterways provide the main open spaces. But in the neighbourhoods that have been built in the past century, buildings, water surfaces and green areas intermingle. Very obviously, these areas have been shaped by the work of the city government and its planners, providing a living exhibition of ideas that planners have held at various times about neighbourhood life. The neighbourhood of Buitenveldert was initiated in the 1950s and 1960s, during the time an internationally famous modernist planner, Cornelius van Eesteren, led the Amsterdam planning office. It is one of a ring of neighbourhoods of this period, built especially for the city's industrial workers who, after 20 years of economic depression and world war, were in desperate need of better housing (see Box 2.2).

As noted in the example, many such planned neighbourhoods have not been as successful as Buitenveldert in providing liveable and sustainable urban environments. What makes this neighbourhood different? The answer lies partly in the location. It is in the city's southern zone, long recognised as more affluent than the western, eastern and south-eastern city suburbs. It is also very accessible by car, train, bus, tram and metro from Amsterdam city centre and from the huge employment complex of Schiphol airport, which is emerging on the neighbourhood skyline to the north. The city planners responded to this location in the 1950s by providing for layout and buildings to be slightly more spacious than in the other post-war neighbourhoods. So Buitenveldert is positioned in a largely middle-class housing market. Nevertheless, it is not only a 'one-class' suburb, as in many UK and US cities. There is a mix of types of housing – houses, apartments, low-rise and high-rise – as well as of tenures. Housing for rent to lower-income families is provided in friendly courtyard layouts,[2] centred on playgrounds, near shops, schools and parks, all managed by a housing association. And the buildings themselves are often of mixed use, with shops below and apartments above, and a layer of offices included in the tower blocks. Finally, despite the 'linearity' of the neighbourhood layout, it has been designed to provide routes for walking, including smooth surfaces for pushchairs, zimmer frames and wheelchairs, and for bicycling, separated from cars, with careful attention to access to public transport stops and to connections by all forms of mobility to areas outside the neighbourhood.[3] In all kinds of small ways, the neighbourhood attests to close attention to details of design, layout, construction and management.[4] In effect it provides an expression of what are now called 'sustainable' urban design principles and promoted by the American 'new urbanism' movement (see Duany et al. 2000, Talen 1999 and Grant 2006). So, with a mixture of location and design, a neighbourhood created 50 years ago has settled into the urban landscape, now much greener with mature trees softening the original grid. There is every likelihood that it will last at least another 50 years as a very 'liveable' urban neighbourhood.

The physical form and arrangement of places are thus often shaped by deliberate action. The motivations for this may be various, reflecting the diverse purposes introduced in Chapter 1. Sometimes politicians want to create a new physical expression of a new life, or a newly established power. New political regimes have often planned their capital cities to become a physical statement symbolising nationhood (see for example Brazilia in Brazil, Taipei in Taiwan, Colombo in Sri Lanka or New Delhi in India). In 1960s Newcastle, politicians wanted to create the 'Brazilia of the north' (Smith 1970). In Amsterdam the ambitions were less grandiose, being focused on creating better living conditions for working people. But such a deliberate shaping has always been done in conjunction with other forces: the inheritance that natural systems provide; the resources of landowners, property developers and infrastructure providers; the particular structure of local land and property relations over the centuries; the efforts of all kinds of people to improve their own surroundings; the calamitous and insidious ways in which planetary dynamics erupt and surround human endeavour. Government intentions have not always been benign and the resultant places have not always been judged as 'good'. But government interventions, including those inspired with planning ideals, have had a pervasive, physical impact on how places have developed.

A major challenge for such deliberate interventions in the physical fabric of cities has been to grasp the relation between an image of urban form and the impact of such a form once created in the urban landscape. What impacts will it have? What meanings will it carry? How will it relate to the specifics of land and property relations, to people's daily life habits, business opportunities and the flow of natural systems? In the rest of this chapter, I introduce the discussion of these questions by considering first, the interaction of people and places and the dynamics of sociospatial relations; secondly, how place qualities are produced; thirdly, how places have been imagined by planners and others; and fourthly, how our concerns with particular places bring into play the connections we have with other people and other places.

Towards the 'good life': People in places

In Chapter 1, I argued that a key value carried by the planning project should be to make a contribution to improving the liveability and sustainability of places. General principles in the abstract, such as the pursuit of 'social justice' or 'sustainable development', can help us think about what we should care about, but they do not go far in themselves as a guide to designing and performing interventions that might help to shape particular place futures. We all live and move around in and among specific places, with widely varying qualities, which we invest with all kinds of diverse meanings. But with all this variety, how can what is an 'improvement' be discerned? What does it mean to seek to increase the possibilities for different people in different places to 'flourish', to lead a 'good life'? What do 'social justice' and 'sustainable development' mean when they are 'at home', related to the fine grain of lived experiences? In Chapter 1, I suggested that the idea of planning, as now understood in a progressive way, carries with it an orientation to the future, an emphasis on liveability and sustainability, an emphasis on interdependences and connectivities, a grounding in knowledge about the interactions between people and place and a commitment to transparency in policy making. But what do such values mean in actual contexts? What should political communities actually *do* to promote them? In the later chapters in this book, I answer this challenge through looking at examples of practices. Here, I draw out more general considerations raised by the challenge of our human co-existence in places.

The challenge of this co-existence raises difficult issues about the relation of individuals to society and to nature, about which philosophers have argued over the centuries.[5] At one level, we all, as humans, share some needs, responsibilities and entitlements to consideration. This perception has inspired declarations of human rights, campaigns against oppression and for the just provision of 'basic needs' for all. The campaign for human rights in Western societies has generated deliberate action to promote place development and management that encourages the provision of a decent physical home for everyone, as well as access to work, health and education, whatever our gender, physical ability, cultural background or income. This objective deeply informed neighbourhood development projects such as those in Amsterdam (see also cases in Chapters 4 and 5). Beyond these basic needs and rights, we vary a lot, depending on our particular 'position' in a society – old or young, parent or child, resident or worker, landowner or tenant, professional worker or manual labourer, teacher or pupil, politician or voter, and typically several of these at once. Such differences feed the idea that everyone has a set of interests and makes 'rational trade-offs' among their particular preferences, in the language of conventional economics. What one person prefers may be in conflict with the preference package of another, generating all kinds of tensions.

However, we are not just economic beings, pursuing our material interests. We are social and moral beings, living in social worlds that shape what become our economic interests and preferences and mould the way we think about our moral identities, how we 'ought' to relate to others and the worlds around us. We are not merely 'situated' in social worlds, but come to our view of what is a 'good life' through our interactions with others and our reflections on ourselves in relation to others in these social worlds. As social anthropologists and social historians can show us, what has been understood as 'the good life' may have some commonalities across the globe and through the centuries. But there is also enormous variety in how the idea of a 'good life' has been interpreted by different peoples in different times and places. In the twenty-first century world, with its high mobility of people, goods, information and ideas, bits of social worlds flow about and collide, allowing people to have multiple identities and to operate in different places at once.[6] Nevertheless, this very mobility may still lead to clashes between very different cultural conceptions of place qualities.

Hillier reports another kind of clash in a case from South Australia. Here developers and municipal leaders were keen to build a new bridge and marina, to exploit an island for a tourist development project that promised economic spin-offs in the locality. But indigenous islanders saw the landscape as a sacred expression of their ancestors and the way in which present and future generations could connect to the cosmos. Such knowledge, being sacred and passed down only among tribal women, could not be revealed in the deliberations and legal proceedings of the South Australian government system. Because they could not do this, their concerns were dismissed by some politicians and local media commentators as a fabrication, merely a ploy in a struggle between interests, rather than a deeper clash between cultures and traditions (see Hillier 2007:Chapter 4).

These days, it is hard to find places untouched by these flows and collisions. They break up the close attachment between a group of people, their place of physical dwelling and their material and moral concerns: the communitarian *Gemeinschaft* of German sociology (Tonnies 1988). One consequence is that those with a 'stake' in what happens in a place are not only local residents, or citizens of a specific administrative-political jurisdiction. 'Stakeholders' may come from other places, but be concerned about qualities in a particular locale, or the impact of what people do there on other places about which they are concerned. The webs of relationships that produce and are affected by the qualities of a place are thus potentially very various in spatial reach and temporal span.

Further, the recognition of multiple flows, identities and stakes implies that, without abandoning a sense of our common humanity and relation to the natural world, what constitutes the good life, and what is valued about place qualities, is always potentially contestable. Any collective action to shape place qualities thus demands choices between different values about place qualities and between different groups of potential beneficiaries of any action. National governments may enact programmes to promote particular place qualities, but such general prescriptions may then clash with other perceptions of what is important about particular places as these general ideas are rolled out in all kinds of different situations. The processes through which choices are made and legitimated between conflicting viewpoints then becomes as important as which choices are made. This is expressed neatly by geographer David Harvey in his search for a specification of 'territorial distributive justice', as a 'just distribution justly arrived at' (Harvey 1973:98).

What is understood to be the good life cannot therefore be taken readily off the shelf in some formulaic way as a set of place-structuring general principles, and then implanted through government action on how people live their lives. Approaching place development and management in this way was one of the major mistakes that twentieth century planners and policy experts tended to make. Instead, such activity pursued with the intention of promoting the liveability and sustainability of conditions for present and future generations needs to find ways to open up awareness of diverse conceptions of the 'good life' and work out what is broadly shared and where deep conflicts lie. In Vancouver, this awareness was developed neighbourhood by neighbourhood as planners and residents worked together to develop an approach to managing neighbourhood change that recognised this diversity – among residents and within the urban complex as a whole (see Chapter 4). They sought to foster a plural conception of what liveability and sustainability in places can mean, one that encompassed the diversity of views among the many and was able to evolve as conditions change, rather than holding on to a narrow and singular conception of 'our place'. To expand on Harvey's words, this means considering what is a good place-management intervention, arrived at by a good collective action process, legitimated by what is understood as good by all those with some kind of stake in a place.

Place geographies and place qualities

But how are we to understand the idea of 'place'? Those trained as planners, often in architecture and engineering schools, have tended to see 'places' as physical materialities, the form and arrangement of objects in the physical and natural environment. Yet the above discussion emphasises that places and place making are deeply social and political concepts and activities, in which meanings and values are created in interaction with lived experiences and, often, with available formalised scientific evidence, as in the Greenpoint/ Williamsburg, Brooklyn case in Chapter 1. The social meaning of a place thus cannot easily be read off from its physical appearance. A so-called slum area in a burgeoning Asian city may contain a quite different social, political and economic energy from that of a low-cost housing 'estate' in a British city, which continues to deteriorate despite repeated physical improvements (see UN-Habitat 2003; for the UK experience, see Hanley 2007).

A place and its qualities thus refers not only to the availability of particular material things: affordable housing, available opportunities and facilities, well-designed connections and so on. It also encompasses the meanings and values that people invest in what is around them and their perceptions of their ability to influence their surroundings. Contemporary geographers, such as Doreen Massey (2005), emphasise that places are not just physically 'there', collections of objects positioned on a surface or in a container to make up a neighbourhood, or city or rural region. They are brought into existence by our experience of them, the way we infuse them with meaning. We do this by the way we flow through places in our daily lives: getting daily necessities, going for an evening walk, taking the kids to school, going to work, discussing with fellow workers, visiting family and friends, chatting with people we meet in bars, in places of religious assembly, in shops and streets, on public transport and in car parks. We comment about and compare one place with another, and experience comfort, wonder and excitement about some aspects of some places; shame, fear and entrapment in others. Place qualities are formed through encounters between our material experiences of our life surroundings and the meanings we make of these.

In using the term place,[7] I focus not on some kind of objectively present reality, although we all have a sense of the materiality of places – their buildings and landscapes, the streets, paths, parks and facilities, the way in which people and vehicles interact. Nor do I consider 'places' as necessarily coterminous with any particular administrative jurisdiction, such as a municipality or province. Things may be co-located, and relations may overlay each other in physical spaces, but they may not create a 'sense of place'. We get such a sense when we feel that we have arrived somewhere, when we sense an ambience, when we feel that we are at some kind of nodal space in the flows of our lives. So a sense of place and of place quality can be understood as some kind of coming together of physical experiences (using, bumping into, looking at, hearing, breathing) and imaginative constructions (giving meanings and values) produced through individual activity and socially formed appreciations.

We all give meanings to the 'where' of our worlds and often convert the 'just thereness' of things into a sense of a place with particular qualities. But how we do this is affected not only by the social worlds in which our identities are formed, but by the span (or reach) in time and space of the relations we have with others. Like the rest of us, city leaders do this in many ways. Those involved in place making in Newcastle in the mid-nineteenth century, for example, drew on Georgian Edinburgh for an image of what a city centre should be like. Their successors in the 1960s made comparisons with a South American new capital city project, Brazilia. By the 1980s, Boston had become for Europeans a model of urban regeneration practice. By the 1990s, Barcelona had such an iconic status.

However, citizens also have knowledge and experience of other places. In twenty-first century life, we may get ideas about how places should be through our direct experiences, through our various social networks, which may stretch transcontinentally even for the poorest of families, and through all kinds of media. In this way, people get to know not only about other places but about how what happens in another place may affect what happens where they are currently living. They get to fear that cheaper labour in emerging economies may be taking their jobs. They see how the principle of the free migration of labour in a transnational polity such as the

European Union creates a new flow of people working on nearby farms, shops and tourist venues. They are upset when relatives from elsewhere comment on how run-down their neighbourhood has become. They get to worry about the impact of the human exploitation of resources on biodiversity and on climate change, and start changing their own behaviour. They worry about their futures and those of their families and friends. Living in a place, in the flow of daily time, people continually bump up against other times: yearly cycles and inter-generational time, as well as the claims of other people in other places across the globe. This is one way in which more general, exogenous conceptions come to bear down on, but also potentially inspire, how people in a particular place think about the qualities of the 'whereness' of their daily life experiences and about how their place might evolve in the future.

So the meanings and experiences of places cannot be understood merely by looking at a standard two-dimensional map. Nor can the qualities of places be easily captured by the image of a place as a collection of assets clumped together. Place qualities are generated and maintained by complex inter-relationships between people in diverse social worlds, which potentially connect them to all kinds of other places and times in dynamic and unpredictable ways. The cases from Nazareth in Chapter 1 and South Australia mentioned above illustrate this very starkly. So collective place-making efforts that aim to expand the opportunities for 'human flourishing' in the places of daily life need to proceed with great sensitivity to who lives where, what they do, what they know, how they get on, how they relate to each other, what they care about and feel that they 'need'. This demands a kind of 'holistic' sensibility, drawing in the various relations and dimensions that affect how a place and its future come to be imagined. But such a sensibility cannot be achieved by treating the 'whole' of an urban complex as somehow self-contained and firmly bounded. For what goes on within large urban areas connects in many different ways to wider worlds and dynamics.

Imagining places

One of the delights of the planning field is to review the imagery that visionaries, politicians and planners have used to bring places into focus. Sometimes these images are drawn from the past, an idealised conception of ancient cities. Or they are imagined future utopias (see Fishman 1977, Boyer 1983, Hall 1988). Such images are often given physical form in sketches and designs. But they may also be expressed in written form, in some kind of 'vision' statement. Some famous utopian texts, such as Thomas More's *Utopia* and Ebenezer Howard's *Garden Cities of Tomorrow* (Howard 1989), were long treatises about a way of life, in which physical form was only one dimension. Such idealised images can be found today in campaigning texts on environmental and technological utopias.

The planning tradition makes much use of designs and sketches, icons, maps and vision statements (see Figure 2.1). These may range from the development site to the city, region, nation and even supra-nationally. For example, spatial planners working at the European Union have in recent years struggled to capture the spatial diversity of a continent in visual representations (Dühr 2007). The value of such images is that they provide a way of connecting the diverse parts and qualities of a place into some kind of holistic representation. They help to draw forward, from the background of people's attention, an idea of place to which different attributes, interests and specific project proposals can be linked. They help to mobilise attention and to generate the 'energy' to translate ideas into action to transform future place qualities. Planning work, which involves translating policy ideas into changes in the built environment, makes extensive use of visual expressions as part of the craft of planning work. In popular imagination, planning work is often associated with the making of a plan. Yet, as Chapters 4 to 7 will show very clearly, a physical plan is only one of the tools that are used in such place management and development work.

However, such expressions of place imagery are by no means neutral in their content and their effects. This is particularly evident when drawings and maps are used to visualise place qualities. They seem to portray the future in final physical form. Such visualisations may have been intended merely as a thinking tool, an imagined possibility. However, sketches and maps can take on a life of their own. They may be just too persuasive, so that people expect them to come about as designed and mapped. Or they may generate hostility, as people feel that their concerns have been neglected in a design produced by a planning office or consultancy group. Or an image, even where produced through discussion with some key stakeholders, may exclude, in a reductive way, many of the 'parts' that co-exist in a place. In areas where people have been systematically oppressed by elites and former colonial powers, designs and plans produced by governments may be treated as the products of alien

Figure 2.1 *Images of the future*

The <u>Vision for Leeds</u> has three main aims

- Going up a league as a city - making Leeds an internationally competitive city, the best place in the country to live, work and learn, with a high quality of life for everyone.
- Narrowing the gap between the most disadvantaged people and communities and the rest of the city.
- Developing Leeds' role as the regional capital, contributing to the national economy as a competitive European city, supporting and supported by a region that is becoming increasingly prosperous.

Source: Vision Statement for the Leeds Community Strategy, downloaded 10.02.09 from www.leedsinitiative.org

a: A vision for Leeds

Vision Statement

" By 2020 the eThekwini Municipality will enjoy the reputation of being Africa's most caring and liveable city, where all citizens live in harmony. This Vision will be achieved by growing its economy & meeting peoples needs so that all citizens enjoy a high quality of life with equal opportunities, in a city that they are truly proud of."

.....As agreed at the Alpine Health Workshop 13-15 May 2001

b: A vision for the Durban area

Région urbaine Marseille-Aix Métropole en projet

c: The evolving Marseille Metropolitan Urban Region (an academic attempt to capture the urban region visually)

Sources: (a) www.leedsinitiative.org (b) Office of the Mayor of Durban (2001) (c) Michael Chiappero.

forces. It may become legitimate in such situations to disregard them (see the Besters Camp case in Chapter 5).

These reactions underline that sketches and images are not merely thinking tools or possibilities promoted for discussion. Ideas about place qualities flow from the realm of discussion into material form. They become embedded in land use and building regulations. They shape the design and layout of development projects. They are reflected in the location of major physical infrastructures, and in the design of public space. These impacts may occur over long time horizons. Ideas consciously adopted in one period, to express the values and concerns about place qualities of a particular political community, may, over time, merge into the background, in the flow of ongoing practices. These may then be experienced by later generations as constraints, as rigidities locked into outdated practices. This often happens in the routine of place management work. For this reason, it is important from time to time to bring these images into the foreground again and to evaluate them carefully. Such open reflection may then provide a challenge to tendencies to narrow and exclusionary conceptions of places and their qualities. However, place imageries that carry a pluralistic conception of a place and its qualities are not easily produced and often do not precede active interventions in reshaping the physical form of places. In Vancouver, it took time to realise what the various neighbourhood guidelines being produced would create at a city scale (see Chapter 4). In Birmingham, the idea of having a city centre design framework co-evolved with work on major development projects in the city centre area (see Chapter 6). This underlines that place qualities and ways of expressing these develop richness and relevance through social learning processes, as participants come to understand what is at stake and what futures are emerging.

Places in wider worlds

So far, I have argued that what we recognise as 'places' are created by the accretion of the material patterning of activity flows in, around and through our surroundings, and by the meanings and values with which we invest these patterns and flows and the encounters they produce. But places are not just individual bits that fit together into a global jigsaw to make a picture of the wider world. Nor are they the smallest unit of a Russian doll of territorial scales or of a map of the nodes of a central place hierarchy. They are the product of the coming together, the conjuncture, of social relations, which pass through and, to varying degrees, 'inhabit' a place (see Graham and Healey 1999, Amin 2002, Healey 2004b, Massey 2005). It is through these social relations and the encounters that they produce that people develop a sense of what is 'at stake' and what stake they have in a place and its qualities. They get to recognise how the stakes in one situation may be related to other stakes, identities and commitments.

Sometimes attention is focused on place qualities because of conflicts among those with a stake in a place. Some may favour a new development, others may feel that it threatens their experience of a place. Some may wish to see an area conserved, to protect wildlife or built heritage. Others may worry that yet more restrictions will limit business opportunities or their freedom to do what they like with their property. Such conflicts reflect the diversity of values and ways of life that may co-exist within a particular place. But in many situations, threats and challenges to place qualities arise from outside a particular locality. Localities may become sites for major investments seen as vital to nation-state interests, such as airports, motorways and major rail routes, which are then driven through or planted down in specific places with little consideration for existing place qualities. Inner neighbourhoods in Kobe, Japan suffered in this way (see Chapter 4). Urban highway building in many North American and European cities in the 1950s and 1960s also provided a major spur to local political movements to challenge and change such practices (see Vancouver and Kobe in Chapter 4, Boston in Chapter 6, and Portland, Oregon in Chapter 7).

In the Netherlands, a political culture has developed that is much more attuned to reducing conflicts through seeking out common ground between economic, social and environmental considerations. In this situation, a municipality and its planning staff may carefully take on a specific role in limiting the domination of national political and economic priorities. Politicians and planners in the municipality of Haarlemmermeer, near Amsterdam, tried to balance powerful economic pressures to allow Schiphol international airport and the logistics complexes related to it with the promotion of liveability and sustainability for those living in the area (see Box 2.3). Haarlemmermeer's politicians and planners thus had to work on several levels at once, positioning themselves nationally as well as locally, paying attention to street-level living conditions and the international dynamics that created work opportunities for people in the area.

Box 2.3   National pressures and local place quality in Haarlemmermeer

Erik Van Rijn, a graduate of Amsterdam University, now works in the planning department of Haarlemmermeer municipality, on the western edge of the Amsterdam area. He explains:

"For Haarlemmermeer, having an international hub within its territory is about finding a delicate balance between two obvious dimensions. On the one hand Schiphol is an economic engine. It attracts businesses and creates jobs, it accelerates investments in roads and public transportation and raises the welfare level. It has positive direct and indirect economic effects on a regional and national scale. On the other hand, Schiphol has a negative impact on the quality of life in terms of noise nuisance, emissions, safety issues and spatial restrictions, mainly concentrated around the airport and its air traffic routes. As an airport region, Haarlemmermeer has a political responsibility to balance the wider-spread economic interests with the need for sound living conditions and quality of life for the residents living in the vicinity of the airport. In the view of our Council (the Mayor and Aldermen), there is a sense of urgency to seek a balance between the further growth of aviation and connected land-side investments, as well as solid investments in measures decreasing noise nuisance for a majority of the residents. In our philosophy the development of the mainport Schiphol is as important as the reduction of noise nuisance and improvement of liveability. However, the latter goal is under pressure. Therefore one of the main focus points of the current municipal policy is recovering the balance and improving liveability in Haarlemmermeer.

Haarlemmermeer is of course only one of the many actors in the decision-making process for the future of Schiphol. Besides major actors such as the Schiphol Group (the airport's owner/operator), air traffic control, KLM (the airline), the city of Amsterdam and the Province of North Holland, important decisions about the expansion of the airport (additional runways, capacity agreements and noise contours) are primarily made by the national government, usually after an extensive consultation period. In the current decision-making process for the medium-term development of Schiphol airport (up to 2020), in which every major actor is involved, we realise that both our goals (economy and liveability) should be pursued."[8]

It is often argued that 'local communities' should be given much more power to determine what happens in 'their place'. As later chapters will emphasise, there are many good reasons why the views of the people who live in a place should be given a lot of attention when collective action to enhance or change place qualities is considered. There are moral reasons relating to the rights to a 'voice' that people should have where their daily living environment is affected. There are also instrumental reasons, relating to the detailed knowledge people have about where they live, as the residents of Greenpoint/Williamsburg in New York emphasised (see Chapter 1). The residents of Ditchling (see Chapter 1) felt that their views should carry much more weight in the deliberations of the formal planning system about the future of their pub. The cases of neighbourhood management practices in Vancouver and Kobe in Chapter 4 provide examples where the views of residents were put at centre stage.

However, the communitarian ideal, where people living in a place control what happens in their locale, is not always benign in its effects. One reason for this is that some people come to play dominant roles that enable them to impose their conception of what a place should be like on everyone else. This may lead to extreme situations. In the United States, some municipalities used zoning ordinances to exclude people of different backgrounds and even in some cases people with children from particular neighbourhoods (Ritzdorf 1985). In other parts of the world, in very poor communities, local mafias and warlords may control who gets access to shelter and water. Those who promote development management with a planning focus often encounter tendencies in these directions. Vancouver planners struggled to prevent affluent neighbourhoods from becoming too exclusionary in outlook (see Chapter 4). Those working for a community development project in a very poor neighbourhood on the outskirts of Durban, South Africa, struggled to find ways to distribute development opportunities fairly, in the knowledge that other ways of distributing resources were at work in the area (see Chapter 5).

Another reason places should not be seen as autonomous, self-contained and self-governing communities arises from the links people in one place have to all kinds of other places, through social, economic and political relations. The environmental systems that flow through places set up connections with several different spans of space and time. People buy and sell to many other places. They have friends, relatives and all kinds of other contacts in all sorts of other localities. Water systems connect people in the same water-shed area (river basin area), which may even cross national boundaries. Climate systems circulate around the planet as a whole. Place management and development activity cannot therefore merely be a matter of 'acting locally'. A wider world of interactions and responsibilities has to be drawn into such work. Place management and development work that seeks to promote the progressive values of the planning project thus has to balance not only the demands and claims of different groups, and the different fields of life in places, but different levels and scales of relations and impacts.

A key challenge for such work is to find appropriate arenas where initiatives and disputes about place qualities can be discussed and balances between different claims and arguments worked out. One function of a formal 'planning system' is to provide such arenas, sometimes also linked to principles to be used when resolving particular disputes. Such systems typically apply within particular administrative jurisdictions, such as a nation state, a region or a municipality. Often such systems are developed as a kind of nested hierarchy of authority, with issues of a broader spatial reach being resolved at higher levels of government. In the case of South Tyneside, UK, discussed in Chapter 5, the municipal department charged with responsibility for development management always had to keep in mind what regional and national policy had to say on a whole raft of issues. Its ability to influence these higher-level demands was limited. In the Netherlands, the relations between levels of government reflect a stronger sense of partnership. The politicians and planners in Haarlemmermeer, and in the Amsterdam case discussed in Chapter 7, felt that their job was to give a strong voice to place qualities valued locally, to make sure that they were not ignored in wider arenas. In other planning systems, localities may have a lot of power, but within constraints that are expressed in law. This has long been the case in the US, where law courts have become major arenas in which balances between competing claims and values about place qualities are worked out. Increasingly, European Union law has come to play an important role in the planning and environmental field, while internationally, human rights law may constrain how place management and development work proceeds in a locality.

The situation is made even more complicated when it is recognised that the linkages that people in one place may have with those in other places may stretch across administrative and jurisdictional boundaries. The linkages of a large urban region such as Milan in north Italy stretch into Switzerland. Cities across the world may form partnerships with one another to promote their interests. Pressure groups promoting greater attention to particular environmental issues may work energetically to connect local struggles to global campaigning. These challenges create great difficulties for place-governance (see Chapter 3).

The challenge of finding a governance mechanism for relating local knowledge, ideas and values about place qualities to wider considerations raises another difficult issue. Daily life experiences of places are full of 'habits' and customary ways of doing things undertaken by people we know – people we can 'put a face to'. But wider relationships are often experienced more indirectly, as 'systems' and 'structures' that bear down on us, sometimes clearly visible, and sometimes so embedded in our taken-for-granted ways of thinking and acting that we barely notice them. A major preoccupation of sociological thought in the twentieth century was how to identify such systems and relate these to our lives as active agents. Systems are often perceived as the worlds of 'them' as opposed to 'us' (see Chapter 1). Anarchists and communitarians search to escape from all kinds of 'systems' and the interdependences and responsibilities they produce. Nineteenth century thinking about 'good places' and how to plan them was deeply influenced by both traditions (Hall 1988). However, these utopians were much less aware of the collective impact of human action on the global environment. They did not appreciate how far they depended on systemic relationships or how the actions of individuals and small groups can build up, over time, to produce significant changes and wider impacts. These days, it is widely understood that no community dedicated to self-sufficiency can survive if the river system on which it depends dries up. Anarchists may seek to live without acknowledging what economic organisation, government systems and the various social arrangements of civil society offer them, but yet they depend on these arrangements being available. Entrepreneurial innovators may offer new products and ideas, but how far they are noticed and carried forward depends significantly on the wider sets of relations within which they get developed and used. The international banking crisis of the late 2000s provides a revealing example of how unregulated entrepreneurial action within a system may destroy the conditions of its own survival.

Systems of relations thus shape the opportunities available to people as active agents, and how people respond to these in turn shapes these systems (Giddens 1984). Many examples can be found in the work of place management and development, such as systems of land tenure; water rights; rights to develop and use land and property; the various employment rights that may make it easier or more difficult to employ 'local' people in 'local firms'; mechanisms for redistributing tax incomes to different categories of people and places within nation states; or the way in which land and property markets work to shape the prices that have to be paid for particular sites and buildings, and the impact this may then have on who gets to live and do business in a place. Planning 'systems' are amalgams of laws, policies, formal procedures and organisational arenas created to provide ground rules for place management and development activity, enabling proactive initiatives and limiting narrow, self-interested exploitation.

So place management and development with a progressive planning orientation leads not only to ongoing development management activity, to major projects to refashion parts of cities and to strategies for enriching the future potential of an urban area. It also leads to the creation of 'planning systems' – processes, rules, norms, arenas and organisations, charged with responsibilities for particular place-shaping activities. To advance the planning project as outlined in Chapter 1, particular care is needed in designing such systems to promote both a pluralistic sensibility to the multiple ways in which places are experienced, imagined and valued, and a recognition of the complexity of the overlapping systems of relationships and responsibilities that connect specific local actions to wider relations, impacts and responsibilities.

Place making as a deliberate activity

In this chapter I have emphasised how what we recognise as 'places' get produced in the flow of human activity, as we go about doing things and as we reflect on and give meanings to the 'where' of things in our lives. These 'places' are not static, physical objects stuck on a fixed natural surface, but are as mutable as ourselves, our lives and the worlds in which we live. The clashes and conflicts, dilemmas and challenges, opportunities and potentialities of a 'placed existence' arise partly because of the diversity of what we do and what we value, but also because the various forces that shape these diverse dynamics move to different rhythms and timescales and our understandings have difficulty in keeping up and keeping track of it all. Should we then give in, and just let places and their qualities emerge? Why not leave it to the powerful elites to get on with their projects, while we rest content to live in the environments that result? Should a deliberate, progressive approach to place management and development slip out of collective attention? Or should we, as political communities in some form or other, try to take hold of how place qualities are emerging around us and seek to mould them so that they are more likely to foster an inclusive potential for human flourishing in more sustainable ways over the long term? The progressive planning project argues for the latter case. But what does it mean to engage in place management and development activities that seek not only to work for a better future, but to do so in knowledgeable and transparent ways; that is, informed by the values linked to the planning idea in Chapter 1?

A distinction is often made in the planning literature between interventions that aim to maintain place qualities and interventions that seek to transform them (Friedmann 1987). If we conceive of place qualities as continually evolving, then this distinction is less easy to make. Instead, it is helpful to think of two spheres of inter- vention initiative. In the first, the emphasis is on shaping the routine flow of on-going changes to the built environment. This involves paying attention to the ways in which people value qualities of places, promoting some qualities and resisting the emergence of others that are seen as likely to damage present and future potential- ities and values. This fine-grain work is what many people in devel- oped societies encounter as the 'street level' of planning systems, when they, or neighbours, seek a permit for some alteration to their buildings, or when they worry about rumours of a nearby develop- ment that threatens to disrupt a local view or route or to undermine an important local business or cultural facility. Experiences of this on-going work of shaping and managing neighbourhood change are presented in Chapters 4 and 5. The second sphere relates to deliber- ate transformations, either through creating new or redeveloped parts of cities or landscapes, or by promoting a new mixture of economic, social, cultural and environmental dynamics in an over- arching strategic effort. These areas of planning work are presented in Chapters 6 and 7.

Conceptions of planning as place transformation and place development are closely linked to the broader discussion of the conscious development of societies. In the twentieth century, there was a vigorous political argument about whether the state (govern- ment agencies) or the market (the initiative of private businesses) was more effective in producing development. There were also arguments about which dimension of development should take priority, with a strong tendency to privilege the economic over all other dimensions. It took some time before it was recognised that what constitutes a society is a fuzzy and multifaceted phenomenon, which emerges through complex processes in which many factors are at work. Thus no one force or agent can be called on as the primary mechanism through which development occurs. The forces that shape human life and the environments in which we live are multiple, combining economic, social, environmental and political dimensions in different ways in specific times and places (see Chapter 1).

In the later twentieth century, new debates about development emerged from the environmental movement, especially in conceptions of 'sustainable development'. These debates are infused with notions of the 'good life', which emphasise the importance of meeting basic needs in inclusive ways but at the same time not damaging the environmental inheritance that is passed on to future generations. Within this conception, there are all kinds of proposals for what living the good life should involve and how societies should change to meet the various utopias put forward.

From these debates, a concept of development has emerged that is much more complex than that held by the confident planners of the first half of the twentieth century. The old idea was that societies were on a linear development trajectory propelled by the power of economic dynamism and technological innovation, which produced 'growth' that could be distributed around a society. Places might vary according to where they were positioned on this growth trajectory. Some might be held back by temporary realignments, such as a shift in their economic base. Others might be restrained by weak governments, or temporary imbalances in the provision of infrastructures or the supply of qualified labour, or other key production factors. Exogenous forces might be needed to strengthen a local economic base, or to create value from local assets, in situations where endogenous forces were not creating their own growth dynamic. Place development interventions then meant corrective actions to help set local development trajectories back on their growth pathways.

Newer ideas, however, have abandoned such simple notions of linear development trajectories. Serious questions are being asked about the desirability and sustainability of 'growth' as an objective, especially in situations, such as in northern Japan and Eastern Europe, where populations and economies have been 'shrinking' in recent years rather than expanding. Instead, development is seen as a multidimensional concept, focused on broader concepts of what human flourishing involves and with a much stronger sense of responsibility to other peoples and future generations. We are less confident, more uncertain and more cautious in ventures that seek to shape evolving futures. We may say that we live in a 'knowledge society', where a great deal of knowledge has accumulated about how the world works. Yet this has shown us how much 'at risk' we are, how much we don't know about, from the accumulated effects of our own actions to the natural forces over which our control is limited. The project of 'mastery' over our destiny, so confidently expressed by many western thinkers a century ago, has now been replaced by a sense of the 'mystery' of our future. In this context, initiatives in place development are less about getting back on track and more about shaping possibilities for an emergent future, the shape and challenges of which may be hard to see (Hillier 2007).

Such a commitment motivates many activists, politicians and professionals in their engagement with planning, development and community development practices. However, those arriving in a locality full of inspiration to pursue fine ideals all too frequently encounter complex governance dynamics that circumscribe their scope for action. If there is no institutional 'clean slate' from which to embark on the planning project, how can progressive values be achieved in actual situations? How far can the pursuit of the planning project help to transform institutional contexts to enhance the chances of achieving greater liveability and sustainability in urban contexts, for the diverse many and not merely for the elite few? The next chapter provides a context for considering these questions.

Suggested further reading

There is a rich literature in the social sciences and the humanities on conceptions of place and space. Accessible recent contributions include:

Bridge, G. and Watson, S. (eds) (2000) *A Companion to the City*, Blackwell, Oxford.

Massey, D. (2005) *For Space*, Sage, London.

For influential contributions with a continental European perspective, see:

Ascher, F. (1995) *Métapolis ou L'avenir des villes*, Editions O. Jacob, Paris.

Sieverts, T. (2003) *Cities without Cities: An Interpretation of Zwischenstadt*, Spon/Routledge, London.

For material with a stronger emphasis on deliberate attempts to make better places, see:

Moulaert, F., with Delladetsima, P., Delvainquiere, J. C., Demaziere, C., Rodriguez, A., Vicari, S. and Martinez, M. (2000) *Globalisation and Integrated Area Development in European Cities*, Oxford University Press, Oxford.

Madanipour, A. (2007) *Designing the City of Reason: Foundations and Frameworks*, Routledge, London.

Healey, P. (2007) *Urban Complexity and Spatial Strategies: Towards a Relational Planning for Our Times*, Routledge, London, Chapter 7.

Chapter 3

Understanding Governance

Place-governance with a planning orientation

People manage and develop places in all kinds of ways as they try to improve the environments in which they live. However, one person's initiative can easily get in the way of another's. All kinds of ways of managing and developing place qualities to deal with the challenges of sharing a place with others are therefore to be found in large urban areas. Sometimes these involve providing a framework of ground rules. Or a proactive orientation may be taken, mobilising energy to undertake major projects, or enhance specific place qualities, or provide for neglected needs. Action to deal with shared problems may emerge to protect valued locales, facilities or particular qualities. Such activity is motivated by a recognition that one person's concerns are shared with others, and helps to create a 'public' that has a collective stake in what happens in a place. It reflects and constitutes a 'public interest' that those who make up such a public have in the qualities of a place.

Such activities undertaken to promote collective concerns of some kind constitute the 'governance' arrangements of a particular urban complex. The term governance is now widely used in the literature on urban and regional development and planning, although not always with the same meaning. I use the term with a broad meaning, to cover all kinds of collective activity (see Le Galès 2002, Cars et al. 2002). Others in recent years have used it to describe a shift from collective activity articulated within the arenas of formal governments – national, regional and local – and those that take place outside the so-called public sector. These may be centred in the arenas of economic activity, or in sociocultural life, or in the practices of politics that lie outside formal administration. Such a shift certainly took place in European countries in the later twentieth century. My usage of the term governance does not, however, refer to such a shift, but includes government as a part of

49

the overall deliberate collective activity involved in place management and development. The role of formal government in the governance arrangements of urban areas is very variable, nevertheless. There are many parts of the world where formal government has been largely absent from the management of urban place qualities (see the Kobe case in Chapter 4), or so distrusted that nongovernmental collective activity has come to dominate (see the Besters Camp case in Chapter 5).

All urban areas have some form of place-governance; that is, deliberate collective arrangements for place management and development. But not all of these arrangements have a planning orientation. The planning project, as I characterise it in Chapter 1, gets its particular justification by challenging place government practices to consider a broad public, with multiple stakes in a place, both now and in the future. It promotes a specific way of doing collective work, oriented to the future as well as the present and to the concerns of the many, not the few. It encourages attention to how people are connected to each other, and promotes informed and transparent discussion about collective concerns.

However, just as there are complex debates about how to understand spatial connections and place qualities, so too is there an enormous literature about the nature of collective activity, government, governance, the public interest and the public realm. This is, of course, the essence of political activity, understood in its wide meaning, rather than as merely the arrangements by which the control of the machinery of formal government is exercised. In this chapter, I expand on these debates as they affect the potential for place-governance with a planning orientation. I discuss, first, the relation between formal government and citizens. I then locate this in wider conceptions of how society is organised. I move on to consider where the power and authority to establish the public interest lie and the checks and balances on that power. I next review issues relating to the distribution of responsibilities among different levels and sectors of formal government, creating the arenas and procedures that shape how government activity is practised. Finally, I review the various instruments used to pursue collective place management and development, how these relate to each other and how they are used in collective action programmes.

Formal government, citizens and place-governance

A major issue in the debates about governance processes is the relation between formal government, wider governance processes and political communities. In the ancient Greek *polis*, the city, the state and the citizens (actually rather few of the total city population) were merged into a single conception of a 'polis' or polity, which was as much a spiritual entity as a physical structure and a device for collective management (Madanipour 2007). The practices of collective life were intertwined with the principles for the layout of the city. As Greek culture was rediscovered in Europe in the Renaissance period and began to shape both the political ideas that matured during the eighteenth century and the development of scientific inquiry, increasing tensions and criticisms built up against the authoritarian state forms of much of Western Europe, with its complex patterns of empires, nation states and city states. This critical thrust was given especial energy by the expansion of capitalistic forms of economic organisation, both in relation to the expansion of commerce (mercantilism) and the development of technology-driven industrialisation. In the eighteenth century, with the rise of a middle class (the bourgeoisie), governments were criticised for their arbitrary exercise of authority, for their corruption, for spending taxes on grand projects or on great wars, and for disregarding private property rights in the interests of promoting the projects of kings and elites.[1]

Out of these struggles a new conception of human rights developed, reflected in the developing notion of political communities organised as democratic societies, in which all adults living within a territory, eventually including women, had the right to a vote and a voice. Within Europe, this led to movements to reconfigure the control and administration of formal governments. The key arena for articulating the public interest as an expression of legitimate collective values, interests and action programmes came to be the parliaments and other elected chambers of national, regional and municipal governments. Once this change in state form was won, the focus of political conflict shifted. Different classes and factions in the society struggled for control over the agendas, laws and tax redistributions that such arenas of government could command. This class struggle could then be translated into battles over whether the needs of the working classes, or the demands of the industrial barons, or the greed of landowners and property developers, should take precedence. In Barcelona in the 1970s, political activitists could feel that they had won a harsh struggle against capitalist dominance when the dictatorship fell in Spain, creating space for a new social democratic era, committed to promoting working-class interests (see Chapter 6). In Amsterdam, municipal government was informed by the perspectives of ordinary working people for most of the twentieth century (see Chapter 7).

Within the US, the struggle between classes was less prominent. Instead, the image of the small, pioneer community seeking freedom from the oppression of authoritarian states in Europe had been established in the early days of colonisation. The protection of private property rights was embedded in the American Constitution, which became the major reference point when ideas for government-backed action to regulate private property rights in the wider public interest have been promoted (Cullingworth and Caves 2003). Within Europe, anarchist movements that resisted the idea of formal government generated all kinds of communitarian initiatives, including one of the most influential books in the Anglo-Saxon planning canon, Ebenezer Howard's *Garden Cities of Tomorrow*. Howard also promoted the idea of a self-organising urban community, carefully managing the renting out of land in order to create the resources to invest in public amenities and facilities (Hall 1988).

Despite these alternative views, the twentieth century has come to be considered as the age of big governments, centred around the nation state as the framer of laws and provider of resources for welfare services – health, education and housing for all citizens; and for major programmes of investment in physical infrastructures – transport, energy, telecommunications, water supply and drainage systems. This set up an organisational dynamic that created great bastions of government centred on each service, around which policy communities developed linking public officials, professionals and key lobby groups.

Over time, it was these policy communities that tended to shape political programmes, rather than political ideology or political representation of citizen concerns. The democratic welfare state, for all the gains in welfare that were achieved, seemed itself to have become a new form of oppressive bureaucratic state. And its organisation into functional 'sectors' made it very difficult to co-ordinate state interventions in specific areas, or even in relation to people's daily life existence. Socialist states, too, in theory dedicated to providing for the needs of the working classes, seemed to have grown into inefficient self-serving behemoths.

By the late twentieth century, the economic and political deficiencies of many socialist states had been glaringly exposed. In parallel, the idea of the democratic nation state as a benevolent and legitimate mechanism for establishing the public interest and undertaking programmes to pursue such an interest was once again an issue of critical debate (Cunningham 2002). Assumptions that the nation state was a benign mechanism for articulating the concerns of all kinds of citizens into a majoritarian collective agreement have been undermined by many factors. These include the diversity and conflicts among groups, the way policy communities drifted away from citizens, the increasing impact of supra-national government arenas, and the emergence of multinational companies working directly with regional and municipal governments. For many citizens, formal governments and the wider governance mechanisms that have grown up around them have become a distant realm, apart from daily life worlds. This unsettling of the model of a democratic welfare state raises all kinds of questions about the rights and responsibilities of citizenship, and about whether the mechanism of representative democracy (periodic voting) is sufficient in itself to establish the legitimacy and accountability of public policy programmes. In this context, citizens have sought to assert their 'voice' in other ways than through periodic voting for political representatives. This is evident in the rise of pressure groups and protest movements. The challenge by the end of the twentieth century was to find ways of giving more attention to citizen voice and initiative, while retaining the capacity to initiate and manage complex development programmes justified by a generalised collective purpose.

In this context, and especially given the diversity of citizen's voices, the planning project has much to offer. The difficulties of responding to the concerns of the many, and not only the few, while engaging in development programmes is especially acute in the arenas of deliberate place management and development. The governments of the twentieth century, with their sectoral organisation, did not find it easy to address issues surrounding place qualities, especially where such governments were large and centralised. Attention to place qualities inherently cuts across sectors. People are concerned with how to access health, welfare, education and leisure services and facilities, and realise that where they live and what transport options are available make a difference to their lives. To address their concerns, formal government organisation needs not only to work out how to link together the various sectors as they relate to a specific place. It may often be necessary to co-ordinate action between different government jurisdictions. So those promoting a planning approach to place management and development have often encouraged governments to break out of their traditional boundaries and make links with others. This raises issues about how formal government relates to the wider social organisation of a society.

Understanding governance dynamics

A commonly used conception of society identifies three spheres of life, formal government,[2] civil society and the economy. Although there are various interpretations about how to make such distinctions and what they precisely refer to, this conception is not merely a description. It seeks to identify different driving forces that shape how a society evolves (Urry 1981). Whereas some analysts in the Marxist tradition emphasised the primacy of economic drivers, other theorists argued that internal movements in the sphere of government and in civil society could also act as drivers for change. There were also debates about how the spheres related to each other. In the 1970s, a vigourous debate emerged in Western European critical social science over the relative autonomy of the state, understood as the sphere of formal government. Some argued for the primacy of the economic driver. Others said that the welfare state was pursuing its own dynamic. This made a difference to how planning work was considered. Some argued that planners and public officials generally were little more than workhorses of the capitalist system, smoothing out conflicts in order to enable capitalist-owned industrial production to expand (see Castells 1977, Cockburn 1977). Others claimed that the welfare state could be an arena or institutional site where more progressive policies could be pursued. Some of the cases in this book were initiated by social movements inspired by this latter idea.

These debates about the relation of formal government, economy and civil society moved into a new phase in the 1980s, inspired by the realisation that capitalist economies were changing from that associated with the steady expansion of industrial production towards a much greater sophistication of the commercial and financial dimensions of economic activity operating on a global scale.

Many places experienced new development pressures or the decay of their economic base. Governments were encouraged to shift to a more proactive approach, to revive economies through promoting the assets of particular places. David Harvey wrote of a transition from a 'managerial' to an 'entrepreneurial' state, to reflect this economic shift. This implied a new focus on the economic 'competitiveness' of places. By the late twentieth century, the pursuit of economic competitiveness had become a key plank of what is often referred to as a 'neo-liberal' agenda. This aim was linked to reducing the size and responsibilities of governments and enlarging those of business and communities. In the planning field, some extreme neo-liberals argued for the removal of all but a minimum regulation of urban development initiative.[3]

These conceptions emphasise the on-going struggles between the spheres of government, the economy and civil society over the control and delivery of collective action programmes. They highlight the importance of broad forces that structure these struggles. However, they tend to analyse the sphere of government as a cohesive entity, distinct from economic and social-cultural life. Yet governance activity may arise from the spheres of business and civil society, and is likely to be affected by forces both within and across the spheres. Place-governance of any kind, in this conception, is positioned within these shifting forces. Other social theorists see such struggles in terms of a tension between 'abstract systems' embodied in governing rules and practices, and people's daily life experience as active agents. The continual challenge for those committed to promoting human flourishing, in this conception, is to resist the debilitating penetration of the systems of the economic sphere and the government sphere into the life world (see Giddens 1984, Habermas 1984). This conception locates much planning activity at a critical interface between system and life world. Later chapters provide illustrations of what such 'acting at the interface' involves.

However, others have argued that our daily life worlds cannot avoid being interpenetrated with broader social forces, abstracted from our current conditions. Social theorist Michel Foucault argued that our lives are shaped by practices and beliefs that we mostly take for granted as we go about the flow of life. He suggested that we need to engage in 'archaeological' or 'genealogical' work to bring these assumptions to the surface and critically evaluate their dynamics. Others examining the sociology of the production of scientific knowledge and artefacts emphasise that 'system worlds' have their own daily life routines and modes of behaviour. This has encouraged analysts of public policy to look carefully at the 'discourses' that surface in policy programmes and ideas and in the way governing practices are performed. The aim here is not merely to unpack logics and values within a discourse, but to identify the 'mentality' – or, to use more anthropological language, the cultural perspectives – that lies behind the assumptions embedded in a discourse (see Latour 1987, Hajer 1995, Dean 1999).

Such conceptions encourage a shift of attention from a focus on broad abstractions about what structures the dynamics of government activity to give more attention to the micro-dynamics of governance processes. But once we make such a shift, and look carefully at 'micro-practices', the boundaries between broad categories of social organisation – such as divisions into the realms of the state, the economy and civil society – seem much less definite. Individual people have identities in all three spheres. A public official is also a consumer and a citizen, and lives with others in a particular place, travelling along routes shared with many others. A factory worker may also be a local councillor, or involved in an environmental pressure group. A parent may also be a school governor, or actively involved in a community group to develop better facilities for teenagers. All of these people mix up their personal, private and collective identities and domains of living in complex ways. Thus people have identities within different spheres of society and engage in all kinds of relations that connect them across whatever formal and analytical divisions are set up. Further, those involved in governance activity, including formal government, have their own daily life and networks built around doing such work. As later chapters show, these social networks often cut across the levels and boundaries of formal politics and administration.

These complex possibilities for the organisation of collective action imply that how planning activity takes place is not necessarily defined by the formal structure of a national planning system. Nor is the relation between the declaring of planning policies and strategies and what actually emerges into material form a straightforward linear relation. Policies are reinterpreted as they shift from one arena to another. They may be given new meanings. Each arena is shaped by a different balance of forces. The arenas of policy formation and those of policy 'implementation' may be shaped very differently. The result is often referred to as an implementation gap or delivery failure. Such 'gaps' arise because what governments do is just one force affecting what happens. Government actors do not have an autonomous capacity to control events, or to determine the relation between government policy and action. The arenas of policy making and government practice are sites of continual struggle, on both the big stage of political debate and in the micro-politics of the daily life of doing governance work (see Chapter 1). For the planning project, this means that planning ideas and practices cannot just be taken from some template of 'good designs'. They are not easily transferable from their specific context. New ideas will interact with existing governance practices, and how they work out will depend on how they co-evolve with the dynamics of particular governance contexts.

The relations between citizens, state and governance

A key issue for the planning project is to establish what exactly is and should be considered as relating to the public interest, part of the public realm, and therefore an appropriate focus for collective action. What people understand as appropriate boundaries between the realms of the private and the public, citizen and state, life world and system world, are fluid and porous. They are always subject to interpretation and redefinition. Further, the institutional sites, or arenas, where these interpretations and definitions are made are not static, but shift between levels of government and the spheres of society. How then do citizens, or firms, seeking to engage in collective action with others, or to influence the machinery of governments, get access to significant arenas where decisions are made? What checks and balances operate on those arenas and the actors who perform there. And how, in turn, do those who populate the worlds of formal government and other governance agencies relate to the wider society? It is necessary to look more closely at specific governance arenas and their micro-politics to explore these questions.

Place management and development activity affect people's rights to the unfettered enjoyment of a site or a building. One person's proposal to build an extra storey in red brick can disrupt a valued street scene of stone-built terraces. Another's preference for multistorey apartment living can upset neighbours who prefer houses with gardens. Addressing these conflicts was a key motivation for developing Vancouver's practice of neighbourhood design guidelines. In Kobe, Japan, some people did not want to leave their property, even though it was very run-down and most other neighbours wanted to pool all their sites to create a larger development area on which to build modern housing with much better facilities (see Chapter 4).

One of the characteristics of formal planning systems is that they provide legally based ground rules for balancing the rights of formal government, of property owners and of citizens in regard to how the public interest in land and property development is arrived at and how this is manifest in relation to particular development projects. These formal rights can then be challenged in arenas created for the purpose, such as semi-judicial inquiries, or in the courts. In other words, it is acknowledged that a decision by politicians in parliament or council chamber is not enough. These formal mechanisms are supplemented by all kinds of other checks and balances. In some countries, such as Switzerland, and in some American states, such as Oregon (see Chapter 7), specific development issues are addressed through citizen referenda, although single-issue referenda make it very difficult to identify and debate how one issue relates to another. In the twentieth century, the complexity of place management and development issues encouraged the growth of specialist expertise, and, in some countries such as the UK, a profession of planning experts. These became the staff of municipal planning offices and consultancies advising them. Expert advice then became a check on political decisions. But, as technical expertise became more disputed and less trusted, experts themselves might be seen as creatures of politicians, or of powerful lobby groups seeking to promote particular projects. In many societies, all kinds of pressure groups and lobby groups have developed within the spheres of civil society and economic activity to influence, contest and challenge decisions made in formal government arenas. Such groups and formal agencies use the media (newspapers, television, websites, blogs and so on) to publicise and debate their positions.

Governments have responded to this vigorous place-focused politics by creating formal opportunities for citizens, and all kinds of other stakeholders, to shape government policies and programmes for place management and development. These opportunities have included rights to be consulted and to object to proposals, and rights to attend inquiries held to assess issues and conflicts over projects and plans. In this way, the formal machinery of representative democracy has evolved, in the field of place-governance, into a complex multilayering of political processes. In these processes, citizens and firms have a range of potential rights and opportunities to access and influence place management and development activities, but it is often quite unclear how to use them. This leads to potential and actual inequalities among citizens and others with a stake in what happens in a place. The rights and voices of those less knowledgeable in the ways of a particular practice culture are often sidelined by those who have managed to become the 'key stakeholders' in the practice.

This has raised challenges to the way deliberate place management and development work is performed, as will be illustrated in the chapters that follow. However, these shifts, complexities and struggles also raise questions about the responsibilities of citizens and firms, as well as their rights in relation to government action. When should citizens trust the 'system' and let it get on by itself and when should they engage in mobilisation to get alternative voices heard? When should those outside the formal system try to do more by themselves? As several examples in later chapters show, protest movements from the 1960s were important in transforming government agendas and practices from the 1970s. In the later twentieth century, when initiatives to empower local communities were being widely promoted, citizens had to consider how far they should respond to formal government invitations to take on more responsibility for local place management and development initiatives. An enthusiastic engagement emerged in Brazil in the 1980s, where a movement that had begun as a challenge to dictatorship gained power in many cities in the country from the later 1980s, and finally, in 2002, the national Presidency. The movement was spearheaded by the new *Partidos dos Trabalhadores* (Workers Party, PT). This placed a strong emphasis on open and transparent government, strengthening local control of urban affairs after the heavy centralisation of the dictatorships, encouraging new channels for citizen participation in governance. It emphasised redistribution of urban resources away from benefiting elites to projects valued by the very many poor communities. One now iconic example (see Box 3.1) is that of Porto Alegre, which invented a process of 'participatory budgeting'[4].

Such initiatives have shown that groups of citizens and groups of firms can often find the imagination, organisational capacity and energy to take on governance work. But yet such work is full of potential difficulties. Resources may be difficult to come by in a sustained way. Conflicts may be difficult to resolve without recourse to formal mechanisms. Only some people may stay committed to an initiative over the long term. Keeping such governance work going is often sustained by people committed to working for the public interest. They may act as monitors of what is happening, as citizens were asked to do in Porto Alegre. They may also become intermediaries

Box 3.1   Participatory budgeting: The Porto Alegre experience

In Porto Alegre, one of Brazil's major cities, there had for some time been a tradition of neighbourhood leaders co-operating with other neighbourhoods to form loose coalitions, making demands on the municipal government. The PT came to power in the city in 1989, committed to a redistributive agenda and to expanding the participation of citizens in governance processes. The new political leaders realised the importance of doing this in practical ways through which citizens could see that their voice had a real impact on what happened. They therefore focused on the processes for determining the city's capital investment budgets, although initially there was little such investment to redistribute. Previously, investment projects had been driven by the concerns of the local elite and their alliances with higher government actors. The new Porto Alegre leaders sought to change this. But rather than creating the agenda of projects themselves, they invented a process through which people across the city got involved in identifying projects that were needed and debating how to set priorities between the demands of different neighbourhoods. Citizens were encouraged to form neighbourhood groups, in loose, informal ways, to identify and prioritise needs. They had then to elect representatives, to carry their view to forums composed of groups of neighbourhoods. These then elected representatives to what became a municipal council for setting the budget. At each level, projects were discussed and prioritised. After a while, groups involved in city-wide services, such as transport, education, health and welfare, also participated. Neighbourhood groups were asked to help in monitoring the progress of the projects that were agreed as a result of this process. These various groups and representatives did not become entrenched, as each year anyone could participate and each year new representatives were elected. As Brazil decentralised more functions and finance to municipalities, Porto Alegre municipality had greater resources to spend, and the process could be seen to have real effects in terms of providing improved conditions in the poor urban neighbourhoods that had hardly been considered part of the city until then. One commentator has calculated that, after seven years of operation, 14,000 citizens had an active involvement in the process, and significant budget redistribution occurred. The process was also not opposed by the middle classes and businesses. Instead, they appreciated the introduction of 'clean, efficient government' (Abers 1998:53).

between one arena, policy community or network and another. They may have important roles in brokering 'deals' that enable a valued project to proceed. As the later cases in this book will illustrate, politicians and officials based within a formal government context may play an important role in sustaining these initiatives and in keeping an eye out for potential difficulties – whether of the 'capture' of a local initiative by a narrow group, or the ebbing away of civil society energy. But those in other positions may also make a contribution.

This emphasises that the relations between citizen and state in the planning field are not just about the distribution of citizens' rights, or even only about responsibilities and the distribution of checks and balances on any kinds of place management and governance activity. What is important is what kind of governance practices dominate in particular contexts, and what kind of institutional culture, or way of thinking,[5] shapes expectations of what goes on and who deserves respect and trust. These practices are not static, but are continually being remade and changed through the enactment of governance practices, including planning activity. In this way, governance capacities, or civic capacities (Briggs 2008), are developed and changed.[6] The next section looks more closely at what such 'enactment' involves.

Power dynamics and governance modes

The worlds of politics and government are often presented as a stage on which individual actors with a lot of power play out their games. These dramas present such themes as heroic ambitions mired in failures, or grand rhetoric that conceals manipulation and spin, or struggles to be top dog masquerading as issues of great principle. But this front stage of political performance and media representation pushes into the background much of the daily life of governance activity and formal government.[7] Here we encounter a complex array of intersecting and competing arenas and policy communities, only some of which play out in public on the front stage of political performance and media representations. The front stage and the various back stages of government activity not only connect with each other in complex ways. Different parts of such activity may operate by different ground rules, motivated by different issues and struggles. Such different rules of the game have already been introduced in Chapter 1. Some see the arenas in which collective action work is done as a battleground between competing classes, others as an interplay of a plurality of interests within a politics structured by an accepted legal framework. More recently, the big struggles have been presented more in terms of development ideologies: the pursuit of economic competitiveness versus the search for environmentally sustainable strategies, the promotion of entrepreneurial innovation versus social cohesion and distributive justice. However, governance is not only about struggles to control the machinery of government with the aim of pursuing a particular agenda. It also involves mobilising the power to act. This means releasing positive energy, the power and capacity to do things. A key dimension of governance capacity for deliberate place management and development with a planning orientation is the ability to combine powers to control and regulate what happens with the proactive power to achieve specific projects and programmes (Briggs 2008).

Governance practices, therefore, are shaped by what are accepted by those involved as the rules of the game; that is, the way of doing governance work. These rules often clash with each other. A famous example from Chicago in the 1950s illustrates a clash between two different kinds of government practice. A key issue at the time was the allocation of sites for low-cost housing. The ruling politicians were primarily interested in granting favours to their voters and consolidating their voting power to ensure re-election. They were playing the game of what is known in the US as 'pork-barrel' politics, focused on sustaining their power base so that they could stay in charge of city government. So they approached the location issues with these objectives in mind. The planning staff, among the leading professionals of their generation, believed that sites should be allocated on the grounds of need, identified by careful analysis of living and working opportunities and access to facilities. They were motivated by their interpretation of the planning project, with its stress on knowledge about the needs of the many and its concern for a transparent and carefully reasoned way of arriving at public decisions. In the end, the politicians won (Meyerson and Banfield 1955). But pork-barrel politics, also to be found at the time in cities such as Boston (see Chapter 6), was itself criticised by political movements in the 1960s, which challenged a governance culture focused on delivering benefits to specific supporters, a culture often referred to as clientelist politics.[8] Critics showed how this could lead to longer-term environmental problems and social injustices.

There are many possible ways of playing the games of politics.

Only some of these, as the Chicago advocates of the planning project found out, sit comfortably with a planning orientation. Yet during the twentieth century, elites and citizens have come to value open and efficient government, which has the capacity to deliver on its programmes. This demand has grown in importance as public administration has become much larger and more complex in its range of activities. In this context, several modes of governance have emerged through which public policy programmes are articulated and delivered. Each of these could have a role in deliberate place management and development activity with a planning orientation, as the cases that come later in this book illustrate (see Table 3.1).

In the first two modes, the worlds of political struggle and debate are separated from that of executive action. The model of bureaucracy is underpinned by European administrative law (see du Gay 2000). This sought to take political values, as expressed in the chambers of representative democracy, and convert them into rules of conduct that officials should follow. The ambition was to squeeze corruption out of public administration. The rules provided an apparently transparent way to translate policies into legitimate government action. In the planning field, this led to the practice

Table 3.1 *Modes of governance for delivering public policy*

Mode	Examples relevant to place-governance
Bureaucratic administration	Legal land-use zoning schemes Laws defining environmental standards
Goal-driven rational analysis of action possibilities	Step-by-step procedures for preparing strategic plans that set out the connections between goal setting, analysis, evaluation and choice, often called managerial or technocratic
Ideological advocacy	Orienting all public policy initiatives by values such as the promotion of social justice or environmental conservation
Proactive, entrepreneurial initiatives	Undertaking development programmes and projects to transform localities and reconfigure local economies
Deliberative, collaborative governance processes	Involving many stakeholders in developing goals and action agendas, through open-minded processes of collective inquiry and public reasoning, often called participatory

whereby a 'master plan' for the development of a city was converted into a legal scheme defining land-use zones, norms and standards. Property owners could thus develop in line with the norms without having to establish a right to develop in the first place. Such an approach emphasised the values of certainty and transparency.[9] However, the approach had two real difficulties. First, a master plan that became fixed into a zoning scheme was often unable to keep up with the dynamic evolution of urban activities. Land-use allocations, norms and standards required continual amending. Secondly, the practice of amending plans provided an opportunity for a new kind of corruption, whereby politicians and officials could speed up plan 'variation' processes in return for some kind of personal bribe or political payment.[10] Thus, the bureaucratic model promotes formal transparency, but was undermined by a conception of the future as a fixed blueprint, rather than an unpredictable evolution. The concept of converting policies into legal rules remains a powerful influence across Europe, not least in the European Union, where rules expressing civil rights and environmental goals have now to be respected in all member states. Such rules have become significant structuring elements in the way in which place futures and spatial dynamics interrelate.

In the US, as illustrated in the Chicago example above, the idea of a 'rational planning process' was put forward as an alternative to both bureaucratic inflexibility and political clientelism. It drew on ideals about the development of knowledgeable democratic cultures, in which scientific knowledge and robust expertise available to government agencies would guide both politicians and officials. Rather than converting policies into formal rules, in the rational model skilled and knowledgeable policy experts translate politicians' policy goals into strategies and programmes of action to realise the goals. Specific decisions can then be judged not on their precise conformity with the rules embodied in a legally approved plan or development scheme, but in terms of their coherence with the argumentation of a strategy. Rather than a process of checking conformance, the emphasis shifted to performance, justified by transparent reasoning processes. Clearly, this was a challenge to practices exemplified by the bureaucratic model, but also, as is clear in the Chicago story, to political manipulation.

The planning literature is full of stories about how this rational process did not work out in practice. Yet the idea of such a process became hugely influential in the second half of the twentieth century, as government activity expanded and took on ever more difficult tasks. In Western countries it penetrated into institutional cultures in ways that led citizens to evaluate governments in terms of whether their programmes did actually deliver what they said they would. Policy initiatives thus became surrounded and informed by critical, knowledgeable debate. However, in many instances, and very evidently in the planning field, the initial ideas of a knowledgeable process of open and transparent argumentation were subverted into more formulaic practices. Plans and strategies came to be produced following templates of procedural steps in which the arguments connecting issues, policies and actions tended to get lost, and the text of plans came to be little more than records of agreements reached. Also, after ambitious attempts to develop a robust scientific basis for modelling the dynamics of urban and regional change so that futures could be predicted, it became clear that the complex choices about values and risks could neither be merely the preserve of political representatives nor grounded in agreed science.

A different approach was suggested in the 1960s. This argued that, since facts and values could not be separated, what was needed was a stronger emphasis on ideological commitment. This aimed to bring politics and executive action more closely together. Politicians should hire officials and experts compatible with their perspectives, or even, as in Italy, of the same political party. Paul Davidoff (1965), a socially committed planning lawyer in the US in the 1960s, argued for a form of 'advocacy planning' in this context. He thought that policy experts addressing place management and development issues should become cause-committed officials and advisers. His concern at that time was with social justice and in particular the plight of those living in poverty in inner cities in the US, who also suffered severe racial discrimination. The politicians and planners involved in Vancouver, in Barcelona and in Portland, Oregon (see later chapters) were deeply infused with this way of thinking. Today, environmental advocacy has been added to this agenda, sometimes in a combination referred to as 'environmental justice' (see Haughton 1999, Schlosberg 1999).

Nevertheless, how such advocacy fares as a mode of governance depends on the wider governance context. As the Chicago case just referred to shows, politicians may not be interested in the ideas that planners advocate. And advocates who speak from the community to city planners may also not be listened to. Robert Goodman, a follower of Paul Davidoff's advocacy planning ideas, describes such an encounter with Ed Logue, the Boston planner we will come across again in Chapter 6 (see Box 3.2).

Box 3.2   Neighbourhood advocacy in mid-1960s Boston

"We had gone to Boston's redevelopment office one summer morning back in 1966 to explain why our group was helping a neighbourhood organization oppose the city's official plan. That plan would have removed the neighbourhood in order to build a new city-wide high school. Our small contingent of four planners made our presentation to Edward J. Logue, the agency's director, in his office overlooking the demolition and reconstruction of downtown Boston. We said neighbourhoods should be able to choose their own planners and explained that such a process would make planning more democratic. He listened with a patient smile, asking only a few questions as he sat facing us from the end of his large conference table. When he finished, his smile vanished. 'So long as I am sitting in this chair,' he said, 'there's only one agency doing planning in this city, and that's this one!'"
(Goodman 1972:60–61)

Such cause-committed government action may be very successful in mobilising attention and capturing command over powers and resources. But ideological commitment may also have a blinkering effect, making it difficult to see new opportunities and challenges in emerging futures. And the advocacy struggle may lead to polarisation and alienation among some groups involved in governance activity, which may make access to relevant powers and resources difficult to achieve. Nor is it always easy to move from broad general principles to the precise ways in which principles such as liveability and sustainability might be achieved in a specific instance. Careful discussion and argumentation in a specific instance may be more productive in working out what really would advance key values in a particular instance.

In any case, delivering policy programmes and projects is about more than a struggle over priorities. It involves proactive work in mobilising investment and managing complex development projects. Whether on a large or a small scale, such projects can never be fully defined in advance. Politicians, citizens and other stakeholders may try to define the parameters within which a development project should proceed, but these are always liable to shift as a project proceeds. Chapter 6, which focuses on major development projects, illustrates why this is the case. In such projects, it is particularly difficult to specify in advance what the costs and benefits are likely to be, and what contribution a project will make to the public realm. It is often only when a major project gets underway that citizens and other people come to realise its implications and what is at stake.

The final mode has grown in importance as citizens have come to demand a greater voice in the delivery of government initiatives, as well as in articulating what these initiatives should be.[11] It reflects a steady shift from an understanding of democratic practice in elite terms to more participatory conceptions of democracy (see Cunningham 2002, Westbrook 2005). The central ideas of this governance mode are that purposes, strategies and specific action programmes of governance activity should not be just the work of political elites and technocrats, but that all those with a 'stake' in a place should have some kind of voice in shaping policy making, and that this should be done through discussion and deliberation, not only through technical analysis. In this way, the worlds of politics and executive action are opened up, to allow the knowledge, experience and reasoning of the political community at large to have a stronger influence on establishing government agendas and practices. The arenas for this mode of governance may then widen out significantly from formal government parliaments, cabinets and council chambers to all kinds of sites of collective discussion about future possibilities and how to develop them. The potential of a deliberative and collaborative governance mode has been developed strongly in recent years in the planning field, as it offers a way of developing a place focus in governance systems that have been organised to focus on service functions rather than on place qualities. It works by persuading many people of the value of a place focus. As the cases in Chapters 4 to 7 show, working in this way has made a valuable contribution to shaping places now considered as exemplars of liveable and sustainable urban areas. However, it is not a simple matter to develop such a governance practice. Also, if too much emphasis is placed on forming a stable agreement or consensus around a particular agenda, this may close off further discussion and close out those with different viewpoints. The Porto Alegre participatory budgeting process tried hard to limit this tendency to the capture of participatory processes by specific groups, but others who have tried to follow this example have been less successful.[12]

These different modes of doing governance work are sometimes used as abstract normative models, statements of how government work should be done. But modes of governance also exist as practices and as mental constructs that particular actors in a governance context hold in their heads, creating expectations of how government is, or should be, done. Conflicts over strategy making, project development and place-management practices are often as much about these process questions as about matters of substantive policy or impacts. Yet these modes are not necessarily exclusive. As the cases in subsequent chapters will show, modes may be combined in different ways in different situations. In recent years, governments promoting deliberate place-management and development initiatives have often sought to combine a proactive orientation with bureaucratic robustness and citizen 'empowerment' and 'engagement'. These combinations often co-exist uneasily. Nevertheless, this does not mean that place-governance with a planning orientation should be exclusively linked to a particular governance mode.

The 'where' of governance: Arenas, levels and divisions

For those struggling to understand the governance dynamics that influence deliberate place management and development, the challenge is not only to work out what rules and norms are in play. It is also important to know where the game is being played and how to get access to these arenas. Formal government systems, such as planning systems, may set up such arenas, but there are often informally constituted ones as well. Working out where the critical arenas for policy making, project development and routine place management are located in any situation thus requires careful institutional 'scoping'.

One dimension of such scoping relates to issues about levels of government. The concept that levels of government were arranged in a neat hierarchy, which could be paralleled in the design of a planning system, has already been mentioned. These days, although such hierarchical power is still often asserted, the situation is more confused. Faced with resource constraints and with a potential overload of responsibilities, national governments have often sought to devolve responsibilities over place management and development matters to subnational tiers, or to encourage more joint working between and among different levels. Such a devolution initiative provided a background to the Porto Alegre budgeting experiment (see Box 3.1). In Vancouver, the municipality already had substantial powers (see Chapter 4), in contrast to the much more limited power and authority available to South Tyneside in the UK (see Chapter 5). In recent years, there has been a widespread emphasis on devolving more formal government capacity to municipalities and other subnational levels.[13] Yet the nation, or a supra-nation such as the European Union, is still often the locus for passing laws about environmental impacts or civil rights issues. Commenting on the emerging European landscape of formal government, some political scientists have claimed that what is emerging is some form of 'multilevel' governance. This is understood as a kind of network governance, in which linkages are developed between some key government arenas, which may cut across government levels (see Gualini 2004, 2006, Sørensen and Torfing 2007). Such a development parallels the recognition of the complex social, economic and environmental networks that connect people and activities in one place to another. It acknowledges that formal territorial jurisdictions may not be coterminous with the key relations that need to be mobilised to address particular place-management and development problems and potentialities. The examples in Chapter 7 highlight the difficulties this can create for developing strategies for large, expanding urban areas. But this construction of 'network power' (Booher and Innes 2002) makes it much more difficult to identify where key arenas are located and how they connect to each other. So there is a loss of transparency.

Formally, the creation of networks and arenas between government bodies is held in check by the accountability of each body to its elected politicians and its legal specification of powers and duties. But many governance initiatives these days involve joint action between formal government and other stakeholders. These may be businesses, non-governmental organisations (NGOs) or other civil society groups. In Kobe, Japan, neighbourhood development was initiated by a residents' group (see Chapter 4). In Boston and Birmingham, major projects were carried out by an informal partnership between municipal government and private developers, underpinned by specific contracts between them (see Chapter 6). The situation is made more complex where tasks such as physical infrastructure provision are carried out by private firms within regulatory parameters set by formal government. Arrangements that are outside formal government, or that involve some combination across government boundaries, raise difficult questions about accountability. Yet such arrangements may be necessary where the power to act is spread across the spheres of government, the economy and civil society and demands some form of co-ordination.[14]

However, this does not solve the co-ordination dilemmas of place management and development. Within the traditional welfare state, as noted earlier, there were always distinct divisions of government, each with their own set of tasks and policy communities. Many of these divisions remain today. In the later twentieth century, influenced by neo-liberal ideas of making government smaller and more market driven, some tasks in some countries were handed over to the private sector. This was markedly the case as regards the provision of infrastructures: transport, water, energy and telecommunications (Graham and Marvin 1996).

The situation gets even more complicated where special place-management and development agencies are created that are semi-autonomous of formal political control. This is the case with many specialist government agencies, which are only loosely connected to a formal ministry or government department. There is also an increasing array of partnership bodies set up to link the energy of business, and/or non-governmental agencies or community groups, to government agencies. Partnership bodies are often promoted for instrumental reasons, as they increase the capacity to do things. But they are also criticised because they create yet more arenas and networks, to add to the existing array. This raises questions not only about the accountability of such arrangements but about their contribution to developing the overall governance practices and culture in an area. A partnership may achieve significant material outcomes, but it may also create hostilities and suspicions that undermine the creation of future task-oriented special-purpose agencies. It may fail to achieve material outcomes where connections with other agencies needed for a programme to succeed cannot be successfully negotiated. Keeping track of where deliberate place-management and development work is being undertaken is thus no easy task, either for outsiders or for those who work within the governance practices involved. Where key arenas are located and how they work has to be specifically investigated in each instance, as the cases that follow in later chapters will show.

The instruments of place development and management

In this chapter, I have focused on the processes of governance and the relation between formal government and wider governance processes. I have sought to emphasise how government is not some homogeneous mass but a tangle of complex relations and arenas, in which particular actors come together. Some of these arenas are played out in the public eye, in the front stage of public attention or at least scrutinised by the possibility of such attention. Others are situated in less accessible and sometimes hidden places of governance and are difficult to hold to account. In these encounters, actors struggle over how governance power should be exercised and used, over who and what should be the beneficiaries of their activity and over who has the power to decide between conflicting positions and viewpoints. But what exactly are these struggles about? What specific governance instruments are deployed in deliberate place-management and development work?

At a very general level, sociologist Anthony Giddens discussed this issue in relation to how to make a connection between the world of systems or structures and that of life worlds or agencies (see Chapter 2). He argued that the critical linkages are those related to the exercise of authority, those related to the allocation of resources and those related to the mobilisation of ideas, knowledge and information. In relation to place management and development, where land and property issues become very significant, this general idea can be made more specific[15] (see Table 3.2). The exercise of authority includes the legitimate use of force, but also the power to change legal rights, responsibilities and entitlements. Resource allocation covers direct public investment, but also financial incentives in the form of grants and tax relief. The mobilisation of ideas helps to shape the attention of relevant actors, providing framing concepts within which routine activities are evaluated, major projects shaped and ideas for spatial strategies developed.

However, as I have emphasised earlier, planning activity does not work with a clean slate as regards the tools available to pursue planning tasks. The work of development management, the promotion of major projects and the production of spatial strategies have most of the time to make do with what is available. This typically involves putting together a package of instruments. Regulating who can build where needs to be linked to what infrastructure provision will be available to support development. This in turn may be related to struggles over how much government should invest and how much can be provided by landowners and developers. Regulatory rules may need to be justified in their local application by reference to some kind of policy statement, strategy or plan. And in many parts of the world, the rules available in formal planning systems are systematically disregarded or deliberately subverted.

Table 3.2 *Instruments for place-governance*

Type of structuring linkage	Instruments of place-management and development activity	Examples
Authoritative	Regulatory restrictions	Norms and standards to which development must conform, for example in a zoning scheme
	Regulatory requirements	Developers' contributions to ameliorating adverse impacts on surrounding areas and to supporting local community development
Allocative	Direct provision by government	As in the building of physical and social infrastructures, or the construction of housing by government bodies
	Acquisition by government	Purchase, by agreement or by legal force, of land and buildings needed for 'public interest' development
	Financial incentives	Provision of grants, tax rebates etc. to encourage particular developments
	Incentives to encourage joint working etc.	Partnerships with developers, community development partnerships, community trusts etc.
Ideas	Knowledge and information	Studies and surveys, focus groups
	Key principles/criteria	Statements and images in master plans, policy guidance statements, design frameworks
	Frameworks and strategies	Strategic plans, indicative area development plans and briefs

The art of effective place-governance work centres on figuring out how to use the available toolkit to the maximum effect in a specific situation. This may, in time, lead to the creation of new tools, as experience leads to pressures to change the design of planning systems, to alter the way funding regimes work, to revise key regulations governing rights and relations with respect to access to place qualities, and so on. Such work involves continual judgements about when to 'make do', when to 'invent' and when to struggle with some authority to get regulations changed and resource flows altered. How such judgements are made, however, reflects the ideas that direct place-governance activity. Later chapters show examples of all these responses. Place management and development with a planning orientation may deploy all the instruments in Table 3.2, but it is how they are combined and directed that expresses the orientation.

Achieving the planning project

In this chapter, I have emphasised that deliberate place management and development oriented to collective purposes takes place as a response to place-management and development problems and issues about which people are troubled. Such activity is inevitably located in specific contexts formed by past governance practices and in response to pressures and forces acting at the time. The institutional dynamics of governance have structuring power to shape what people think it is important to do and how they go about it. In analysing, critiquing and undertaking place-governance work, it is always important to pay careful attention to these dynamics as they are manifest in particular situations. This also implies a need for great caution about transferring lessons from one situation to another. I have identified some key aspects that help to focus such careful attention.

However, governance dynamics are not fixed and static, though sometimes they seem so. They are themselves the result of a historical evolution of struggle between citizens and state – over modes of governance, over the division of responsibilities and arenas and over the design and use of instruments of government action. These struggles happen in the visible macro-arenas (parliaments, national government executive offices) where laws get passed and resources are accumulated and distributed for public purposes. They also take place in the fine-grain, micro-practices of the daily life of governance work. They are reflected in how individuals and work teams perform the tasks they are set, or set for themselves. The implication is that the planning project needs to pay attention both to the level of the design of formal systems for place-governance and to the practices through which such systems are brought to life.

As I stated in Chapter 1, planning is a political project. It is part of the governance resources of a political community. It contributes to the governance capacity of such a community. But it is not just any governance activity. The project promotes a specific orientation, as outlined in Chapter 1 (Box 1.1). Its value lies not only in encouraging conditions that may enhance the potential for human flourishing through promoting the inclusive liveability and sustainability of places in ways that recognise interdependencies and connectivities. It also emphasises the importance of creating and sustaining a vigorous, active and inclusive political community, in which a politics of place and spatial responsibilities can be articulated. It stresses the importance of considering long-term potentialities and threats, not just immediate problems and issues. It focuses attention on the linkages between issues. It emphasises not merely the role of multiple perspectives on problems, issues and future imaginings – that is, a pluralist viewpoint – but the value of knowledge thus mobilised in assessing and developing strategies, projects and the routines of impact assessment. And it asserts the importance, in a context of knowledgeable and contestable governance activity, of honesty and transparency in making the connections between policies and actions, between the rhetorics of governance intentions and the choices actually made in the flow of action.

I have also argued that the quality and orientation of place-governance are not to be found in debating chambers and great political struggles. It lies in the micro-practices of governance activity. These may be affected by broad structuring forces of various kinds, but how they work out and how people as active agents identify and exploit 'moments of opportunity' to change what has been going on are highly variable.[16] In the chapters that follow, I explore these micro-practices. Chapter 4 focuses on improving the qualities of urban neighbourhoods, through creating both new ways of thinking about neighbourhood futures and new ways of doing governance work. Chapter 5 expands this exploration of small-scale, fine-grain development management work by looking at two quite different situations: the routine work of land-use regulation in a so-called developed world context,[17] and the challenging work of improving living conditions in a poor, 'informal' neighbourhood on the periphery of a developing world urban metropolis. Chapter 6 returns to the developed world, to look at major urban projects that have created new locales valued by both citizens and visitors. Chapter 7 then switches the focus of attention from parts of cities to the production of conceptions and strategies for cities considered as 'wholes'. The cases have been selected because they have been acknowledged as making significant contributions to improving place qualities and as exemplars of the planning project.[18] Through the cases I focus on three issues, to which I return in Chapter 9. I consider how far the planning project, as presented in Chapter 1, has been realised. I examine how it was achieved in each instance, and how the opportunities for such an outcome were affected by the specific context and wider forces affecting the situation. In doing so, I focus also on the active work those involved carried out, not only to bring about better place qualities, but also to enhance the governance capacity to do so in the future.

Suggested further reading

There is a very wide literature on which the discussion in this chapter draws. Each country has its own literature on its political and governmental system. Within political science, the field of comparative politics has approaches and methods for analysing political systems. A particular strand, political sociology, has provided helpful inspiration to analyses of place-governance activity, especially the strategic relational approach developed by Bob Jessop, for which see:

Jessop, B. (2002) *The Future of the Capitalist State*, Polity Press, Cambridge.

There is also a rich literature on forms of democracy, see:

Cunningham, F. (2002) *Theories of Democracy: A Critical Introduction*, Routledge, London.

Nearer to the planning field are two other areas of academic work: the analysis of public policy and urban governance. For helpful material from the policy analysis area, see:

Kingdon, J. W. (2003) *Agendas, Alternatives, and Public Policies*, Longman, New York.
Fischer, F. (2003) *Reframing Public Policy: Discursive Politics and Deliberative Practices*, Oxford University Press, Oxford.

Hajer, M. and Wagenaar, H. (eds) (2003) *Deliberative Policy Analysis: Understanding Governance in the Network Society,* Cambridge University Press, Cambridge.

Rose, R. (2009) *Learning from Comparative Public Policy: A Practical Guide,* Routledge, London.

Within the planning field, there have been contributions to the analysis of urban regimes, see:

Fainstein, S. and Fainstein, N. (eds) (1986) *Restructuring the City: The Political Economy of Urban Redevelopment,* Longman, New York.

Contributions have also been made to the analysis and promotion of particular governance modes and practices, see:

Fischer, F. and Forester, J. (eds) (1993) *The Argumentative Turn in Policy Analysis and Planning,* UCL Press, London.

Healey, P. (1997/2006) *Collaborative Planning: Shaping Places in Fragmented Societies,* Macmillan, London.

Briggs, X. d. S. (2008) *Democracy as Problem-Solving,* MIT Press, Boston, MA.

Innes, J. E. and Booher, D. E. (2010) *Beyond Collaboration: Planning and Policy in an Age of Complexity,* Routledge, London.

There are also rich case study accounts, including two famous studies:

Meyerson, M. and Banfield, E. (1955) *Politics, Planning and the Public Interest,* Free Press, New York.

Flyvbjerg, B. (1998) *Rationality and Power,* University of Chicago Press, Chicago.

Chapter 4

Shaping Neighbourhood Change

Meeting the challenges of neighbourhood change

Neighbourhoods are where we live and establish daily patterns as we move around and beyond them. For some, a neighbourhood is a vaguely sensed backcloth as we scurry along to somewhere else. For others, it is where we relax, chat to passers-by, call at the corner shop, worry about what other people around us do in case they disrupt our living environment with visual or noise intrusions. It is where our intimate private lives bump up against the strangers who are our neighbours (Sandercock 2000). Sometimes the resultant tensions are too great. New people move in with different habits or tolerances. People living elsewhere start using our neighbourhood as a through route. Local green spaces get littered because no one is managing them. Governments propose large projects that threaten massive disruption, which may be temporary or permanent.

The challenge of sharing our living space with others and adapting to continually changing conditions makes the governance of the place qualities of neighbourhoods a key arena for efforts to help improve the conditions for human flourishing. Yet it is also difficult to establish place-governance practices in which attending to micro-level neighbourhood qualities in a planning-oriented way becomes routine. Such practices cannot be performed solely by some well-meaning official or community development worker on their own, delivering services in a paternalist way to beneficiaries. There need to be ways in which neighbours themselves can contribute to shaping neighbourhood management practices, expressing their aspirations and their knowledge of what goes on, as the residents in the Greenspoint/Williamsburg case in Chapter 1 insisted on. This implies that place-management practices focused on improving neighbourhood qualities need to develop a porous and interactive relationship between governance activity and civil society more widely. The two cases to be discussed in this chapter are examples in which residents became actively involved in neighbourhood management practices. They have been selected not only because they brought significant benefits to residents. They also resulted in city-wide improvements, to the quality of the urban environment across the city in one case (Vancouver) and to the relations between civil society and formal government in the other (Kobe). Both provide rich exemplars of the aspirations of the planning project as identified in Chapter 1.

In these two cases, I explore what it takes to create and sustain neighbourhood management and development practices in which those affected get to have a say in what happens in their locality. What arenas become significant? What governance instruments prove necessary? Through this exploration, I examine how conditions for people in neighbourhoods were improved, and how such place-governance with a planning orientation can come to have wider impacts on the larger political community.

The two cases illustrate place-governance practices that have evolved in cities that are experiencing the pressures of urban growth and transformation. Urban growth means not only the expansion of a city onto the areas around. It also involves changes in the position and values of existing parts of cities. Such changes may also happen without overall growth, as city economies and societies shift in their fortunes and values. In such dynamic situations, affluent neighbourhoods may look for ways to protect themselves against intrusion by those seeking to share their advantages. Poorer neighbourhoods may attempt to improve conditions in their own locales or search for ways to protect their neighbourhoods against exploitation by developers who spy an opportunity to 'upgrade' an area for higher-income people. In many cities (such as Chicago and Boston in the 1950s, see Chapters 3 and 6) the result can be a politics of neighbourhood competition, where politicians see themselves as advocates of their electoral area, seeking to maximise their area's share of the municipal budget. Neighbourhoods without economic and political resources suffer in such a context, but so too does the public realm of the wider urban context, as opportunities, services and infrastructures for the overall urban area get neglected.

The first case presented in this chapter illustrates a different approach, which, through a slow evolution, managed to combine detailed attention to the qualities of specific neighbourhoods across the city while keeping the wider public realm of the city and its residents in mind. Vancouver lies on the Canadian west coast, where the Rocky Mountains meet the sea. In formal government terms, it is within the large, resource-rich province of British Columbia, and is an amalgam of municipalities, while the City of Vancouver is one of a group of municipal jurisdictions across which the Vancouver urban area now sprawls (Tomalty 2002). Within this wider urban region, growth has been rapid in recent years. My account focuses on the City Council area. The city's planning approach combined sensitive attention to social conditions, urban design and how to involve residents, property owners, builders, developers and architects in a participative approach to produce neighbourhood development guidelines. They continually sought to understand issues through the daily life experience of residents and other stakeholders (Grant 2009). This case acts as a counterpoint to the stories of Ditchling in South East England and Nazareth in Israel with which this book started. In those cases, the interface between residents and the actions of formal planning processes or formal government initiatives led to increased alienation (in Ditchling) and disruption of residents' sense of safety and security (in Nazareth). In Vancouver, in contrast, the interface was enriched and sustained, while material benefits were delivered and a way of 'living with neighbours' encouraged that enabled individual initiative to proceed, but with some regard for the public realm of neighbourhood life in both its local and wider dimensions.

Producing neighbourhood development guidelines: Vancouver, British Columbia[1]

Today, Vancouver has a reputation as one of the world's most attractive and liveable cities (see Figure 4.1). This is partly a result of its location on Canada's mountainous and mild Pacific coast. But Vancouver residents also know that it is a result of the approach to managing urban development that has evolved responsively and inventively over the past 35 years. The city is a twentieth century phenomenon. There were fewer than 3000 inhabitants in 1900, but over 1.9 million in the wider urban area by 2001, with half a million in the municipality of Vancouver itself, a number that has grown substantially in recent years. As with most North American cities of this period, for many years it grew steadily through the grid-layout subdivision of rural land into road and service layouts and building plots. Major landowners (in Vancouver's case, the Canadian Pacific

Figure 4.1   *A Vancouver overview*

Source: © I-stock

Railway was especially important) and, increasingly, the local council were responsible for the overall grid layouts and the specification of hook-up requirements to services and the regulation of the amount of development allowed on a plot. Individuals then built single housing units, varying in size with individual resources and lot sizes. Design fashions and building materials varied from period to period, but overall the result was a low-density city, with growing problems of traffic congestion and pollution. As the city grew, and changed from a centre for export of primary products (timber and minerals) to a major regional service centre, pressures built up, especially from real-estate developers, for redevelopment of harbour areas and low-density residential areas. This investment was combined with major freeway projects to open up accessibility across the city area.

Vancouver City Council has considerable administrative and legal independence from the provincial government (British Columbia) and the Canadian national government, though it can still access national funding programmes. It can thus evolve its own regime for regulating land and property development rights without having to conform to higher-tier strategies or legal requirements. Initially, as in so many western cities at this time, the politicians and city planning officials facilitated the development impetus, inspired

by ideas about modernist urban design. These design ideas emphasised cities with high-rise apartment blocks and multilane freeways
to accommodate the rapidly developing shift from rail to road as the
favoured transport mode. However, Vancouver residents, as in
many other cities in the 1960s, protested at these disruptions to their
own idea of what their city should be like. They challenged what
they saw as the nexus between the city council and real-estate developers, so common in many cities in the neighbouring US (see
Fainstein and Fainstein 1986, Logan and Molotch 1987). They
focused attention on the values of neighbourhood liveability, citizen
participation and community development activity. Their activites
resulted in a change in government regime and a new planning staff,
given substantial discretion by the new political leaders. The political initiative was supported by a wider social movement in the city
and elsewhere, which struggled for more equitable approaches to
urban development and more participatory approaches to determining planning programmes and projects. The values of the planning
project were carried forward by this movement.

The City of Vancouver as an administrative jurisdiction covers
the core of an expanding urban area. City politicians and real-estate
interests have often worried about whether this core would lose out
compared to other parts of the area. Accommodating growth in the
core meant increasing densities on single-lot sites as well as redevel-
oping the extensive waterfront areas. Yet residents were increasingly
concerned about both the major schemes and the steady shifts in
their localities as plots were split up and apartment blocks were
built, and as people converted their own house units into two (often
by converting lower-storey garage space to a second unit for rent, to
help pay the mortgage). Neighbourhood associations and protest
movements grew up to challenge even very small changes on plots
(see Box 4.1).

What evolved in Vancouver was an open-minded and flexible
way of managing physical change in neighbourhoods, in discussion
with residents and other groups. In effect, a new 'practice culture'
has been invented for managing development change. The result for
living conditions in the city has been a reduction in car use and
ownership, a lively street life, considerable social and ethnic mixing
in neighbourhoods and improvements in people's health. The
approach managed to keep at the forefront of attention the relation
between the parts of the city and the city as a whole, both as regards
social differences in income and lifestyle, and as regards the different places in the city. Since the 1970s, there have been political and

Box 4.1   Developing neighbourhood guidelines in Vancouver

Until 1970, the provincial government had held the power to draw up zoning regulations.[2] However, a residents' association in an affluent neighbourhood persuaded the City Council to negotiate greater autonomy from the province, to allow the council to develop its own approach to zoning. Residents had hoped to protect their properties from intrusion by neighbours who wanted to increase the numbers of dwelling units on their plots, either by new building or by turning large houses over to multiple occupation. The City Council initially attempted a revised zoning code that struck a balance between these neighbours with competing interests, and allowed the neighbourhood association to initiate prosecutions of those who violated the code. But the association, dominated by preservationist interests, hired its own consultants, who proposed a plan that would have cut off all opportunities for those seeking to change the way in which plots were used. A newly elected City Council, committed to a participatory approach, then looked for a way to pull back from this polarised position. Working with neighbourhood association members, an approach was developed that provided a zoning framework that allowed for smaller lot sizes and some subdivision and redevelopment,

$\rightarrow$

staffing changes in the city council and major changes to the social composition of the city. In 2000, less than half of residents had Anglo-Canadian backgrounds and a quarter spoke Chinese as their first language. However, the commitment to a responsive and creative approach to promoting the liveability of the city has helped to convert a political and planning ideal into what is now an appreciated daily life context for residents of a cosmopolitan city, as well as a pleasurable city experience for visitors.

It is not all good news in this 'liveable city' and there is a lively climate of critique of planning activity. The city also has some of the worst areas of concentrated poverty in the whole of urban Canada. Homelessness, drug addiction, unruly and neglected children are very evident on the margins of Vancouver's city centre, in Downtown Eastside. This neighbourhood accommodated a population of restless, homeless former panhandlers, drug addicts and psychiatric patients, along with different ethnic groups, some with well-established businesses and some more recent migrants. There are many reasons for this. However, it must be acknowledged that

→

but within a framework of design principles and place-management guidelines that sought to maintain the overall ambience of the area. The consultation process encouraged all parties to think carefully about what kind of area they wanted their neighbourhood to be.

Soon, other neighbourhoods wanted similar 'guidelines' and the practice developed and evolved across the city. Different neighbourhoods had different conditions and all were subject to changes, so that the guidelines differ too. Some parts have become predominantly Asian, with very different ideas about what an urban ambience should be like, while others are very mixed, so that single dwellings are interspersed with multistorey apartment blocks even in the same street block. Nevertheless, the emphasis on the overall 'feel' of the area, its landscaping, the relations between streets and interior spaces and easy movement in and around an area is to be found in all the statements. This is linked to a general expectation among residents, developers, architects and builders that they all should have a say in how a neighbourhood might develop and should respect one another's demands. The city planning team is trusted in its efforts to achieve a result that promotes liveability and quality in the overall urban environment. Developers and architects have come to work creatively and profitably within this expectation.

one factor is the neighbourhood planning approach itself, which has tended to reduce the amount of low-cost rental accommodation, often produced in the past by substandard division of larger units, at a time when house prices and rents overall have been rising fast. In line with its neighbourhood-based, community development approach, the City Council has been working with voluntary initiatives to sustain and improve conditions for low-income residents and resist upscaling pressures. This has involved encouraging developers of new build projects to provide community facilities and social housing, promoting social enterprises of various kinds, assisting other initiatives and attempting to resolve conflicts between the various groups that co-exist in these areas.

In the Vancouver case, then, the City Council, with its planning department, became a key arena in which the energy and philosophy of a social movement took up residence, sustaining the commitment to promote liveability in diversity in a rapidly changing west coast North American city. Learning through experience but focused by a commitment to the planning project as understood in this book, a city planning team, learning along with residents, helped to create not only a city of liveable neighbourhoods. They also helped the growth of a political community that valued paying attention to place qualities, in both its neighbourhood parts and the city as a whole. Politicians of all parties express their support for this kind of planning, because they know that their constituents value it (Grant 2009). Similar commitments informed cases to be discussed later in this book, particularly in Barcelona, Spain (Chapter 6) and Portland, Oregon, (Chapter 7).

The value of making connections between the fine grain of the urban fabric and the overall qualities of a city has been underlined in the work of US urban designer Jonathan Barnett (2003, 2006). He cites a case from Omaha, Nebraska, in the US Midwest. A proposal for a new Wal-Mart superstore was being discussed at a public hearing in the city of Omaha, and someone asked Wal-Mart's architect why the building being proposed looked so much less attractive than a recently built Wal-Mart in a nearby town. The architect replied that this other town had design guidelines, while Omaha did not. This exchange set the city leaders thinking. They began to wonder how having design guidelines might not only defend themselves against poor-quality proposals from developers, but, as in the Vancouver case, promote more attention to place quality across the city. This resulted in an initiative encouraging all neighbourhoods to develop their own thinking not just about design guidelines for their areas, but about how their part of the city related to other parts. In this way, citizens across the city became involved in specifying the guidelines for each other's neighbourhoods and in shaping an understanding of what Omaha itself as a place could be (Barnett 2006).

In cases such as these, politicians, planners and citizens have all, at one time or another, acted as guardians of values and issues that concern them all; that is, of the expression of their interest as a public. But the central institutional site in Vancouver for sustaining the commitment and orientation to the planning project over decades was the city planning office. Some planners working for the City Council dedicated most of their career to the project of reshaping their city, its development community and its political community. However, it is not always the planning office that plays such a role. In some cases, it may even impede this kind of project. I now turn to a very different situation, where activists from civil society had to work much harder and much longer in a struggle to get the formal government authorities to pay attention to neighbourhood living conditions.

Civil society takes the initiative in Kobe, Japan[3]

Kobe, at the western end of Japan's enormous central coastal urban belt, is a city of some 1.5 million people. Port and industrial areas fringe the coast, with mixed commercial and residential areas in and around the old urban core, and newer residential areas spreading up hillsides towards more mountainous areas to the north (see Figure 4.2). By 2007, it was one of 13 cities in Japan designated to have a high degree of municipal autonomy in policy areas, including on social welfare, public health and urban planning. It is also located in an earthquake zone and suffered a very serious earthquake in 1995.

At the turn of the century, any visitor to the area interested in urban governance would have been struck by the very vigorous involvement of citizens in neighbourhood planning and the provision of welfare services and cultural facilities. 105 groups of residents were registered with the city council in the form of *machizukuri* councils,[4] and a study in 2000 found a total of 200 civil society groups involved in all kinds of activities (Funck 2007:141). Many are linked to a particular neighbourhood, but some provide services or promote an activity across the city. Some draw up neighbourhood development guidelines, of a similar nature to those in Vancouver but reflecting a very different urban reality. In older parts of the city, the emphasis has been on environmental improvements, especially creating more open spaces and green areas in a very crowded city, on expanding the amount of social housing,[5] and on the reorganisation of a structure of very narrow streets and tall buildings. There is often a concern to provide modern facilities (access for ambulances and fire equipment, as well as cars), and some people are interested in preserving the traditional urban character. In some areas, the emphasis is on reducing the scale of pollution in an area. Many such groups have started up in response to urban planning projects initiated by the municipality, sometimes at the municipality's request but often in critical opposition. Others have focused on managing public spaces and providing community facilities. These *machizukuri* councils co-exist in Kobe with long-standing neighbourhood associations, and are sometimes in conflict with them. In addition, there are some associations of shopkeepers that manage shopping streets and promote their interests. All this suggests a very active civil society focused on urban management. The Kobe experience exemplifies Sorensen and Funck's comment that 'many Japanese people demonstrate an enormous willingness and talent for working together with their neighbours in common

Figure 4.2   *The city of Kobe*

Sources: Map: Kayo Murakami. Photo: City of Kobe.

projects' (2007:277). Where, then, is formal government positioned in all of this?

In Vancouver, the City Council and the planning department had a key role in encouraging and working with community initiatives, but this grew out of local protest movements in the late 1960s. In Kobe, too, protest movements in the 1960s led to changes in local government. However, the power of the municipality in the Japanese government structure was much weaker than in Vancouver. It was possible for municipalities to prepare land-use plans using a few use categories designated in national law.[6] These gave property owners rights to develop according to the use category specified. In 1968, municipalities were given the power to approve such plans themselves. It was only in 1980 that they gained the power to prepare 'district plans' that specified area layout details and were legally enforceable. Such plans could only be prepared where there was a high level of agreement among those affected, which limited their use to small areas (Sorensen 2002).[7] It is only since 1999 that municipalities have gained the power to pass their own legally binding ordinances using their own specifications of norms and standards, with the continuing requirement for a very high degree of consultation and agreement among all parties. And until 1998, there was no general law that allowed civil society organisations to exist as formal legal entities independently of central government approval.

Kobe municipality has been a pioneer in Japan in promoting both citizen-generated ideas about neighbourhood development and welfare provision and in providing mechanisms to enable civil society groups and non-profit organisations to exist (Watanabe 2007). In Kobe, such a pioneering civil society initiative has been on-going since the 1960s, and provided a model in the 1990s to other cities and campaigns seeking to reduce the autocratic and paternalist power of national government and to strengthen municipal government. Some accounts of Japanese urban management suggest that, at the end of the twentieth century, a kind of suppressed energy was released in civil society focused on improving the daily life experience of what is now a highly urbanised nation. Does Kobe provide a model for advocates of community self-governance and citizen empowerment?

Just as the Vancouver 'achievement' is not so easily transferable, the Kobe experience also has a very specific history and was unusual even in the Japanese context (Evans 2001, cited in Sorensen 2002). Japan's government traditions have for centuries reflected a high degree of centralism. This was reinforced in the twentieth century, which saw a massive expansion of the national state and the bureaucracies that served it. The national government operated hierarchically, with lower levels of government (prefectures and municipalities) organised to ensure compliance with national directives and aims (Sorensen 2002:157).[8] This top-down system was disrupted after the disaster of Japan's military project in World War II and the subsequent US occupation, but came to be reconstituted from the 1950s. It proved an effective vehicle for the new national project of rapid economic development, pursued especially by the promotion of industrial development and major infrastructure schemes across the country. Later commentators have come to refer to Japan as the 'development' or 'construction' state, as the major construction companies that grew from this policy thrust had very strong connections to the political elites of the dominant Liberal Party. As the national project gained momentum, the country, already highly urbanised, saw massive urbanisation and the growth of the enormous megalopolis that stretches from Tokyo in the east to Osaka and Kobe in the west. Some of this was in the form of planned settlements (Sorensen 2002, Ishida 2007), but much consisted of sprawling suburbs enabled by very weak land-use regulation. The 'construction state' was little interested in liveability or environmental consequences, urging citizens to put up with poor living conditions for the sake of the national project.

Living conditions in cities grew steadily worse. As Sorensen records:

> By the early 1960s, the enormous scale of industrial investment and lack of controls on pollution emissions resulted in some of the worst concentrations of air pollution in the world, and high levels of waste emissions into rivers and streams. In addition, the weak zoning regulations meant that many of the worst polluters were situated in close proximity to high-density residential areas. (Sorensen 2002:201)

This led in the 1960s to an assertion of citizen power, as people protested about the impact of rapid economic development and infrastructure investment on environmental quality and living conditions. One of the very first *machizukuri* councils emerged in Kobe in 1963 as a voluntary initiative to protest against the impact of road traffic growth and the quality of the public realm in the area of Maruyama. This was promoted by labour union leaders and did not last beyond the late 1970s, but another initiative, in the Mano area in Kobe (see Box 4.2) and set up in the mid-1960s, continues to this day. Its origin lay in concerns about the impact of air pollution on children's health. For some years it fought the local government authorities, but later came to work with the municipality, helping to shift the approach to managing the built fabric in older parts of the urban area from a focus on redevelopment to rehabilitation. Ideas about local place management developed slowly, with citizens working with the municipality and with outside expert advice, eventually funded by national and local government, to produce informal guidelines for future development. (These outside experts were often also involved in progressive groups, and/or were academics working with their students.) When national legislation allowed municipalities to produce their own district plans in 1980, Kobe municipality became one of the pioneers in making use of it.

It is partly this history that accounts for the large number of civil society organisations to be found today in Kobe. The building of such governance capacity has taken time to evolve, but has provided a robust mechanism for interrelating local government and civil society initiative, capable of addressing the fine-grain routine and the extreme challenges of post-disaster reconstruction. Kobe's experience was paralleled in other Japanese cities, as the political and economic troubles of both the national and local governments set in during the 1990s.[9] This wider context fostered a climate and a moment of opportunity for a strong movement to strengthen the powers of municipalities, particularly in the area of urban planning and development. The movement was fuelled in part by citizens' concerns about the quality of their place of living and their increasing distrust of distant and paternalist government. However, it is still not clear how far these concerns have really been taken on board by government bodies. Moreover, the promotion of development elsewhere in the city, particularly in the city centre and the waterfront areas, has led to significant social shifts in the population of inner neighbourhoods. Many people also moved away from inner urban areas in the immediate aftermath of the earthquake and never returned. Building structures may have been improved, but the old social fabric has suffered. And the city council does not always pay attention to what its citizens demand (Hirayama 2000). Some commentators on these developments in Japanese society wonder if the momentum for civil society involvement will persist into the future without the energy of women, many more of whom are now themselves part of the workforce. Yet the practice of collaborative

Box 4.2   Mano machizukuri in Kobe, Japan

Machizukuri ('community-making') groups began to appear in Kobe and other areas in Japan from the 1960s. One of the leading such groups emerged from the Mano neighbourhood in Kobe. A *machizukuri* study group was formally established there in the 1980s, involving 27 community members (including neighbourhood organisations, shopkeeper and industry organisations and others), four academics and four city government officials

(Sorensen 2002:272). It built on an earlier neighbourhood activist group that had been working on local improvements since the 1960s. These earlier experiences helped both citizens and municipal politicians and officials to learn a new practice together. The group included women, traditionally excluded from political organisations. It is the women and children who, until recently in Japanese society, lived most of their daily lives in their home neighbourhoods, men being much more socially involved in their workplace networks (Funck 2007). In 1981, Kobe municipality took the pioneering step of enacting the first *machizukuri* ordinance, a set of policies and

Earthquake devastation

guidelines about how the local administration would relate to these voluntary groups. This gave more status to *machizukuri* councils. The local administration set up an 'expert despatch system' to provide technical help to these councils, and allowed formal agreements to be made between the City Council and the *machizukuri* councils over local development and environmental management issues

Discussing a new housing scheme

→

→

Post-earthquake rebuilt housing, with setbacks

(Watanabe 2007:51). By 1995, 12 *machizukuri* councils were registered under Kobe's 1981 ordinance, and a further 16 had some degree of recognition (Funck 2007).

Then, in 1995, a massive earthquake struck the city. Over 4000 people died, highways collapsed and a great deal of injury was caused to people, place and property. In Kobe and across the nation, this disaster focused a spotlight on urban living conditions and how to manage them. One lesson was that the 'construction state' had not been as technically good at construction as it claimed, and the story of the collapsed highways unravelled to reveal poor technique and corrupt contracting practices. A second lesson was that civil society across the nation responded with a surge of volunteer effort to provide assistance to the stricken area. Thirdly, the national government was slow to organise a relief effort. Finally, organisations such as Kobe's *machizukuri* groups were the most effective agencies organising initial relief and were able to act as key players in the longer-term reconstruction effort. The networks they had built up in their local areas, and their connections within and beyond the municipality, provided a mobilisation and organisation capacity that helped reduce the spread of fire, rescued the elderly and infirm, and provided shelter. The *machizukuri* groups in areas such as Mano, by this time formally recognised by the City Council, then did significant work in developing reconstruction plans and guidelines, drawing on the practices that had built up within the city since the late 1970s. As the reconstruction effort has been completed, the councils have continued to act to pay attention to the quality of local environments and promote conditions for improved liveability, in a fluid relation with the work of the municipal council. As a result, many people in Kobe have come to participate in active ways in local place management and development.

Source: Taken from a series of newsletters (1995–96) called 'Mano-ke Ganbare' (Cheer-up Mannoko!).

neighbourhood organising also builds on deeper roots in Japanese culture, where the formation of individual identity is understood as deeply interlinked with the wider relations of social life, and with the natural environment (see Hamaguchi 1985, Nishida 1921/1987).

In this case, an old paternalist blurring of the boundaries between government and civil society has been replaced by a remoulding driven by practices initiated within civil society. It was residents' concerns about the quality of their living and working environments that provided momentum for the transformation of governance practices and cultures. Rather than a rapid transposition from a social movement to a formal government arena and practice, the capacity for place management in Kobe has been developed through on-going mobilisation by activists and concerned residents. These groups have continually challenged the municipality's claim to be the sole representative and guardian of the public realm of place development. Their approach to liveability has been able to integrate social welfare and physical development concerns in a productive way. They have both represented and been an active force in changing Japanese urban governance practices, although the overall gains in urban living conditions have so far been limited (Hirayama 2000), and changing the governance cultures of urban administrations is itself a long-term project. In contrast to the Vancouver case, those promoting the planning project in this instance were as much the citizen activists and the expert advisers on whom they drew, as they were city officials formally charged with planning functions. Their concerns co-exist within the City Council's declared vision with the promotion of the international profile of Kobe through major projects (see http://www.city.kobe.lg.jp/foreign/english/index.html). And sustaining citizen activism over a long period is always hard.

Key capacities of 'street-level' place-governance

Both these cases show that governance institutions are not fixed, monolithic government structures, but are themselves continually evolving. The citizens of Vancouver and Kobe helped to create the formal local government organisation and practices that they now have. Civil society energy carried transformative power into the government sphere. Collective concerns about the liveability of neighbourhoods were critical in energising these political transformations.

The experiences show how attention to the street level of governance activity increased knowledge of residents' material needs and concerns. They developed understanding of how particular place-management instruments, such as Vancouver's design guidelines, could work out. In Vancouver and Kobe, the combined efforts of residents, officials and stakeholders helped not only to create real material improvements to the qualities of places, but also place-management practices with the capacity to meet new challenges in which residents, by and large, could place their trust. In this way, inspired by a planning orientation, ideals were made active elements of place-governance capacity.

In both cases, there were pre-existing practices of place management. Vancouver had a simple system of land-use zoning rules, designed to expand urban areas by a process of regulated subdivision. Kobe had been given higher-authority regulations about appropriate land uses and building norms for particular areas. The challenge for the activists in Kobe and the city planners in Vancouver was to work through, in and around the inherited practices, to create new ways of doing things. They did not draw unthinkingly from academic texts or best-practice manuals, although such knowledge was sometimes a useful aid or inspiration. Instead, such activists and professionals working at the fine-grain interface between government and civil society paid careful attention to the particular context and the daily reality of power dynamics – the affluent pressure groups in Vancouver, the tensions with a hierarchical formal government system in Kobe. They knew how to listen to 'local', street-level knowledge and translate this into arguments relevant to wider issues and policy debates, in a similar way to the resident activists in Greenpoint/Williamsburg, Brooklyn in Chapter 1. Through this listening, learning and experimentation, new governance capacities were created (see also Briggs 2008).

In both cases, and in the Omaha case also referred to, a key capacity was the ability to relate local action and local place qualities to wider concerns. This not only demanded shrewd political work, connecting networks and mobilising attention at different levels of government action. It also meant a good awareness of the dynamic geography of the urban complexes in which neighbourhoods and cities are situated. The neighbourhoods in Vancouver were not self-contained, nor were the administrative areas of the city councils. In Vancouver, the changes manifested in neighbourhoods as 'pressure for development' and 'new kinds of resident' resulted from growth in the wider metropolitan area and in shifts in global geopolitics, through the city's links with flows of people and invest-ment capital from East Asia. In Kobe, intense pressure for develop-ment and a strong national promotion of industrial development and major infrastructure projects unhindered by consideration of local impacts created the conditions against which local people mobilised their efforts. Kobe activists needed good knowledge of urban dynamics, and looked to sympathetic university academics and other experts to help them understand the wider forces that affected them.

In addition to an experimental attitude and an awareness of the need to relate street-level concerns to wider forces, the key players in these cases also understood that doing without formal government was not an option. They needed the authority of government-backed instruments to underpin the actions they promoted. When dealing with how land is used and developed, and how changes to the built environment take place, those doing place-management work enter a complex area of property rights. Striking appropriate balances between individual and collective rights and responsibilities is a major challenge in such situations, which is one of the reasons plan-ning work gets so tangled up in legal questions. So in addition to a value-oriented commitment and a participatory practice, it was also important to make sure that the bureaucratic work of following legally correct procedure was undertaken appropriately.

In Vancouver and Kobe, a key concern was with the rights of individuals with respect to their properties, rights to determine the character of a street and rights to demand attention to public realm qualities. In Vancouver, a key quality that slowly developed as part of the prevailing governance culture was a recognition that individ-ual rights needed to be balanced with respect for the rights of others and for the overall public realm of the city they all shared. The chal-lenge was to resist exclusionary attitudes among some affluent and long-established residents, who wanted not only to improve the 'look' of their streets but to restrict those living there to 'people like themselves'. This meant that Vancouver City politicians and profes-sionals had to establish the legitimacy of governance attention to the quality of the public realm of places, in the face of well-defined indi-vidual property rights. In Kobe, the position of the individual prop-erty owner was also strong. A key motivation behind the development of collaborative *machizukuri* practices was to persuade individual owners that they were better off working together on area improvement projects than trying to go it alone.

However, in both Vancouver and Kobe, it was recognised that the traditional land-use zoning plan or scheme was an impediment. Such instruments give legal rights to property owners to develop in line with a legally approved zoning ordinance, prepared according to legally specified procedures.[10] They provide the legal justification for limiting private property rights and demanding some degree of site allocation for public realm purposes. However, standard zoning tools typically provide only a two-dimensional specification of the distribution of land uses, where public facilities such as roads, schools and welfare services are to be located, along with a specification of norms of building heights and standards, road widths and so on.

In Vancouver and Kobe, the challenge was to manage changes to the existing built fabric, fitting in individual changes in neighbourhoods that were themselves transforming. Traditional zoning instruments designed to guide urban expansion were no longer adequate for this task. In Kobe, the *machizukuri* process was used to develop more sophisticated policies and layout guidelines, specific to particular areas and backed by local stakeholders until a legal basis and local government capacity were in place. The Vancouver innovation was to generate a flexible approach within the context of a zoning tradition, based on design principles rather than fixed zoning rules. A flexible approach puts much more weight on judgement in the light of local circumstances rather than rule-following behaviour, but this then requires sufficient trust in the governance arenas and the people who make the judgements to underpin its legitimacy. It demands officials trained in making such judgements in legally and ethically robust ways.

The changes in neighbourhood management practices that evolved in Vancouver could not have happened without the energy of the wider society, both as reflected in the social movement dynamics of the 1960s and 1970s and through the work of all kinds of community groups and individuals, focused more on their particular neighbourhood conditions. The political community in the Vancouver area was itself transformed, generating new foci for public attention and a new governance culture. This was held in place by the active monitoring of local groups and residents. In Vancouver, there is widespread awareness of what is in a design guideline, with residents alerting the City Council to deviations. This culture in turn carried structuring power, which shaped not just the games of politics but also how private developers behaved. That is, it shaped markets too. In Kobe something similar began to happen. Citizens noted breaches of plans and called on Japanese traditions of solidarity to shame people into conformance. Nevertheless, such community monitoring, where residents and other community stakeholders come to act as intermediaries between civil society and local government, only develops where residents feel that they have some trust in and political 'ownership' of their local government and do not fear reprisals from other members of a locality. There is also a lurking danger that such monitors may become a kind of community police, enforcing conformity with only one way of life. This was the danger that the planners in Vancouver sought to avoid, as they negotiated their first design guidelines with affluent residents.

The management of neighbourhood change in Vancouver and Kobe thus reflects the evolution of the kind of interaction between citizens and administrations that all who promote the progressive role of local governments have in mind. How it works depends not merely on what politicians or planning staff do and how they act. It results also from the energy and outlooks of the many diverse groups and individuals within civil society. In such contexts, the guardianship of place quality, that is, of the public realm of individual neighbourhoods, has a pluralist quality. It is spread among many arenas. Later examples in this book will highlight the value of an active, pluralistically critical civil society in maintaining attention to place quality and in limiting introverted tendencies within city administrations. However, in both Vancouver and Kobe, such work by active civil society groups was not enough by itself. Both needed more expertise. The Vancouver transformation would not have occurred without committed and skilled planning staff. In Kobe, expert advisers outside formal government provided a valuable resource.

The kind of local political culture and place-management practices that emerged over time in Vancouver – and may perhaps emerge in the future in places such as Kobe and Japanese cities more widely, where civil society is developing much greater confidence to assert its role in promoting liveability and sustainability – is not easy to replicate. It cannot be created merely by inserting a new process or 'good-practice' formula into a governance context. Like the Porto Alegre case cited in Chapter 3, the experiences of Vancouver and Kobe described here grew out of very specific circumstances. The energy of local activism made a difference, but the moment of opportunity (see Chapter 3) in Vancouver was more capacious than in Kobe, and formal government arrangements gave the City Council much more autonomy than in countries with a more centralised government, such as Japan. In Kobe, local activism within a civil society context had to be sustained for well over a decade before it began to affect formal government arenas and practices.

Yet these experiences may still carry hope for those seeking to pursue planning-focused place-governance in situations where moments of opportunity are narrow and transformative energy less dedicated and concentrated. Governance cultures and practices grow from particular contexts and specific circumstances. They are changed by the way those charged with official responsibilities and those who live, work and are politically active in a locality bring to the foreground of attention what they feel is going wrong, about their place qualities and about the prevailing practices of dealing with them. They mobilise collective action; they campaign for attention; they draw on other experiences, but honed to the challenges of the particular situation they face. Where such energy is to be found, new practices for managing change in the liveability and sustainability of neighbourhoods can be brought into being and, over time, may come to have transformative effects in a wider sphere. These may become a major force in changing the place qualities and governance culture of a city. In the next chapter, I look at situations where the scope for governance innovation in place-management practices is much more limited.

Suggested further reading

The literature on governance initiatives to promote better-quality neighbourhoods expanded in the later twentieth century as governments in Western countries developed 'urban' and 'housing' policies to address concerns about poverty, social exclusion and insecurity in troubled parts of cities, despite general increases in affluence (see Imrie and Raco 2003, Murie and Musterd 2004). In the US, and to an extent in Europe, this literature overlaps with that on social segregation and racism as this affects urban living environments (see Galster 1996, Madanipour et al. 1998, Wacquant 1999) and has links to the wider literature on community development (see Taylor 2003). In parallel, there is a literature on the design of urban neighbourhoods (see Barnett 2003, Grant 2006). The references cited below provide helpful introductions to this range of material.

Barnett, J. (2003) *Redesigning Cities: Principles, Practice, Implementation*, University of Chicago Press, Chicago.

Galster, G. (1996) *Reality and Research: Social Science and U.S. Urban Policy since 1960*, Urban Institute, Washington, DC.

Grant, J. (2006) *Planning the Good Community: New Urbanism in Theory and Practice*, Routledge, London.

Imrie, R. and Raco, M. (eds) (2003) *Urban Renaissance? New Labour, Community and Urban Policy*, Policy Press, Bristol.

Madanipour, A., Cars, G. and Allen, J. (eds) (1998) *Social Exclusion in European Cities*, Jessica Kingsley/Her Majesty's Stationery Office, London.

Murie, A. and Musterd, S. (2004) Social exclusion and opportunity structures in European cities and neighbourhoods, *Urban Studies*, 41, 1441–59.

Taylor, M. (2003) *Public Policy in the Community*, Palgrave, Houndmills, Hampshire.

Wacquant, L. (1999) Urban marginality in the coming millenium, *Urban Studies*, 36, 1639–48.

Chapter 5

Managing Neighbourhood Change

Managing at the fine grain

This chapter moves from experiences in which significant transformative changes in neighbourhood management practices were achieved, to situations where contextual conditions make it much harder to achieve such changes. No political momentum among residents in the locality created the energy for change. A planning orientation was maintained in the first case by local government planners, doing what they saw as what their profession demanded. In the second case, a charitable non-government agency (NGO) initiated a neighbourhood improvement project, which was realised by staff with backgrounds primarily in community development work, a field of activity that shares many values in common with the planning field. In the first case, citizens were not discontented with their City Council, largely accepting the services delivered to them as part of the flow of 'normal life', though they were very concerned about their neighbourhood environments. In the second case, any formal government activity was experienced as remote and inaccessible, associated with a history of a repressive and racially discriminatory regime. Although the case spans the collapse of this regime and its replacement by a democratic one, people still associated 'government' with their past difficulties.

Both the experiences examined are presented from the point of view of those working within agencies charged with place-governance tasks. One looks at the work surrounding the quintessentially bureaucratic task of granting development rights. What does it take to perform such work with a planning orientation? How can an activity that needs to be performed with careful attention to the possibility of legal challenge and with sensitivity to the fine grain of how a new project fits into the existing environment be combined with creating timely and resource-efficient procedures? The other case is an example of a community development initiative in a very turbulent context, where outside agencies sought to bring benefits to a very poor locality. Here, sensitivity to beneficiaries has to be combined with accountability to funders. How can sufficient trust in professional agencies among residents be created to enable benefits to be distributed fairly and transparently?

For many people, formal planning systems and the practices to which they give rise are experienced as a remote, constraining and incompetent bureaucratic apparatus. Regulations about how land and property can be used and developed intrude on our ideas about how to rearrange buildings and make use of land, if we are fortunate enough to have rights to make changes to either. At the same time, it often seems as if other people, by some influence denied to us, can get the liberty to do what they like. This was what upset the residents of Ditchling (see Chapter 1). It was such attitudes and experiences that the planners, politicians and citizens of Vancouver sought to break through, by developing collaborative ways of creating rules and practices for guiding neighbourhood change. These collaborative ways encouraged more responsive and interactive relationships at the interface between the state and civil society. In Kobe, in response to sustained citizen activism, something similar began to evolve.

The ambition was not to displace bureaucratic routine or remove the need for regulating how land was used and developed in complex urban situations. Instead, the challenge was to create new, more relevant regulations and new ways of undertaking regulatory work. To sustain such new practices requires continual attention to the quality of their performance. In Vancouver and Kobe, this was achieved by a complex mix of individual commitment to public service, reflective understanding of what serving the public means in relation to a particular field of activity, and careful management of the service in question (see also Chapter 8). The experiences presented here are very different. Both focus on the fine-grain management of small-scale changes to local environments. In both cases, committed staff sought to create service-delivery routines that were accessible to, and trusted as fair, by those using and otherwise affected by them. The management challenge was to deliver street-level governance practices in locally sensitive, knowledgeable and inventive ways.

Such work demands a complex mixture of practical technical capacity, deep knowledge of local dynamics and commitment to public service among those who become key actors in place-governance. This is a hard demand to meet and is often undervalued, little noticed and underpaid. This 'daily life' of street governance is barely noticed when it goes well. It is when problems crop up that people look around for someone to blame, a 'they' who should have been attending to the public realm on their behalf, a government official who should have been taking care of their interests. It is these intermediaries who for most people provide the personal embodiment of public action in the flow of daily life, the ones we talk to and contact when we have a problem with what is going on where we live, the ones who negotiate the ambience at the interface between our daily lives in places and the systems of governance that affect place qualities and connectivities. How such people perform their work has a significant impact not only on the achievement of a specific outcome, but on the trust and engagement people have with local area governance processes.

This kind of work is continually threatened by pressures to subvert its focus and ethics. Politicians and officials may come to enjoy being in charge and see themselves as ruling their patch. Or officials may relax their reflexivity and see themselves as merely guardians of the rules, without considering whose rules they are, what they are for and whether they still have relevance. Or they may focus so much on individual cases that they fail to see the wider picture, or that their caseload backlog has built up. More seriously, politicians and officials within public agencies charged with under-taking regulatory work may be seduced from a commitment to public service by the lure of private gain or political advancement. Because a development permit is often very valuable, there are always opportunities in the regulatory side of planning work for receiving bribes or allowing friends and relatives privileged access to regulatory permits, or even completely to breach the regulations expressed in publicly available planning schemes, master plans, zoning ordinances and such like. So place-governance with a plan-ning orientation in such situations demands good-quality bureau-cratic procedures. The challenge is to combine these with sensitivity to local circumstances and a facilitative attitude towards people's own initiatives.

The two experiences discussed here centre on the work of a municipal planning office in England[1] and a special agency involved in upgrading an informal 'squatter' settlement in South Africa, funded by a non-governmental agency. I selected the first case because it has been judged in the English context as an exemplar of good development management practice. The second case was selected from many other possibilities because of the difficulty and hope of community development initiatives in the 1990s in the

South African context.[2] The ambition in the first case, a metropolitan district in the North East of England, was to combine attention to treating every application for a planning permit with sensitivity to the specific circumstances of applicants, their neighbours and the site, with external demands that the planning service achieve nationally defined performance targets and internal pressures to adjust to shrinking municipal budgets. Its practices were shaped by the UK's long-developed, sophisticated approach to regulating land use and development change, in a context where, especially in England, government is highly centralised. How can local sensitivity be combined with the continuing demands of a 'heavy' central state? The second case is from the Durban area. In South Africa, a systematically oppressed majority is struggling to overcome a history of extreme colonial rule and racial discrimination, with its consequences for poverty, marginalisation and distrust of formal government and law. Here, an externally funded community development agency was charged with funding improvements in the quality of living conditions with as little displacement as possible. At the same time, agency staff sought to distribute access to new opportunities and resources in ways that were seen locally as fair, in a context in which government services had been experienced as unfair and unjust, and where informal ways of getting access to a scrap of ground on which to build a hut depended on who you knew. Both cases show committed agency staff acting as intermediaries between citizens, small enterprises and more powerful forces, struggling to prevent these larger power structures crushing and displacing sensitivity to street-level aspirations.

Delivering a quality planning service: South Tyneside, Northern England[3]

South Tyneside is not a prosperous area like Vancouver and Kobe, though there have been recent improvements. Nor is it experiencing rapid urbanisation, having had such a period in the nineteenth century. Since then, the challenge has been to improve the quality of the urban environment and the fairness of people's access to it. It is an area with considerable relative poverty compared to the rest of the UK and the rest of Western Europe, but few struggle for basic needs, as do those in the South African neighbourhood to be presented next. In the UK, the inheritance of a welfare state lives on, with a recognition that everyone is entitled to some basic minimum of housing, health and welfare services, infrastructure and income. There are continual initiatives to improve conditions for social groups and areas that experience conditions well below the average. These include area-upgrading projects, referred to over the years as urban/area renewal or regeneration programmes, as well as policies focused on more specific elements of the urban environment, such as improving the condition of the housing stock or providing more green space and managing it better. In an area such as Tyne and Wear, there is also a strong policy emphasis on helping and attracting firms, to replace the employment opportunities lost through de-industrialisation.

In the UK, as in north west Europe generally, formal government is strong and involved in very many areas of activity, from education, health and welfare provision, safety and security, economic support, land-use regulation, environmental management, the promotion of sports and leisure provision, and tourism opportunities. Local government in England consists of large, multifunctional municipalities, along with a regional tier of agencies mostly with powers delegated from national government. Although co-existing in a single authority, municipal functions have tended to build up their own departmental 'silos',[4] each linked in its own way to a national government agency and policy community of active stakeholders. This makes integration between departments difficult. There are also many other agencies, some public and some private, which provide and promote public services, in the context of regulatory requirements set by national and European governments. Despite these levels and agencies, compared to other European countries the English state is strongly centralised. Municipalities and agencies that deliver public services and infrastructures are all, despite a frequent rhetoric of devolved power, closely tied to the national state for funds and for legislative authority. South Tyneside municipality thus exists in a paradoxical governance context, where a heavy national government combines with fragmented governance activity within localities (see Rydin 2003 for an account of the British planning system).

There are many agencies and departments of a local authority that have a role in what happens in a neighbourhood or other urban zone. However, the role of formal guardian of the public interest in local environmental quality has, in the UK, been given to a well-developed planning system. This is defined in national legislation. The heartland of national government, especially in England, is centred in the South East of the country, around

London, and conditions in northern areas are often ill understood. The planning system, created in its present form in the mid-twentieth century, is continually being adjusted, as new and often contradictory demands and expectations are placed on it. In terms of local area management, the primary role of the planning function is to co-ordinate development initiatives, to pursue agreed strategic policies about where development and major infrastructures should be located, and to ensure that the public realm implications of private development initiatives are given adequate attention while generally facilitating development activity. It is also expected to respond to resident and business concerns about local environmental quality. The main tool for this task is a form of land-use regulation that relies on discretionary judgement on the part of officials and politicians, rather than on legal zoning plans (Booth 1996). In the UK, no land or property owner has a 'right' to develop land as they wish. Instead, that right formally belongs to the state, and it is up to national and local governments to give development permits. The decision about whether or not to give a permit is governed by national legislation, which requires a combination of attention to national and regional policies, local policies (given legitimacy in a formal 'development plan') and 'other material considerations', which can range from emerging national policies to very specific local matters.

For many decades, this activity was known colloquially as 'development control'. It involves consideration of every project above a certain threshold 'on its merits', but in the light of a complex battery of national and local plans and policy statements that limit local discretion. Often in the past, 'development control' has been seen as a low-status activity, in contrast to the apparently more exciting work of preparing urban and regional strategies or promoting major urban transformation projects (see Cullingworth and Nadin 2001, Rydin 2003). Yet once the public sector ceased to be the main developer of the urban fabric (in the 1950s), the development control offices and planning subcommittees of local authorities became a key interface between formal government and all those with a stake in a particular project. As a former Chief Planning Officer from Manchester City Council comments: 'the development control process is probably the part of the planning service that is most involved in a continuous interaction with its customers'[5] (Kitchen 1997:101).

South Tyneside Metropolitan District Council covers part of a much larger urban complex, which stretches from the North Sea coast along the south bank of the river Tyne. Much of it was urbanised in the nineteenth century, but there are substantial areas of newer development. This resulted from replacement after damage in World War II, the redevelopment of areas of very poor-quality housing, the redevelopment of industrial and port-related areas for newer industries or reclaimed as new green spaces, and some areas of expansion onto undeveloped areas on the margins of the built-up area. However, such expansion is continually kept in check by a national, regional and local policy consensus that urban sprawl across undeveloped countryside should be kept to a minimum. For many years, sprawl has been contained by the designation of a 'green belt' around towns and cities (see Hall et al. 1973, Elson 1986). In South Tyneside, the local authority has always been in the hands of the Labour Party, but this has not meant a continual cohesive political direction, as at times the councillors have had stronger allegiances to their local areas than to the council as a whole. A 'South Tyneside' identity competed in politicians' minds with the identities of the former urban district authorities, which had been amalgamated in 1974 to form the larger district. There have been times, too, when councillors wanted to keep a tight control over the granting of planning permits, seeing themselves, rather than professional officers, as the only legitimate guardians of local environmental quality. In the 2000s, however, the council was winning national accolades for both the competence of overall council management and for the quality of its planning services.[6]

Local authorities in England have complex political and administrative structures through which to conduct their affairs, and they are continually exhorted by national government and various lobby groups to improve their management (Wilson and Game 2002). Formally, an elected council makes all decisions, advised by its technical staff in different departments. In practice, there is considerable delegation to officials. South Tyneside has 54 councillors, but the key decision-making arena has been the cabinet of a few councillors in charge of various areas of responsibility, under the guidance of a 'leader' and deputy from the main political party, to which committees report.[7] The council in recent years has been attempting to achieve an integrated approach to all its activities, but is continually challenged in this ambition by the separatist tendencies of service departments, and by changing national policy directions across all its services. The official side of the authority is headed by a Chief Executive and, in the mid-2000s, it was divided into three large super-departments in an attempt to increase a more integrated approach. The Planning Service is located in the department that deals with urban regeneration projects, and the

---

Box 5.1   Managing a regulatory caseload

In the mid-2000s, the Area Planning Group (APG) was dealing with around 1500 applications for a planning permit per year, with 1600 pre-application inquiries. 22 of the planning cases in which it was involved were major developments and it had negotiated 14 'agreements' with developers over key public realm issues.[8] The permit applications ranged from house extensions to major development projects. National policy also demanded that particular attention should be given to developments that increased the supply of housing. All new development was expected to meet 'sustainability' criteria, in terms of energy use, building materials, flood damage mitigation and the promotion of diversity. Meanwhile, the APG was committed to providing a service that was seen as a helpful experience by applicants, the agents who advised them[9] and others who wanted to give voice to concerns about particular applications. The group had long had a commitment to achieving local environmental benefits when considering a development proposal, combined with an attitude of maintaining a good relationship with local people and local agents. Officers were well networked and were out and about in their 'patches', getting a feel for what was at stake in any development project and how it could be addressed.

However, this practice was time consuming. It came under pressure as municipal budgets were reduced, with consequences for staffing. National government put pressure on municipalities to complete the processing of planning applications within a short timescale. Eventually, national government provided additional funds for local authority planning work, but this was tied to performance targets, linked to the speed of application processing. The driver for this policy was to reduce 'bureaucratic delay' in development projects.[10] In South Tyneside, however, the consequence was a recognition that the planning service was not achieving its

$\rightarrow$

Area Planning Group, which performs the development control function, works alongside other groups focused on strategic planning and urban regeneration activity. The group reports to the senior executive officials in the council and to the councillor who chairs the planning committee. Box 5.1 summarises what they do, how they relate to other areas of the local authority's work and how the management of the service was revised in an attempt to retain a quality of service appreciated locally while still meeting national government expectations.

By the mid-2000s, South Tyneside's Area Planning Group had met all its targets without serious compromise to its tradition of

→

targets and therefore would not be able to access the national funding. Along with a major effort to transform the council's overall management in the early 2000s, efforts were therefore made to reshape the development control service. An audit was carried out to review practice and procedure, and a new group leader for the service was appointed. The challenge was to combine meeting national efficiency targets, to sustain funding, while maintaining good relations with users of the planning service and all those concerned with the quality of a development.

The APG gave more administrative support to professional officers, while ensuring that all officers kept performance targets in mind as each managed their own caseload. This meant that professionals were expected to see their time as a finite resource to be accounted for. Councillors were persuaded to give the officials much more discretion, with fewer applications needing to be decided by the committee, as a way to speed up the service. Committee meetings where applications were discussed were made open to the public. Initiatives were taken to make potential applicants and the agents who advised them much more aware of the public realm issues to which they would be expected to pay attention, and regular discussion meetings were held with agents. More attention was given to enforcing compliance with the terms of a planning permit, as breaches of permits could cause much resident concern. A great deal of effort was given to making other municipal departments and other agencies with development interests aware of the need to consider the wider public realm implications of the projects they were promoting. This in turn encouraged better overall co-ordination of municipal activity around the area. It also helped developers with larger projects to have clearer initial expectations of what would be required from them.

considerate treatment of individual projects, in a way that was sensitive to applicants and other stakeholders. This was achieved by careful attention to detailed management, networking and community connections, along with a focus on securing good-quality development, paying attention to local concerns about development impacts and finding ways to secure wider policy considerations. However, complacency about their achievement was not an option, as neither national government nor regional policy frameworks were stable, and funding pressures were becoming even more severe.

High levels of customer satisfaction are reported in City

Council surveys. In the South Tyneside area, the relation between state and civil society at the local level has settled into the lived practice of the formal model of representative democracy, underpinned in North East England by Labour Party and trade union linkages. In contrast to many other parts of England, there are fewer active residents' groups and amenity societies, and those that exist are more likely to be linked to neighbourhood regeneration initiatives. If people have a problem about an issue in their neighbourhood, they tend to look to their ward councillor to take it up for them. This locally specific cultural expectation, reinforced with a continually critical media, is met in South Tyneside by a practice culture among planning and administrative staff that emphasises a professional commitment to delivering a quality service to local stakeholders and achieving quality development. This orientation is combined with a pragmatic recognition of the need to meet national targets and adjust to national and regional policy initiatives that keep changing the context in which officials work. Local government officials are thus positioned in this case as intermediaries, managing the interface between a heavy state and an inherited social-democratic working-class culture. They acted, with their technical expertise and professional ethics, as a key guardian of the quality of local place management.

Upgrading an informal settlement and innovating new governance practices: Besters Camp and the Inanda Development Trust in Durban, South Africa[11]

The interaction between efforts to create capacity for neighbourhood management in already built-up areas and wider transformations in politics and administration is starkly evident in this next case. Urban development in Vancouver, Kobe and South Tyneside proceeded in the twentieth century through an interaction between land and property development activity, regulated by private and administrative law (that is, through formal market processes). Individuals and firms bought land and properties, divided up sites, constructed buildings and often provided services. The struggles that led to citizen protests focused on establishing the limits of private rights over what property owners could do, in order to safeguard collective concerns about the quality of the public realm dimensions of local environments. In many other parts of the world in the late twentieth century urbanisation occurred very rapidly, with people on low incomes flocking to cities in search of a better life, without the means to buy or rent a dwelling of any kind through formal market processes, partly because of low incomes and partly because the stock of properties and services simply could not expand fast enough. In this context, all kinds of informal settlement development and management arrangements grew up. These include situations where residents 'squat' on sites and gradually build some accommodation for themselves.

These informal, 'squatter' settlements have often been celebrated for their flexibility and innovation. However, such informal settlements are created initially without basic services (water, drainage, energy supply), or consideration of access within and beyond neighbourhoods, or provision of health, welfare and education facilities, let alone nearby work opportunities. They are merely footholds to an urban life. Since the 1960s, all kinds of initiatives have been promoted to upgrade such informal settlements, retro-fitting them with basic services. These initiatives have been facilitated by aid agency funding and an international movement spreading ideas about upgrading practice across cities where informal settlement is commonplace. In many cases, through time, with and without such initiatives, such informally developed settlements become a part of the established urban fabric. In other cases, they grow and merge into vast slum areas in exploding cities. This is where, in the early twenty-first century, a large number of the world's population are anticipated to spend their lives. The upgrading of such areas has therefore taken on greater urgency in urban policy debate in the developing world (see Gilbert 1998, UN-Habitat 2003, Mitlin and Satterthwaite 2004, Payne 2005).

In some ways, such upgrading programmes have echoes of urban neighbourhood regeneration initiatives in Western cities in the later twentieth century. These focused on islands of poverty found in most larger cities, characterised by high unemployment, poor health, social difficulties and poor local environments. There were several neighbourhoods in the South Tyneside Council area that registered on national statistics of very poor neighbourhoods. Vancouver had such a neighbourhood in Downtown Eastside (see Chapter 4). The initiatives often initially focused on refurbishing the built stock, but then extended to wider and more integrated community development programmes. They were commonly organised through special agencies, set up with time-limited funding, in the

hope that an injection of funded activity and new governance practices could somehow kick-start the energy for longer-term, self-
sustaining efforts to improve neighbourhood conditions. Such
special agencies have often been inspired by the kind of philosophy
that guided the planners in Vancouver. Funders and agency staff
often hoped to displace bureaucratic and paternalist practices, which
were seen to encourage residents to be dependent on their governments. They thought that they should promote arrangements where
residents became more active partners and participants in neighbourhood improvement programmes. Sometimes these programmes did
achieve substantial physical and social improvements, with enduring
effects on neighbourhood conditions and local governance cultures.
However, the experiences have been very variable, depending on
wider contexts and local circumstances. Upgrading programmes in
informal settlements in developing-world cities have also had very
variable outcomes for the same reason. But in these cases, the provision of basic needs has had a much higher priority and the availability of economic resources has been much less. Moreover, the relations
between citizens and their formal government have often been
complicated by struggles to escape from political regimes that have
oppressed their populations in other ways. In such a context, trust in
formal government may be very low indeed.

From among a great many experiences across the world of such
upgrading initiatives, I have selected one from Durban in South
Africa. It illustrates what was considered an innovative programme,
funded by a non-governmental agency, outside the formal government structure. Its period of operation spreads across a major transition in South Africa, when white minority government with its
policies of the social and spatial segregation of races (known as
'apartheid') was finally overturned, to be replaced by a democracy led
by the African National Congress party. The initiative achieved significant short-term improvements and inspired other upgrading projects
promoted by the City Council and the national government in the
post-apartheid era. Much of the philosophy that guided it has been
formally adopted in later City Council strategic documents (Breetzke
2009). Nevertheless, for the residents it remains a very poor area
within a city in which extremes of affluence and poverty still co-exist.

Durban originated as a major port city in the late nineteenth
century and became known in South Africa a century ago for its
explicit policies of racial segregation. The majority black population
were not allowed to live permanently in urban areas, but yet they
were expected to work there. Not surprisingly, many came to live

informally in urban areas, wherever they could find a space. In the 1960s, large numbers of people were displaced from a complex socially and racially mixed area known as Cato Manor in an attempt to assert the apartheid policy (Edwards 1994). This aroused intense protest. Riots broke out in Durban over the lack of adequate urban housing provision. Local community leaders, often with some tribal authority, took the lead in organising invasions of state-owned vacant land. The case that follows centres on one such area, Besters Camp, on the urban periphery to the north of Durban. It is part of a large area of informal settlement that originated through invasion processes, led by tribal and political leaders. Formal government was a remote, alien and oppressive force, deliberately limiting opportunity for the black, Indian and coloured majority. People in areas such as Besters Camp relied on informal arrangements and connections with tribal leaders, underground political parties and other warlords[12] for their security and welfare. A dwelling for them was typically a wattle-and-daub shack, a single room of 10–12 square metres.

Besters Camp is now in an area known administratively as INK (Inanda–Ntuzuma–KwaMashu) in the e-Thekwini (Greater Durban) municipality (see Figure 5.1). The municipality as a whole has a population of around three million, divided since the early 2000s into five 'area management' zones. Back around 1990, the INK area had about 750,000 people. Besters Camp itself housed approximately 50,000 people on hilly land on the urban periphery. Dwelling units were clustered closely together for security reasons, with networks of pathways between them, the urban structure evolving as the settlement itself grew. Plots had no direct power source, water supply or sewerage connections.

It was in this context that a large-scale programme was initiated by a non-governmental organisation (NGO), the Urban Foundation Informal Settlements Division. This was an organisation founded by South African corporate businesses in the 1980s, concerned about providing better conditions for the urban labour force. The Besters Camp project drew on prior experiences and debates, and for a while became an exemplar for other upgrading projects in the Durban area and in South African cities generally. As one of those involved in the initiative recalled:

the implementation of large-scale shack settlement in-situ upgrading was without precedent in South Africa at the time ... [and the project] was initiated during a state of emergency in a

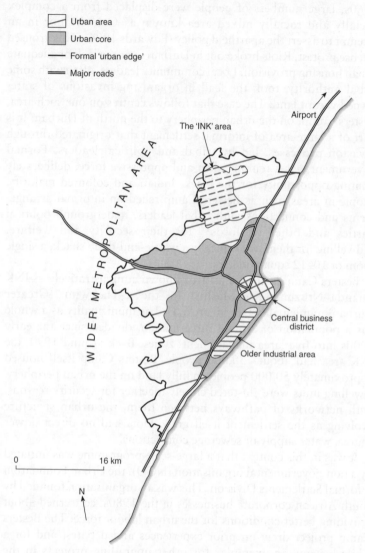

Figure 5.1   *eThekwini Municipality and Greater Durban*

Urban area
Urban core
Formal 'urban edge'
Major roads

Airport

The 'INK' area

WIDER METROPOLITAN AREA

Central business district

Older industrial area

0   16 km

N

settlement undergoing violent conflict between political parties with competing vested interests in it. (van Horen 2000:391)[13]

The project worked steadily for about five years. The NGO had the support of the then Durban City Council, but the area stretched into other jurisdictions, notably those controlled as Kwazulu tribal homeland areas. Substantial physical improvements were achieved in this time: there was an improved network of paths and roads, so that people did not have to keep walking through each other's plots; a spread of water standpipes and garbage skips was provided across the area; while every plot was given electricity connections and latrine pits, along with a hotplate for cooking. Each shack occupant was given a small basic grant for improving their dwelling. Some community halls, health centres and school buildings were also provided. Disruption to sites was kept to a minimum as routeways and community facilities were inserted into the existing, informally developed urban fabric. Very few people had to be found replacement dwellings. Around 6500 households in total benefited from improved conditions by the end of the project period (1989–95). What made this initiative different was that it grew out of intensive discussion with all the households involved.

In many other upgrading projects up to then, experts had been called in to prepare new layout plans, to regularise the higgledy-piggledy accretion of plots that arises when people informally find access to a site and then subdivide it for family members and often for rental to increase family incomes. An assumed benefit from such regularisation was that residents could then get formal tenure to their site, and maybe use this as collateral to raise funds for improving their dwelling. However, this assumes that residents have the resources for such improvements. Further, such regularisation can also cause a great deal of hostility among residents, when traditional communal arrangements are displaced by creating individual land and property claims.[14] In the South African context, hostility was likely to be exaggerated by the long history of oppression by formal government. People relied much more on informal governance processes linked to tribal and party connections.

The approach adopted by the Besters Camp project worked in a different way. The starting point was not to get land rights sorted out. Instead, community development workers met with groups of residents and held intensive discussion processes to work out new alignments for their plots and clusters, and the relation of these with pathways through the settlement (see Box 5.2).

As van Horen (2000) notes, the intensive processes did not create overnight a new governance practice, nor were the governance practices that emerged driven by the concerns of local residents. This was a time of intense political change in South Africa as the country recreated itself as a democratic country based on complete adult franchise. In this period, there was energetic encouragement of participatory

Box 5.2   Working with residents on neighbourhood upgrading

Together, local knowledge and sensibility were used to work out collectively how basic infrastructures could be provided to each dwelling, and how routeways through the settlement could be realigned to improve access. In this way, alterations to paths and plots could reflect norms and practices that residents themselves had evolved to survive in such conditions. Small-scale governance processes were developed with residents, including small area committees to address particular functions such as water supply and health and to co-ordinate activity, along with workshops and mass meetings (van Horen 2000:396). Through these intensive discussion and adjustment processes, routes and locations were decided and some kind of plot layout produced. Only towards the end of these processes were these arrangements consolidated into a plan. This mostly confirmed site locations and boundaries, with adjustments where needed to accommodate collective facilities. Some funds were made available to help people improve their dwellings, but as these were tied to having formal legal tenure, take-up was low. Residents had few resources for improving their dwellings. They felt they already had security of tenure through their informal governance processes and were not attracted to the idea of engaging with the formal state, which in any case involved costly paperwork and an expensive trip to a distant office. What they now had were better services and accessibility opportunities, and more clarity about where the boundaries might lie between the private part of their plot and the needs of public access.

Source: van Horen, B. (2000).

processes in housing provision and community development, which provided a very positive context for the Besters Camp initiative. However, these processes were also arenas for the development of the political parties of the new democracy. In the Durban area in the early 1990s, there were complex struggles between different political groupings, played out in different governance arenas, both within the framework of formal government and outside it. The Besters Camp area had grown up not merely outside the framework of formal land laws, but with very few connections to any kind of formal government. Yet the upgrading project needed to create some kind of agency with a legal status, through which funds from aid agencies could be provided. It was hoped that the upgrading work could be continued once the initial Urban Foundation funding was used up. It was also thought that a local development agency could help to develop on-going relations between local people and the wider governance environment. The result was the formation of a legally autonomous Community Development Trust for the wider area in which Besters Camp is situated, the Inanda Community Development Trust (see Box 5.3).

The achievements of the INK Trust attracted widespread attention. In a very difficult context, it pioneered a flexible approach to place management and development, grounded in a combination of local knowledge, local capacity building and technical skill. The

Box 5.3   The Inanda Community Development Trust (INK)

Much of the work of the Trust was spent on negotiating arrangements with the municipality, by this time the Greater Durban Metropolitan Authority, and the funding agencies on which the Trust relied. It also sought to make contact with all kinds of local organisations that had some role in local area development. However, a proactive movement among residents prepared to engage with the Trust did not develop. This left the Trust as the guardian of resident concerns, as expressed in the intensive discussions over the upgrading work. At the same time, Trust members acted as intermediaries, carrying residents' concerns upwards through the complexities of a wider politics and bureaucracy.

However, the work of upgrading continued and spread out to other parts of the INK area under the aegis of the Trust. When it became clear that people were too poor to upgrade their dwellings, the focus shifted from a 'sites-and-services' orientation to the construction of basic housing units. Funding was limited, but enabled the provision of an 18 m² two-roomed starter house, which people soon began to improve with their own labour. The Trust staff helped to make access to funds quick and simple by careful attention to keeping good records, working closely with field workers and monitoring small-scale transactions. This helped to contain costs and promote good-quality construction. People got paid within two days of doing the work, which helped them with cash flow, while tendencies to corruption and clientelism were kept in check.[15] The Trust also worked hard to develop strong links with the beneficiary communities, encouraged community-based enterprises producing building materials and security personnel, and enabled the provision of a school.[16] Wherever possible, Trust staff were drawn from among local residents, who were provided with appropriate training.

Trust was promoted as a 'best-practice' exemplar of citizen involvement in area upgrading in South Africa. Yet Besters Camp residents
themselves began to feel that they had been short-changed, as the
quality of their own dwellings was much lower than the starter
homes provided by the INK Trust.[17] The Trust was also continually
struggling with formal government and funding bodies to gain
recognition of the need for very careful management and funding
flexibility. Attempts were made to extend the approach elsewhere,
but few of these have been able to achieve sufficient operational
freedom to produce significant benefits.

The problem here, as in many other such upgrading initiatives, is
that the governance landscape is fragmented among many arenas,
which compete with each other in expressing and shaping public
realm concerns about place development. In the Durban context,
this fragmentation was exacerbated by the unstable political conditions that were inevitable as the country as a whole worked out
what kind of political community would emerge in the post-
apartheid era. The commitment of the agency staff working in
Besters Camp and for INK to values similar to those of the planning
project had a major impact on the outcomes achieved. These values
were also vigorously promoted in the national rhetoric of the ANC
Party and officials in formal government bodies such as Durban
municipality. However, this rhetoric co-existed with other governance practices developed during the years of oppression. In the
Durban area, the situation was further complicated by tensions
between the ANC and the Zulu-based Inkatha party for domination. Yet the philosophy of resident involvement in neighbourhood
management projects and of community participation in governance arrangements has not been lost. In the 2000s, it was strongly
asserted by the e-Thekwini municipality. The Council leaders
acknowledge that one area in which achievement has been lacking is
redressing the 'ineffectiveness and inefficiency of inward-looking
local government still prevalent in the municipality'.[18] In the later
1990s, the municipality participated energetically in the national
promotion of *Integrated Area Development*. The INK area became
one of five areas designated nationally for such an integrated initiative. Durban officials looked at international exemplars to develop
their approach. Nevertheless, it has remained difficult to translate
such models of integrated and participatory governance into practice, in a situation in which other political practices are still strongly
present, notably the inheritance of authoritarian bureaucracy associated with the past and the informal governance networks of party

politics and tribal allegiances, which have been carried forward from the resistance days into present practices (Watson 2003). So in Durban's northern periphery, significant material improvements have been achieved in people's daily life circumstances. But it has so far been difficult to produce an on-going governance capacity to maintain and enhance such improvements, let alone create governance arenas that residents trust and participate in.[19]

The routines of street-level governance

The examples in this chapter have explored the routine work of local area place-governance. They are from completely different contexts and the streets in question look and feel very different. In neither case was it easy for officials and agency staff to undertake place-governance work oriented by the values of the planning project. Yet they worked hard to use the opportunities available and to enlarge these where possible. They struggled to help individual residents improve their living conditions and realise their aspirations. They searched for ways to combine a fair and transparent approach, technical quality and a responsive and trust-creating relationship with residents and other users of their services, despite pressures from the wider context that made this difficult. In South Tyneside, the challenge was to sustain a community-sensitive and co-ordinative practice when resources were slipping away and narrowly conceived performance pressures undermined efforts at more integrated approaches. In the Durban area, the initial context was one of extreme alienation between residents and formal government. Here, the struggle continues to create some kind of local governance system in which all residents can trust sufficiently to allow some aspects of place governance to proceed routinely and be perceived as fair.

Both cases focused on the personnel who work at this interface, whether from a background as community activists or trained professionals. Such people act as a form of community development worker, providing a friendly, accessible, trustable and tolerant face to governance processes, combining technical skill with an ethics of concern for the quality of life for those in their 'patch' and the wider society. With this commitment, such personnel provide an important role, along with others such as political representatives and pressure group activists, as carriers of knowledge and demands from the world of streets and neighbourhoods into the complexity of wider governance arenas. Acting at the interface between residents and governance processes is not only about commitment, however. It involves a daily practice that shapes conduct as well as the specifics of action (see Chapter 8).

The officials and agency staff in both these cases were well aware of this. They knew that they had to act out their philosophy of responsive public service as they went about their daily activities. However, the street was not their only front stage. They were also watched by higher-tier authorities (as in South Tyneside) or by funding agencies and a wider political and policy community searching for ways of creating new government practices (in Durban and South Africa generally). In their back office, they had to pay careful attention to management routines that would assist them in performing appropriately on both stages. Routine work for such people is thus not a day-to-day practice of acting by the rules. Instead, it is a process of continual reflexive learning, exploring, experimenting and adjusting. In this way, staff in these cases enacted a bureaucratic governance mode with a human face, while at the same time, and especially in the Besters Camp/INK case, they sought ways of developing a more collaborative way of working with residents and other stakeholders.

Activists and officials who combine a community development sensitivity with an experimental attitude soon develop an intimate knowledge of the social dynamics and development aspirations of their particular area. They develop an eye and an ear for local detail, for the 'word' on the street, and for how local networks connect people in one way and another. But localities are rarely self-contained entities (see Chapter 2). Decades of neglect by alien authorities and national struggles between the African National Congress and the Inkatha party created neighbourhood insecurities in Besters Camp. In South Tyneside, residents and politicians were slowly trying to work out what their localities could be like in post-industrial times. Sometimes powerful outside forces press in so hard on localities that there seems no space for local action, let alone time and space for innovation and experimentation. However, it is also possible for local sensitivity to be crowded out by too much learning from what goes on in other places, at the expense of developing rich, street-wise, local knowledge. Learning from the experience of others is not the same as seeking to replicate that experience or turn it into an off-the-shelf manual of good-practice recipes.

The performance of locally sensitive place-governance work was not only about paying attention to local knowledge and aspirations.

It also involved careful attention to rights, especially to rights to make use of and get value from specific sites, buildings, pathways, facilities and how a place looks and feels. These were important in both cases. In addition, the Besters Camp/INK case raises the issue of people's rights to claim that they are entitled to an improvement in their situation from someone who has resources to distribute. When rights are called into question, attention is needed to where such rights are defined and redeemed. In the South Tyneside case, rights to use and develop sites and properties were defined in the complex law of land and property tenure and in planning system law and procedure. These served to limit what people could do with their property and what the relationship between public and private realm considerations should be. The formal planning system in practice gave municipalities substantial power to constrain what a property owner could do, including when contributions to the public realm were expected. National law required that these constraints were made transparent by clear statements of principles, norms, standards and the areas to which they applied – the plans and policy documents of the planning system. These documents included statements of national planning policy, resulting in a complex array of principles, with national and local statements layering over each other (Rydin 2003). A major challenge for municipal officials was to find ways to explain this regulatory tangle to applicants and those who were concerned about local developments. It is no surprise that people in England more or less accept that there should be such law and regulations, but were continually critical of how it all worked (see the Ditchling case in Chapter 1).

In contrast, in Besters Camp and the later INK project, people had no confidence in formal law and procedure and were very unclear about what rights they might have. In such circumstances, sheltering under the umbrella of a local leader operating through informal power seemed a lot safer. In these conditions, the agencies created by the upgrading initiatives in effect sought to define a new approach to defining people's rights. These combined the formal rights that became available in the new South African democratic state with a commitment to the provision of universal and equitable human rights to fair access to urban opportunities and resources. However, this was not an established approach. It was grounded neither in previous formal government practice nor traditional Zulu customary land-allocation practices. It is perhaps not surprising in such circumstances that the agency's way of operating had difficulty in surviving. Its experience echoes that of the planners' 'rationality' in Chicago in the 1950s (see Chapter 3). Similar examples can be found elsewhere in Sub-Saharan Africa (see Nnkya 1999, Ikejiofor 2009).

Those involved as officials and agency staff in such street-level governance are thus often at the sharp end of structural problems that are not easy to resolve. Without a battery of law and procedure behind them to support their role, they are continually exposed to charges of favouritism and corruption. Overwhelmed by this background, they could easily lose their capacity for sensitive judgement about the merits of particular cases. Yet those working in situations such as those described in this chapter are not merely front-line guardians of the public realm of local place quality. They are the public face of initiatives to promote fair and transparent governance processes, with an inclusive commitment to service delivery and to promoting liveability and sustainability in urban neighbourhoods. The focus of their efforts is to enhance the opportunities for human flourishing in diverse ways, in the streets and neighbourhoods of daily life. Yet in situations of great instability in governance contexts, it is very difficult for sustained efforts to promote the values associated with a planning orientation. In such contexts, local concerns about place qualities can be neglected and localities exploited by outside agencies.

The examples discussed here reinforce the discussion in the previous chapter and underline that sustaining place-management practices that contribute to making local environments more liveable in inclusive and fair ways is not an activity that proceeds by some formula, recipe or rule. For those acting at the interface between civil society and governance processes, it involves a lived philosophy, a daily life of continual learning and pushing at contextual boundaries. It demands the exercise of careful judgement and technical skill. It requires experimenting with new ways of making connections, focusing on issues, identifying what is at stake and who are stakeholders. It is quiet work, often unnoticed in its successes but attacked in its failures. With commitment to such a practice, over time, significant improvements to the conditions of human flourishing can be achieved. What differed between the cases in Chapter 4 and this chapter was the wider impact and what was achieved. In neither South Tyneside nor Besters Camp/INK did the efforts to promote a planning way of doing place-governance expand into significant influences on the practices and culture of the wider political community. Yet within the institutional space available to them, the officials and agency staff in the cases discussed in this chapter were able to achieve significant benefits for local residents and local place qualities, despite continual pressure from forces deflecting attention away from sensitive local responsiveness.

The planning project, understood as I have described it in Chapter 1, is committed to resisting such pressures. It argues for careful attention to the quality of life in places as experienced in diverse ways, and to cultivating attention to the fine grain of the challenge of co-existence in shared spaces. It encourages the creation of institutional arenas for the emergence and sustenance of a culture and practice of place-governance that is committed to human flourishing in the daily life of places. It seeks to foster a kind of democratic practice that engages in both experimentation and innovation, and in careful learning about, critiquing and probing what is going on, in a context where multiple voices and values are respected. In Chapters 4 and 5, I have tried to show that such a project is not simply a utopian dream, but has been brought to life in some places at some times. Nevertheless, it is not easy to achieve and is under continual pressure from forces that will undermine it. In the next chapter, I look at the more dramatic and visible practices of the production of major projects designed to transform built environments.

Suggested further reading

For neighbourhood improvement policy and community development generally, see the references in Chapter 4. For comparative accounts of land-use regulation practices, see:

> Booth, P. (1996) *Controlling Development: Certainty and Discretion in Europe, the USA and Hong Kong,* UCL Press, London.
> Davies, H. W. E., Edwards, D., Hooper, A. and Punter, J. (1989) *Development Control in Western Europe,* HMSO, London.
> Cullingworth, J. B. and Caves, R. W. (2003) *Planning in the USA: Policies, Issues and Processes,* Routledge, London (this has a comparative perspective).

For the UK specifically, see:

> Rydin, Y. (2003) *Urban and Environmental Planning in the UK,* Palgrave, Basingstoke.

On planning in South Africa generally, see:

> Harrison, P., Todes, A. and Watson, V. (2007) *Planning and Transformation: Learning from the Post-Apartheid Experience,* Routledge, London.

There is a rich literature on international development, which covers planning and development experiences in urban and rural contexts. See:

Chambers, R. (2005) *Ideas for Development*, Earthscan, London.

Mitlin, D. and Satterthwaite, D. (eds) (2004) *Empowering Squatter Citizens: Local Government, Civil Society and Urban Poverty Reduction*, Earthscan, London.

UN-Habitat (2003) *The Challenge of Slums: Global Report on Human Settlements 2003*, Earthscan, London.

For a critical angle on this field of practice, see:

Simon, D. and Narman, A. (eds) (1999) *Development as Theory and Practice*, Addison Wesley Longman, Harlow.

Cooke, B. and Kothari, U. (eds) (2001) *Participation: The New Tyranny*, Zed Books, London.

Chapter 6

Transforming Places through Major Projects

Creating urban locales

Our lives are not only lived in the flow of daily routines. We also go to special places, for celebrations, for enjoyment, or because key resources are concentrated there. For firms, there are locales with particular kinds of business climate. For people who like shopping and window gazing, some locales have a special seductive power. For societies and social groups, some places express special qualities about themselves and their cultures in their buildings, landscapes and ambiences. In Paris, the grand, tree-lined avenue of the Champs Elysée connects the old city core with the Arc de Triomphe to the west. In London, people enjoy the walk from Piccadilly Circus through the shopping environments of Regent Street and then beyond Oxford Street up to Regent's Park. Or they may take a short light-rail trip from the old heart of the City of London to a new financial and leisure locale with a completely different ambience at Canary Wharf. And after visiting smaller cities such as Boston and Barcelona, tourists go home with memories of historic waterfronts, where they have been able to idle along among shops and restaurants and attractive public spaces.

The above is partly a list of places that seem to have the qualities of special urban places. We think of them as iconic places to go to in cities, whether we are residents or visitors. They are different to the neighbourhoods where most people in urban areas dwell (see Chapter 2). They are stimulating. They convey some kind of cosmopolitan atmosphere and often aesthetic enjoyment as well. They combine private spaces within a public realm that conveys a cosmopolitan feel, a sense of being in a city, of 'urbanity' (see Amin and Thrift 2002). They make us feel that we are in a real city. But the examples listed above also originated as major city rebuilding projects. They were produced by concentrated, co-ordinated effort, involving complex mixtures of public activity and the mobilisation of private investment over a long time. Such efforts have created new 'pieces of city', new landscapes and ambiences, and new relations between lived experiences and built forms, reshaping parts of urban areas for the 'new times' of their times. Some date from previous centuries, but many have been created in recent years, in response to the challenge of reconfiguring parts of cities that had been sculpted in the service of now outdated forms of industrial production and logistics. The spatial organisation of cities is never static and new locales appear often by the accumulation over time of small changes. However, not all locales can find new qualities in this way. In some, major barriers have to be overcome to release potentials. This is where major redevelopment projects find their rationale (see Box 6.1, continuing the tour of Newcastle City Centre, started in Chapter 2, which already highlighted two major projects, one from the nineteenth century and one from the 1960s/1970s).

This work of deliberate urban reconfiguration, of generating major projects, often now called 'mega-projects' (Diaz Orueta and Fainstein 2008), to create or recreate urban locales, is perhaps the most exciting and visible area of planning and development work. Some politicians and civic leaders like such projects for their potential to symbolise their dynamic contribution to city development and to leave a permanent mark on the urban landscape. It is proactive work, apparently stretching into the future. It involves mobilising all kinds of resources and finding ways through regulatory hurdles. Nevertheless, such projects also attract much criticism (Moulaert et al. 2000). Some projects, as with Hausmann's reorganisation of Paris, become symbolic of a grandiose and elitist political regime (Harvey 1989) or of the over-reaching ambitions of developers who collapse into bankruptcy, as in London's Canary Wharf (Fainstein 2001a). For some critics, the late twentieth century wave of major projects has symbolised 'rampant capitalism' or an urban manifestation of neo-liberal globalisation strategies, bent on extracting the maximum commercial and financial value from redevelopment activity and the promotion of 'consumerist' cultural values. For others, such projects display yet another elitist attempt to open up older parts of cities to the middle and upper classes, to gentrify areas that had become neglected or polluted, congested and socially tense.[1] Or such projects are lambasted as mere displays of architectural flamboyance, responding to local politicians searching for some demonstrable icon or 'flagship' with which to promote their city in a landscape of competition between cities for residents, investment and

Box 6.1 Recreating the quayside in Newcastle, UK

The 'tour' now continues from Grey's Monument and moves down Grey Street, a major project created through a ninteenth-century public–private partnership. By the 1990s this had become very run-down, despite efforts to renovate some individual buildings. It was squeezed between two other major projects, the comprehensive development of the 1960s to the north, and the work of the Tyne and Wear Development Corporation (1987–88) along the riverfront quayside. This latter initiative, funded by national government through a special agency always in tension with the City Council, refurbished buildings and produced a major project along the waterfront, creating a locale of hotels, offices, the law courts, apartments, bars and restaurants, where once there had been warehouses and other commercial buildings. Some of the firms that helped to create this new area relocated from old-fashioned premises in the older part of town, leaving yet more vacant units. To address this, and again using national government funds, a new partnership was created, involving the city council, representatives of business interests and all kinds of stakeholder groups, including the increasing numbers of residents moving into new apartments being created in the area. Its objective was to improve the public realm of streets, open spaces and general circulation, while at the same time attracting private owners and investors to get involved in refurbishing and developing their properties. This Grainger Town Partnership had a significant impact on the local environment and won awards for the quality of its work.

By the 2000s, the walk (or bus drive) from Grey's Monument flowed down refurbished and more lively streets to the quayside, which had been further transformed through imaginative investments by the neighbouring council of Gateshead, funded by national government urban renewal programmes and managed by Gateshead Council. This created a new art gallery in an old storage building, a new music centre to international standards designed by Norman Foster, a public space amphitheatre and surrounding hotel and apartment buildings and, most important of all, an elegant bridge linking one side of the river to the new locale created earlier on the Newcastle side. By the mid-2000s, through this accumulation of project initiatives, Newcastle/Gateshead had become a major location for national arts and music events, while the Quayside had become a much-valued public space within the city (see the last photo in Box 2.1).

tourists. Major projects are also often criticised as inefficient and badly managed, dragging taxpayers' funds into ballooning budgets as politicians pursue grandiose ambitions (Flyvbjerg et al. 2003).

Yet some of the projects noted above have created locales that are now valued, as in the Newcastle case, by citizens and visitors alike. They are accessible to all kinds of people, rather than elite enclaves. Many such projects in Europe and North America in recent years have sought to generate significant social and environmental benefits for a general public, along with creating profits for developers and end users (see Diaz Orueta and Fainstein 2008). They may have a dimension of theatrical display, but that is part of the enjoyment of urban life. They increase opportunities for most city dwellers, rather than displacing one group in favour of another.

The creation of new locales in urban areas with such qualities may come about by accident or it may result from the particular historical or geographical attributes of a location.[2] The transformation of the Newcastle quayside had history and geography on its side, but lacked sustained resources and so proceeded in 'bursts' as national funding became available. However, the creation of new widely valued locales mostly results from careful attention to the creation of positive place qualities by those involved in their development. It demands a planning orientation, infused with a commitment to creating long-term public realm resources.

In this chapter, I will look at what it takes to imagine and create such positive place qualities through major projects. The focus on such projects is not because they create the city. In fact, they are usually only a small part of what produces the built fabric of cities and the complex and shifting ambiences and flows of the social relations of urban life (Salet and Gualini 2007). Their importance lies in the enormous mobilisation of political and economic energy that is required to produce them, their symbolic role in expressing ideas about place, place qualities and the wider society in which they are situated, and their impact on how citizens and visitors view their governments and other major actors in their societies. The challenge is to ensure that concerns – for design quality, the provision of a public realm accessible to all citizens, and attention to making building and subsequent maintenance processes do as little harm as possible to the environment – are kept at the forefront of attention and not lost in the struggle to make such projects economically viable, both during construction and in subsequent use. It is this focus that expresses a planning orientation in which major projects are promoted and realised.

To explore what it takes to create new locales that enhance the place quality of an area and make substantial public realm contributions, I have selected three examples from among many such projects in cities around the world. They are from different continents. One was initiated in the 1960s while the other two are later. They have arisen from different local political cultures and socioeconomic circumstances. Yet they cross-reference each other and, particularly the first two, have served as exemplars for others promoting a major project elsewhere. They have all helped to create new 'pieces of city' in former industrial, commercial and port areas that are now valued by citizens and visitors alike. The first example is the Faneuil Hall Marketplace adjacent to the city centre of the US city of Boston, Massachusetts. The second is the Barcelona waterfront in Spain, where the Olympics were held in 1992. The third is Brindleyplace, around an old canal basin near the city centre of Birmingham, in the UK. They all illustrate a concentrated effort to reconfigure and reposition a part of a city near the city centre and create new locales with attributes of inclusive urbanity (Majoor 2008). In each case, the details of the project are set in the wider context of city politics and socio-economic dynamics, covering a period of a decade or more. Particular people become very visible in these cases, but the emphasis in the accounts is on how the projects were brought into being – how possibilities and project ideas were imagined, how resources were assembled, how ideas progressed from designs to land clearance and building activity, and how attention was sustained for projects that had long time spans from initial idea to completion. Through these accounts, I highlight how a planning orientation, centred on creating public realm benefits, was kept in play through the many challenges that such projects face as they get to be realised. I also underline what it takes to manage such complex projects, with long-term development horizons, during shifts and changes in political and economic conditions.[3]

Faneuil Hall Marketplace, Boston, US[4]

Boston and its Redevelopment Authority (BRA) have already been encountered in Chapter 3. In the 1940s and 1950s, the city had a reputation as a badly governed city in which corruption was rife. Working-class groups struggled against complacent elite families and were themselves divided into conflicting Irish, Italian and

Jewish communities. Investment in city centre improvement and in poorer neighbourhoods was neglected, while industrial firms and the extensive harbour areas declined as the economy changed. Many residents and firms moved out to the surrounding areas, where the State of Massachusetts had been investing in major highways. This encouraged the development of business parks and shopping malls on the urban periphery. Meanwhile, African Americans moved in considerable numbers to some inner neighbourhoods, to add to the existing mix.

In the 1950s, a new regime came to power under Mayor John B. Hynes, committed to less corrupt and more effective government. Many projects were put forward at this time, but few reached the development stage, because of political conflicts and lack of confidence among potential private investors. City development plans were also prepared, proposing substantial clearance and redevelopment of housing, commercial and industrial areas around the city centre. In 1957, the Boston Redevelopment Authority (BRA) was created,[5] being led after a year or two by Director Ed Logue (see Chapter 3). Logue energetically pursued the realisation of projects already agreed in principle. He also encouraged the revision of the city plan, after substantial opposition to the redevelopment plans. In its heyday in the late 1960s/1970s and under the political guidance of Mayor Kevin White, Boston became 'an icon of city planning and reformed progressive city government' (Murray 2006:63). A key issue for Mayor White was to combine neighbourhood improvement, in participation with residents, with projects to promote reinvestment into the city centre and reverse the outflow of people and firms to the areas around.

Faneuil Hall Marketplace is located between the city's financial and government district and the waterfront. It consists now of the old Faneuil Hall, built in 1742 as an assembly hall in the early days of Boston's history, and the former Quincy Market, once the city's major food wholesale market, remodelled into an area of boutique shops and stalls, bars and restaurants, among old cobbled streets, opening across a wide open space (below which is a major road artery) onto a park, apartments in converted warehouses and the sea. Declining since the 1900s, the area around Quincy Wholesale Market was deteriorating rapidly in the 1950s (see Figure 6.1). The central artery highway, built on the surface in the 1950s, divided the area from the waterfront. Boston's City Planning Board, engaged in clearance and redevelopment in other parts of the city, proposed clearing the whole area. However, campaigning planners and architects recognised the

Figure 6.1   *Old Quincy Market*

Source: The Art Archive/National Archives, Washington, DC.

heritage value of the buildings and suggested a different place-development concept. This centred on retaining the historic structures and encouraging retail shopping, to replace the wholesale market. The campaigning eventually attracted the support of both the Mayor and the BRA Director. Studies were set up, involving the local Chamber of Commerce, with an eye to acquiring Federal Government grants for urban renewal, resulting in 1964 in a Waterfront Renewal Plan. This suggested that the Quincy Market building should be restored and the remaining wholesale activities moved out.[6] These were to be replaced by a mixture of shops, offices, small business units, apartments, food retailing and restaurants. (This alternative plan was drawn up by a firm of consultants, advised by the famous MIT urban designer Kevin Lynch.) Thus an idea of a new kind of urban environment for American cities was generated, a locale for leisure and consumption to attract the affluent back to city centres. This concept has since been replicated across the world's richer cities, echoing the lively urbanity of European cities in the eighteenth and nineteenth centuries.

Such an innovative and risky project needed a strong advocate in order to attract private-sector investment interest. In the US, too much state intervention tends to be suspect and the political priority in Boston was to improve conditions in the neighbourhoods. A local architect and businessman, Ben Thompson, one of the advocates of the project and committed to enhancing his city of Boston, took up the challenge, using his contacts to find a developer to carry the project forward. This search led to the involvement of James Rouse, later to become internationally known for his work regenerating Baltimore's waterfront (see Box 6.2).

For Rouse, shopping and entertainment locales within a city were places that drew many different kinds of people together. A shopping experience could thus create a lead activity to attract people back to a neglected part of the city. This required a 'clever use of space' (Frieden and Sagalyn 1991:176). The core idea was to convert the old market buildings into a collection of small units selling all kinds of speciality products, along with restaurants and bars, all interlinked to create an enjoyable strolling experience both within and around the buildings. Rouse's company had financial resources built up from previous projects, and a team with the multiple skills and business contacts needed to take on a difficult, innovative project. Rouse himself was also skilled in purveying optimistic energy, engaging in energetic evangelising for the project. Accounts suggest that this was not mere marketing hype, but that he believed (correctly, as it turned out) that the project would work out well. The development task was thus to release the potential development value that already inhered in the location and the historic buildings. How this was achieved is summarised in Box 6.3.

A decade later, Faneuil Hall Marketplace had become a prototype in the development business as a new kind of shopping locale. Not only was it 'in town' and not in the peripheral suburbs, it promoted the idea of a retail environment as entertainment, with a festival ambience and speciality shopping. Visitor numbers were much higher than expected. By the mid-1980s, 16 million people were coming to the Marketplace each year, more than were then visiting Britain. They were not spending a lot individually, but the high volume enabled the retail businesses to do well and hence pay

> ## Box 6.2   Selecting a developer
>
> By 1970, a developer had been found who was agreeable to the BRA, but deadlines were set that the developer could not meet, especially as the property development industry was heading into one of its cyclical downturns. By 1972, however, a second developer had become interested in the project. This was James Rouse, who had built a major business out of developing suburban shopping malls and food markets. Another local architect-developer also came forward with a scheme. The City Mayor and the Director of the Redevelopment Authority, worried about the continuing decay of the buildings and unsure of the project idea, were thus able to weigh up the potential of each scheme, giving particular attention to the financial returns to the municipality and the managerial capacity of the developers. These, of course, did what they could to cultivate confidence. Rouse, the 'outsider' in terms of local networks, promised to keep Mayor White and the BRA fully informed at every stage in the twists and turns of the project as development proceeded.
>
> In 1973, the Rouse Company was named as the developer. Rouse combined clever politics with a strategic sense of how new urban locales could be created and a good understanding of the complex relations between the design, management and financing of a development scheme. He was also himself a strong believer in the value of creating an open, accessible urban ambience and wanted to experiment to see if the qualities being created in his firm's suburban shopping malls could be adapted and enriched in an inner urban context. In his sense of social responsibility to urban life generally and to making a contribution to the public realm of the city, he was unusual among shopping mall developers of his time.

good rents (Frieden and Sagalyn 1991:176). As a result, the project generated substantial profits and paid around $2.5 million per annum to Boston City Council. Across the US and in Europe, the project and the Rouse Company came to symbolise what creative, energetic redevelopment of older parts of cities could achieve. Within Boston itself, the project helped to generate the confidence for further waterfront development.

In the 2000s, Faneuil Hall Marketplace remains an important public space and leisure locale within the city, for residents and visitors alike (see Figure 6.2). With the sinking of the central artery below ground, the area now connects the city centre to the waterfront. It is well positioned on city-wide networks of walking paths and bikeways, public transport and highways. Over time, the mix of

---

Box 6.3   Achieving a project idea

The deal that the BRA made with Rouse involved some work from both parties. The BRA bought the old marketplace, relocated the remaining wholesale merchants, removed a highway ramp and put in new utility lines. It then leased the buildings to the James Rouse Company. This had the advantage for the company of reducing its initial costs, while politically, the BRA could ward off criticism that it was 'selling Boston's heritage' (Frieden and Sagalyn 1991136). The lease contract established a rental structure through which both parties could share in hoped-for rising rental returns, although a cap was put on the City's share in rising revenues. (This in retrospect turned out to be much too low).

The BRA provided around 28 per cent of the development costs in one way or another, drawing on federal funds for a substantial part of this finance. Although the Rouse Company had its own financial resources, its long-term intention was to sell the project to a property investment company. This required confidence from an investor that adequate rental returns would be achieved. One investor became interested, but did not want to take over the project until it was completed. Local Boston bankers were very reluctant to get involved in financing the construction stage, preferring less risky projects, or at least the promise that a well-known 'anchor store' would locate in the development. The company could not promise a major department store, as this was not the ambition of the project. Instead, a restaurant chain agreed to locate in the project, and, with some 'arm twisting' by the Mayor, local bankers were persuaded to provide construction finance. Rouse also agreed to meet city council social objectives by employing minority contractors and encouraging minority businesses.

Throughout the development phase, the company had to address new issues to do with design, materials and finance. Thanks to the vigilance of the Mayor, and thanks also to the company's own commitment to these values, attention to both design quality and to appropriate management mechanisms for the resultant project was sustained through to completion. Commercially, Rouse recognised that a commitment to quality and attractiveness was critical to the economic success of the project.[7]

---

activities has shifted from high-end shopping to restaurants and bars, but this perhaps reflects shifts in consumer spending patterns. Frieden and Sagalyn (1991:174–5) comment that the project:

> hit a series of themes just right for the time. For a mass public that had just discovered gourmet food, the central arcade served it up in volume and with flair. For a public with a fresh interest

Figure 6.2   *Faneuil Hall Marketplace in 2008*

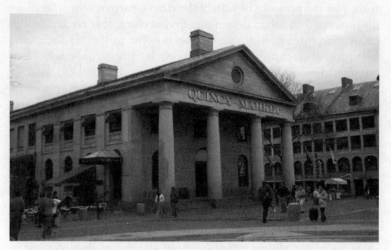

in history, the market presented authentic 150-year-old buildings and cobbled paths rich with historic associations. For a
generation that had discovered sidewalk cafés and bustling piaz-
zas in Europe, the market brought these pleasures home.

However, the project has also been much criticised. Echoing the
general criticisms of mega-projects noted at the start of this chapter,
critics claimed that the project symbolised an escapist consumerism,
a type of 'theme park' environment (Sorkin 1992), rather then a real
contribution to the social and economic regeneration of Boston. It
encouraged a nostalgia for a lost past and did not have much impact
on the rest of Boston's downtown, where some people still lived in
severe poverty. Yet an urban locale was created adjacent to the city
centre where anyone could take a stroll, look at the stalls and out to
the sea. It also helped to attract people back to city centre living.
Thanks to the City Council's neighbourhood renewal strategies of
the 1970s and 1980s, and to the stream of inner-city apartment
projects that followed from this first project, Boston's population
has increased and places like Faneuil Hall Marketplace still provide
locales where people from different backgrounds mix together.

This project was, for the city of Boston and for American cities
generally, an experiment in creating a new kind of urban locale. Its
quality, including the commitment to enhancing the inner-city
public realm, was held in place by the attention of the Mayor, the
commitment of the powerful Redevelopment Authority and

the skills of the James Rouse company. This attention was reinforced by the presence of watchful citizens, particularly professionals interested in urban design and architecture. It is no accident in
cultivating this activism that Boston is home to the Massachusetts
Institute of Technology (MIT), with its prestigious School of
Architecture and Planning, and to the Harvard School of Design in
nearby Cambridge. A further positive factor was the emphasis on
connecting what was happening in this inner-city retail mall project
to opportunities for those in inner-city neighbourhoods around the
city, with their clusters of different working-class communities. And
the location, which combined historic heritage, adjacent to the city
centre and near an attractive waterfront, provided assets waiting to
be realised. As those campaigning against clearance and redevelopment argued, there was a moment of opportunity to be grasped for
creating a significant public realm asset. It was a risky experiment,
but in this case it ended up creating significant and varied development value for all concerned, without significant displacement of
pre-existing firms and neighbourhoods as had happened in earlier
redevelopment projects in the city. As a development approach,
however, it contrasts strongly with the next case, from Barcelona.

The Barcelona Waterfront, Catalonia, Spain[8]

In Boston, the approach to urban development was essentially project driven. The municipality created an opportunity, but much of the
finance and expertise came from private-sector developers and
investors. The City Council expected to share in the returns from
development, both financially and through the creation of public
realm assets. Like Boston in the 1980s, Barcelona became in the
1990s an international model of how to achieve an urban 'renaissance'. However, its development approach has been very different.
   Spain's second city, by 2001 the Barcelona municipality had a
population of around 1.5 million, with 2.8 million in the Barcelona
metropolitan area and 4.8 million in the wider metropolitan region.
In recent years, people have been moving out to this wider region as
infrastructure provision has improved (Marshall 2004). The municipality has substantial tax-raising and income-generation powers,
though it has not historically had a substantial amount of land in its
ownership. It is the capital city of the autonomous region of
Catalonia and in the nineteenth century was a substantial commercial, industrial and port hub within the Mediterranean area, with a

bourgeoisie committed to investing in the city. During this period, industrial and commercial development spread along the waterfront, behind which was the old city. Around the urban core, urban extensions were built to an innovative plan of 1857, drawn up by local engineer Ildefons Cerda. The city was noted for its intellectual and artistic culture, for its commercial prowess and its poor but activist working class. Barcelona was not simply a working-class, industrial city. It was a city of architectural and artistic innovation, symbolised in the amazing forms created by the architect Antoni Gaudí. This heritage, disrupted in the twentieth century by civil war and dictatorship, helped to inspire a new generation of politicians, architects and planners who, in conjunction with civil society protest movements, created a new strategic momentum and new ideas for the city, which shaped urban development activity for the rest of the century.

During the dictatorship period, which ended finally with General Franco's death in 1975, there was very little investment in housing, public facilities and infrastructure until the later 1950s, and most working people found themselves crowded into ageing and poorly serviced housing stock. When Franco's government began to encourage more urban growth, this took the form of poorly built speculative development, filling up vacant land and open spaces, including sites reserved for public facilities such as schools, health centres, libraries and small parks in the prevailing urban plan.[9] This added to the overcrowding and general deterioration of quality of life for residents. It was in these conditions that citizen protest about neighbourhood conditions grew into a wider social movement, with connections to socialist politics elsewhere in Europe, demanding changes in government priorities and politics (Castells 1983). Protest was especially vigorous against proposals to demolish neighbourhoods to make way for new developments. Local architects and urbanists were very much involved in these protest movements.

The dictatorship regime made some responses to these demands for greater attention to living conditions, and an initiative was started to produce a new General Metropolitan Plan for the city. This plan anticipated continued substantial growth in the city, but aimed to reduce densities, increase facilities, public parks and green spaces within the crowded neighbourhoods and improve the city's long-neglected physical infrastructures. There were significant struggles over this plan, reflecting the tense political climate. Citizens argued that it did too little to resist speculative exploitation by developers, while the developers claimed that it was too restrictive. Formally approved in 1976, this is still the prevailing plan.

When the dictatorship ended, these strategic ideas were carried forward by a new democratic municipal council. As in the Vancouver case in Chapter 4, key activists from the protest movements, many with an architectural background, became leading politicians, and also headed up the municipal departments of urban development and architecture. The new municipal regime emphasised the importance of building up a capable administration. In the post-dictatorship period, such administrative reorganisation was made easier as officials from the old regime could be dismissed and a new, more streamlined organisation created. The strategic urban development project of the new administration was to realise the ambitions of the 1976 General Plan, expanded with further urban design concepts. These included consolidation of the important harbour installations in an area to the south west, where there was space to create the new kinds of facilities that the marine container trade demanded. This meant that the old industrialised waterfront area could be turned into a recreation area for citizens. Overall, there was a strong emphasis on improving the physical public realm, in terms of landscaping and public sculpture. A key strategic principle was to create a more urban ambience in the expanding peripheral areas, and to recover the quality of the city centre (Esteban 2004).

While the City Council had enormous popular support in realising these ideas, its first priority was to deliver improvements in the neighbourhoods, for which the financial resources that could be raised locally were sufficient. After 1986, when Spain joined the European Union, Barcelona also had access to EU funds for such neighbourhood improvement work. But waterfront reclamation, not to mention physical infrastructure investment, was another matter, requiring very substantial resources, beyond the capacity of the municipality. It was in this context that the politicians and key officials developed the strategy that they refer to as 'event-led regeneration'. If an event was sufficiently strategic nationally, funding from the national state and from the Catalonia region could be mobilised to combine with municipal funds. It is in this context that Barcelona developed its bid to host the 1992 Olympic Games. The idea was first developed in 1982 within the City Council and approval was formally accorded by the International Olympic Committee in 1986. Antonio Samaranch, then head of the International Olympic Committee, was a project developer in Barcelona (Majoor 2008:164). This kick-started the reconfiguration of Barcelona's north-east waterfront, adjacent to the old city core

Figure 6.3   *Barcelona city centre and waterfront area*

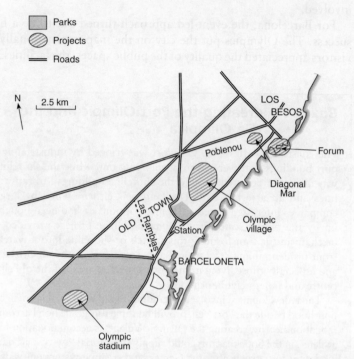

and harbour, where the Olympic Village was sited (see Figure 6.3). It also attracted resources for major infrastructure and other large open space improvement projects around the city. Ward (2002) reports that some people from Barcelona visited James Rouse in Baltimore to learn more about waterfront inner-city regeneration.

The Olympic project had the major strategic benefit of focusing the attention of all levels of government and of the various public agencies responsible for infrastructure investment. This encouraged the co-ordination needed to bring the overall project to fruition. The project was designed and managed by the City Council's architecture and planning department, under the leadership of architect-planners Oriol Bohigas and later Joan Busquets, overseen by Mayor Pasqual Maragall, mayor from 1982 to 1997. There were also a number of special agencies for particular parts of the work, though strongly linked to the Council. The project implied substantial financial investment and the complications of building on complex, polluted sites. It also presented a challenge of making such a location accessible to the substantial flows of people associated with an event such as the Olympic Games. Box 6.4 summarises what was involved.

For Barcelona, the event-led approach turned out to be a huge success. The Olympics put the city on the map internationally, as visitors appreciated the quality of the public spaces, the facilities and

---

Box 6.4   Creating the Port Olimpic and the Vila Olimpica

The coastline north of the Old Port was fringed by industrial and port buildings that were steadily emptying out, while the shoreline was dirty and polluted. Behind the shoreline buildings ran railway lines and an arterial road. The land was either owned by large companies interested in redevelopment options or had been bought up by the public sector. The Olympic Village project provided a mechanism for transforming this stretch of shoreline into a waterfront residential and recreational area to be enjoyed by all citizens, and especially those living in the poor, crowded areas of the old city centre and inner neighbourhoods.

The redevelopment involved upgrading an old working-class neighbourhood beside the Port Vell, providing some top-grade hotel accommodation nearby, creating the Olympic Village as accommodation for athletes, in the hope that this could supply substantial low-cost accommodation for citizens after the Games, and creating waterfront walkways from the old port (Port Vell), past the Olympic complex and on along the north-eastern waterfront, where beaches were created, to impress visitors initially but mainly as a future resource for citizens. The rail lines were cleared away and part of the arterial road was sunk, as in Boston. In addition, the city's sewerage system was improved, so that the shoreline became suitable for swimming.

Intense persuasive activity among intertwined political and technical networks was undertaken to commit all levels of government and public agencies to enable co-ordinated action to a tight timescale. Most of the site was already in municipal ownership thanks to the foresight of some council officials in the immediate post-Franco transition, but the whole site had to be assembled and facilities built to a very tight timetable. Some of the facilities were to be sold off later, but it was expected that much would remain as public facilities to be funded and managed by the public sector. Not surprisingly, this created a huge financial burden for the City Council, leading to subsequent debts and demands on revenue expenditure. One casualty of these financial pressures was that the apartments created for the Olympic athletes did not become available as social housing, but were sold off as private apartments.

Figure 6.4   *Barcelona waterfront in the 2000s*

Source: Ali Madanipour.

the seafront environment, adjacent to the older parts of the city centre (see Figure 6.4). The project impressed subsequent tourists, investors and entrepreneurs, as a reflection of the dynamic energy of the city. Vigorously marketed by leading city politicians, planners and architects, it became an icon of politically-led city regeneration. The citizens too enjoyed the celebrations and the new assets, especially the opening up of the waterfront as promenades and beaches. The City Council was itself surprised by the success. Nevertheless, reflecting the city's lively political culture, there was also considerable criticism. Some argued that the project deflected attention away from the neighbourhoods and gave too much emphasis to external image. The financial burden of the Olympic project meant that the City Council was forced to rely more on private capital and to make compromises that resulted in gentrification. The Olympic timetable led to some projects being built too quickly, with loss of quality in construction and in design. And there were big increases in land and property values in the older parts of the city centre, leading to displacement effects as poorer potential residents were priced out and moved to the periphery of the urban area. Some also argued that the project reflected the excesses of 'capitalist' urban development.

Yet in comparison with Boston and urban development in the US generally, what is striking is that this project was driven and executed primarily by public-sector initiative and capital, informed by social-democratic principles. Politicians, their planning and architecture staff and their key networks were the entrepreneurial 'master developers'.

It had been the City Council's intention, once the Olympic project was underway, to move on to take a more strategic look at overall development directions for the city. A more socio-economic guidance strategy was agreed by the Council in 1992 (*Barcelona 2000*). This identified major infrastructure investments and redevelopment projects, including a northern extension of the Olympic waterfront. However, these projects proved much more challenging to achieve, especially as the City Council was now heavily indebted. The city tried an event-led approach again, but had to create its own idea of an event (a Universal Forum of Culture, held in 2004). This attracted EU funds, but many fewer visitors than expected (Majoor 2008, Majoor and Salet 2008). A private-sector developer from the US funded an apartment and retail scheme (Diagonal Mar), which was successfully completed. But as of 2008, other planned projects along the waterfront were proceeding slowly, with difficulties in attracting finance.

In Barcelona, then, urban regeneration in the waterfront area was driven by the City Council, through major projects and primarily with public-sector funding. It was infused by a strong strategic conception of a vital city centre, a key nodal locale for an urban community. The ambition was to create the city not just as built form but as a social ambience and an expression of the spirit of its citizens (see Maragall 2004, Marshall 2004). In the context of the escape from dictatorship, the project was about creating a democratic city and community. The Mayor and his close advisers saw themselves as the primary expression of this community, and as guardians of the public realm on behalf of the citizens. This relationship was legitimated by the oppositional public created during the Franco era. A large moment of opportunity was thus available within which the City Council could play such a role. However, as time went on, the politicians and their advisers were themselves the focus of criticism from a vocal citizenry used to an active role in public life. Such critical challenge had a valuable role in maintaining the council's attention to the qualities of the public realm and the provision of facilities for citizens as well as tourists and companies. It placed at the forefront of attention the need to balance investment in key urban nodes with improvements in neighbourhoods. It is all these dimensions that infuse the Barcelona model of urban regeneration through major projects (Majoor 2008).

However, 30 years after the transition to democracy, the City Council has to live in more ordinary times. A critical and more affluent citizenry is less satisfied with the political-technical fix that drove the regeneration model and demands new forms of consultation and participation. While the efforts of the City Council created substantial development value and economic opportunities in the city, this also led to social displacement, as richer people moved into city centre locations and lower-income residents moved out to the periphery.[10] In the 2000s the public sector at all levels of government had more limited funds to invest, and co-ordination between the different levels and sectors of government was much more difficult. This meant more competition for funding between major development projects and other demands on public funds. As a result, the City Council began to seek out larger private developers, but this meant learning more about the way they operate. Politicians and planners have also begun to recognise that a generalised strategy expressed primarily through specific physical projects may have its limitations. By the later 2000s, a major effort was being put into developing a metropolitan 'territorial' or 'spatial' plan for the urban region. It remains to be seen how major projects will now be pursued in Barcelona, in a country severely affected by the financial and economic crises of the later 2000s.

Birmingham City Centre and Brindleyplace, UK[11]

Like Boston and Barcelona, Birmingham City Council pursued an energetic, project-driven approach to city-wide place development, combined with a concern to improve living conditions in poorer neighbourhoods. In the 1980s Birmingham found itself in a not dissimilar situation to Barcelona in the mid-1990s. Both were 'second cities' in their countries, and both were financially indebted from major publicly funded projects that aimed to bring their cities to international attention and to revive their city centres. However, Birmingham is a very different kind of place, although it shares with Barcelona a political culture of energetic municipal development activity. It has forged links with US cities and development consultants, including the Rouse Company, and with European cities, including Barcelona. It is Britain's largest municipality, with a million people in 2001, but is surrounded by other urban areas in an urban amalgam, or 'conurbation', built up through rapid industrial expansion in the nineteenth and twentieth centuries. It has no water-fronts, as in Boston and Barcelona, apart from a network of canals created to move raw materials and industrial products in the pre-railway age. These weave their way through the city and through neglect had become forgotten and polluted backwaters, surrounded by factories and warehouses. By the mid-twentieth century, Birmingham was the proud core of a major manufacturing complex centred on car production and skilled engineering, attracting invest-ment and workers from home and abroad, especially through the links with the old imperial British Commonwealth.[12] But during the 1970s, the buoyant industrial nexus steadily weakened and was further hit by the rapidity of the industrial collapse of the early 1980s. Around 140,000 manufacturing jobs were lost in the conur-bation between 1981 and 1987 (Smyth 1994:128). As well as rising unemployment, this left many derelict buildings and sites, some close to the city centre.

Like Boston and Barcelona, the city expanded rapidly in the 1950s and 1960s, extending outwards into the wider metropolitan area, though physically this expansion was held in check by a tight 'green belt'. Within the city itself, the ambition in the 1950s was to equip the city centre for car-based access. This strategy surrounded the nineteenth-century city centre core with a sunken ring road, which created a 'trench' between the centre and the neighbourhoods around. Within the centre, redevelopment was undertaken in the 1950s and 1960s to replace war damage and provide access for a car-oriented local economy and culture. It was generally agreed later that the result was poor-quality buildings and a drab city centre environment. Retail provision lagged behind the demand being created by the growth in population and affluence in the region. By the 1980s, City Council politicians and officials were increasingly concerned about the loss of investment and retail spending in the city core.

However, the municipality has always had a tradition of forward thinking and proactive urban development, though greatly chal-lenged by the strong centralising tendencies of the British state (see Newton 1976 and the South Tyneside case in Chapter 5). By 1980, it had few autonomous sources of finance and, where it had land resources, was being exhorted by national government to privatise these. Its legal resources were limited too, as any plans within the formal planning system needed the approval of higher tiers of government and involved complex negotiations with surrounding municipalities (see Vigar et al. 2000:Chapter 3). As in Boston and Barcelona, the municipality had to deal with problems of poverty and increasing unemployment, as well as safety and security in many of its inner-city neighbourhoods, badly affected by the changing economic climate. A critical dimension of growth promotion was to develop a stronger concentration of 'tertiary' activities in the city centre; that is, commercial, cultural and retail activities. It was in this context that a city centre reconfiguration strategy developed, backed for some years with a broad consensus that allowed the City Council to build an alliance with the local Chamber of Commerce, sustained by the substantial expertise available within the city administration. The City Council also made good use of access to European funds for restructuring areas hit by industrial decline (Smyth 1994). Thus, despite limited formal powers and resources, the municipality had substantial governance capacity and a long tradition of co-operation between business and council activity.

The strategy developed in two phases. Initially, the emphasis was on major publicly funded projects that would position the city internationally.[13] Like Barcelona, Birmingham made a bid for the Olympics. Though unsuccessful, this generated ideas for hotels, a convention centre and a large indoor arena. When the Olympic bid failed, these ideas were linked to the project of city centre regeneration. A strategy emerged for connecting the existing city centre core retail and office spaces around Colmore Row and Victoria Square, across the inner ring road by a bridge to the existing Centenary Square, where the City Council offices were already situated. The main projects were a new, high-quality concert hall (now Symphony Hall, home to the Birmingham Symphony Orchestra) and, opposite, an International Convention Centre (ICC). Beside this, a major hotel, by the Hyatt chain, was also developed (see Figure 6.5). This backed onto a site of 26 acres (11 hectares) of derelict industrial land and buildings, around part of the city's old canal network. Converting this area into a new leisure and entertainment locale was a key part of the strategy. It is this area that, after considerable setbacks, became Brindleyplace, acknowledged by the end of the century as a major example of the successful creation of a city centre locale or new 'urban quarter' (Latham and Swenarton 1999), and a decade later is a vibrant part of Birmingham's lively and dynamic city centre life.

Councillors and officials discussed and visited US examples of convention centres and major hotel projects, and came to know

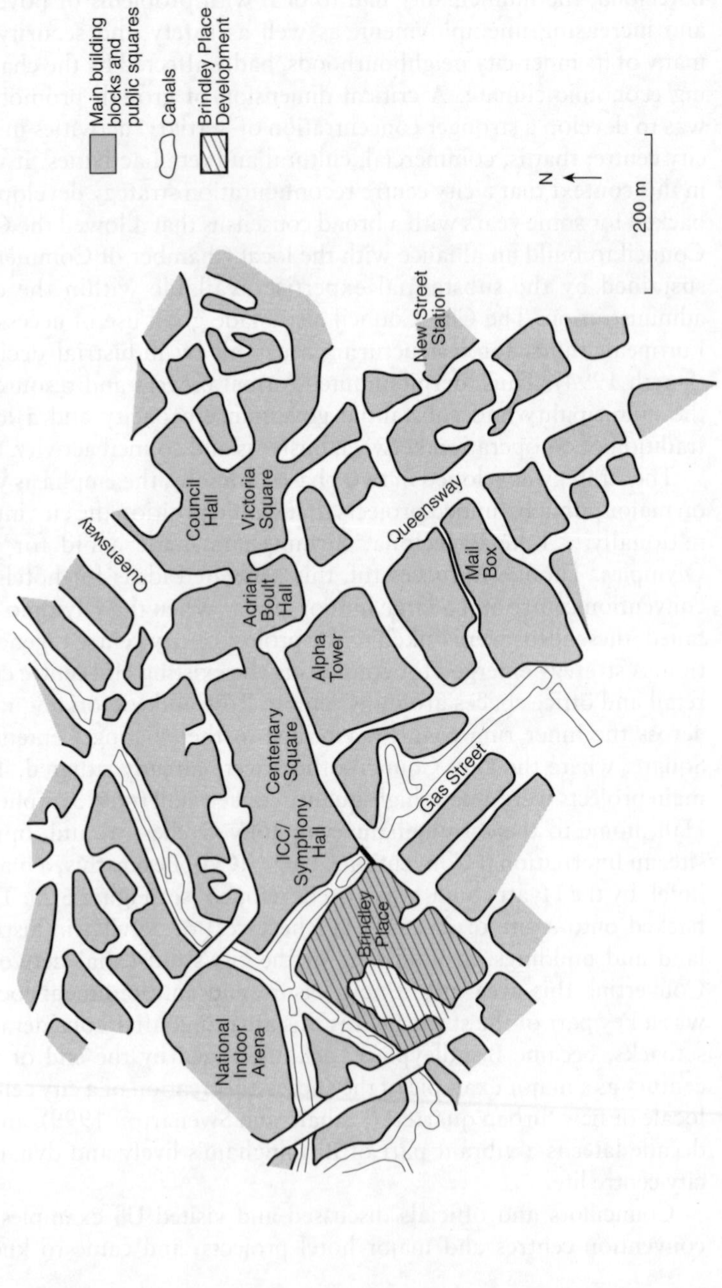

Figure 6.5 *Projects in the Centenary Square and Canalside area*

Legend:
- Main building blocks and public squares
- Canals
- Brindley Place Development

N ←

200 m

Council Hall

Victoria Square

Queensway

Adrian Boult Hall

Queensway

New Street Station

Mail Box

Alpha Tower

Centenary Square

ICC/Symphony Hall

Gas Street

Brindley Place

National Indoor Arena

of James Rouse's ideas about festival shopping as a way to reanimate inner-city locales. The City Council visited Rouse's projects at Baltimore, which grew from the Faneuil Hall Marketplace experience. As part of the overall land assembly for the city centre regeneration projects, which all came to completion in the early 1990s, the City Council slowly brought the Brindleyplace area into its ownership. There had for some time also been initiatives to improve the network of canals that had been rediscovered as tourists took up the canal boat experience. The council's project idea was for a combination of an indoor arena with what was originally to be a festival shopping location, modelled on Rouse's experiences. It hoped to generate the funding for the arena from the sale of the whole site it had assembled to a private developer. By this time, the council's debts were mounting and it was being criticised by local academics on the grounds that big projects were eating up council resources, to the neglect of addressing the difficulties in many of the poorer inner-city neighbourhoods (Loftman and Nevin 1994). At the height of the property boom in the late 1980s, a privately financed development seemed a possible and attractive prospect.

By this time, however, the City Council was beginning to think more strategically about the future of the city centre. During 1987 and 1988, business leaders and design experts helped local politicians and officials produce ideas for a new 'vision' for the city centre. They used an arena created to promote the City's development called the 'Highbury initiative'.[14] With an overall City Centre Vision sketched out, the City Council asked consultants from the James Rouse company to undertake a study of pedestrian movement and urban design options, supplemented by a further study on public realm design. This slowly led to what became the City Centre Design Strategy, which sought to create a lively city centre, with distinct quarters around the core. This helped to fix some of the values of a planning orientation in a way that set a framework within which city council planners negotiated with private developers to achieve what eventually became Brindleyplace. Remarkably, the overall ideas, reworked flexibly as the property development industry went through a major crisis, provided the basis for both a development master plan and legal contracts between the council and specific developers.

In 1987, at the height of the property boom of the time, the City Council produced a development brief for the Brindleyplace area and called for bids from interested developers. The brief required the construction of the indoor arena as well as the development of

Box 6.5   Managing through property booms and busts

The site was sold in the late 1980s for £23.3 million, which the City Council used to subsidise the construction of the indoor arena. The rest of the site development cost, on the remaining 11 acres, was to be provided by the developer, anticipating financial returns through the sale of plots and buildings to owner-occupiers and investors. The indoor arena was built, but by 1990 the property boom had turned to bust. By 1992, the rest of the site was referred to as a 'failed flagship' (Smyth 1994:190). The area had been largely cleared, but the development consortium had by this time unravelled. Laing withdrew once it had obtained its primary interest, which was to build the arena. Merlin also withdrew, as returns from its Darling Harbour project, which it had hoped to use to invest in Brindleyplace, were delayed by litigation in Australia. Shearwater was thus left as the only developer. As British property development companies experienced the harsh winds of a property bust, Shearwater's finances became precarious and Rosehaugh let it go into liquidation in 1990. This left Rosehaugh, with its dynamic chair, Godfrey Bradman, holding the Brindleyplace project. Their primary interest was in single-use office buildings.

The Farrell urban design consultancy was brought in by the City Council to provide an urban design master plan to reflect this change. All this time, the original project director appointed by the consortium, Alan Chatwin, stayed with the project. From 1989 through the difficult following years, although nothing much was happening with

$\rightarrow$

the rest of the site for retail and leisure activities. The City Council received 21 expressions of interest and developers were selected because of their potential for realising the design ideas developed in the City Centre Vision. The result was the sale of the site in the late 1980s to a development consortium, Merlin-Shearwater-Laing. Merlin was a US company with links to the Rouse Corporation and also interests in Darling Harbour, in Sydney, Australia. Shearwater was the retail development arm of Rosehaugh, a high-profile UK company of the 1980s that had developed the Broadgate scheme at Liverpool Street Station in London. Laing was a construction company, primarily interested in building the National Arena (Smyth 1994). However, by this time, the property development industry in Britain and internationally was in a major crisis. Intensive efforts by committed staff working for the City Council and for the developers managed to keep the design ideas alive (see Box 6.5).

→

the site or the project, he met fortnightly with city planner, Geoff Wright, to discuss what could be done to keep the project alive (Latham and Swenarton 1999). The City Council used the master plan to maintain a focus on the quality of the public spaces and the public realm, resisting too strong a shift to offices and emphasising the need for a mix of restaurants, bars, a central square, canalside frontages and bridges, linking the area through pedestrian routes to other parts of the overall city centre complex. Its strategic ambition, shared by Alan Chatwin, was to create a distinctive quarter, with easy and interesting pedestrian flows to other parts of the city centre. It also wanted to increase the numbers of people actually living in the city centre, as part of the idea of making Birmingham more like a typical European city.[15] After negotiation, Rosehaugh's master plan was given formal 'outline' approval under its land-use planning powers by the City Council. Then the Rosehaugh company too went into receivership.

The scheme was put out to tender to see if there was any development interest. Five bidders came forward and, after some negotiations, a relatively unknown company, Argent,[16], was selected because of its emphasis on the public realm. Argent bought the site for £3 million, which became £8 million once all development obligations were complied with. Later, Argent argued that it would never have been able to realise the project if it had not obtained the site at a knockdown price (Latham and Swenarton 1999). Argent continued the close working arrangements with the City Council, which allowed flexible adjustments within the overall master-plan framework.

As the project began to take physical shape during the 1990s and early 2000s (see Figure 6.6), it connected to a major leisure location that emerged along the canalside towards a complex mixed development project, now known as the Mailbox. By the mid-2000s, Birmingham City Council had achieved its ambition of recreating its city centre as an attractive urban core, with an ambience not unlike that associated with other European cities. It had also shown that careful attention to the quality of the public realm was a key attribute of that achievement and that this in turn created value for private-sector property investors and developers. As in the case of Boston and Barcelona, the council was continually having to balance its commitments to its poorer neighbourhoods and the realisation of development opportunities around the city centre. It has not been able to avoid gentrification, as an uplift in property values around areas such as Brindleyplace led to a substantial expansion of

Figure 6.6   *Brindleyplace in 2008*

canalside apartment buildings. Nevertheless, throughout, council politicians and planners have insisted on opening up physical access from the poorer neighbourhoods to the emerging new squares and canalside walkways. As in Boston and Barcelona, an active political community has helped to keep the values of inclusive accessibility to major urban nodes in play.

This case is a good illustration of the complexity of transforming a city centre through mobilising both public and private development energies, making use of different public-sector financial opportunities and nurturing private development activity through the booms and slumps of the property development market. Those involved learned on the job about how to combine good-quality urban design with the specific demands of different kinds of investors, and they developed working relationships that cut across organisational and public/private-sector boundaries. The public-sector actors kept in mind what they believed councillors were looking for in enhancing the city centre. Geoff Wright, who headed up the negotiations, recalls:

I distilled City expectations down to being firstly to achieve restaurants/bars opposite the ICC ..., secondly to achieve a 'people attractor' leisure element, ... thirdly to achieve some housing ..., fourthly to provide a new public square with bridge links. (email from Geoff Wright to Patsy Healey, 17.07.08)

The private-sector actors, in their turn, kept a watchful eye on commercial considerations. They shared a sense of responsibility to achieve a project that would bring value to the city as a whole, to citizens and other stakeholders, as well as to those who used and invested in the properties created. In effect, key people from the organisations involved created an informal but close working part-nership, underpinned by mutual respect and an ethic of commitment to getting a project that would create a valued locale within the city centre. Together, these key actors served as guardians of the public realm. However, they were not autonomous. They worked within the framework of their respective organisations and against the background of critical voices from the wider society. These not only kept the City Council under continual pressure to justify its strate-gies and projects in relation in particular to their impact on poorer inner-city neighbourhoods. Such critical pressure was also felt by the actors in the private sector. Politicians and a critical civil society thus helped to frame the focus and values that the professionals struggled so hard to achieve.

Achieving area transformation

These three cases illustrate the effort needed to accomplish complex mega-projects that transform the physical form of significant areas near city centres and create new places in a city. However, they were not just physical projects. They involved the mobilisation of very large budgets and created new economic values, reflected in prop-erty prices and rents. They added to the public realm inheritance of their cities by creating attractive open spaces accessible to all, adja-cent to their city centres and linked into them by careful attention to the design and landscaping of walkways and cycleways, and to vistas and street furniture. They produced social ambiences, through which new meanings developed as the locales settled into the evolving geography of their cities. Above all, they could not have happened without being taken up as major political projects, in which reversing degradation of the urban fabric was a symbol of a reassertion of city pride and dynamism.

In each case, key actors were committed to creating these public realm qualities. They shared a commitment to revitalise city centres and reverse trends that encouraged people and their spending power to migrate to the suburbs. They also sought outside public funding and needed good project ideas to attract this. In Barcelona and Birmingham, they were influenced by European urban politics that encouraged city leaders to imagine their cities as positioned in a landscape of competition to attract the footloose investments of a globalised economy as the only way to sustain their economies and avoid a 'shrinking' future (Moulaert et al. 2000). These forces encouraged projects to remodel older parts of cities abandoned or degraded as result of industrial change and to reposition them to attract the newly emerging economic activities and social aspirations. They were upgrading projects on a large scale (see Chapter 5), in a physical, social and economic sense. However, rather than focus on urban neighbourhoods, these projects were typically located in areas with few residents, in part because of protests in earlier decades. They were located on sites that, to quote Altshuler and Luberoff (2003), 'did no harm' (see also Diaz and Fainstein 2008).

However, major projects always create some loss and destruction – of memories as well as habitats and familiar environments. They are also full of risk. Outcomes can be hoped for but not easily predicted. Costs and benefits over the lifetime of a major project are difficult to calculate, let alone keep in check. To achieve them, key actors had to sustain sufficient belief and commitment to their value to will them into being. Politicians needed to be kept onside and economic resources mobilised, despite the ebb and flow of property investment cycles. Boston's mayor was cautious about what was involved. It was the developer James Rouse who sustained the belief in retail-driven downtown regeneration. Barcelona's politicians needed the belief in building a new society in the post-dictatorship period to drive them forward. The Birmingham civic culture had a long history of a pro-development orientation and a confidence in its own capabilities. But the experiences of Boston, Barcelona and Birmingham also show that, while the results can be spectacular – more successful than their initiators imagined – such returns are a long time in the making, and the road to realising them is full of unexpected twists and turns, during which politicians may be heavily criticised, developers go bankrupt and poor design quality may be tolerated. And for all the visible successes, such projects have wider impacts on the political programmes they symbolise, on patterns of land and property values in and around them, on financial budgets for other urban investments, and on the evolving spatial dynamics of their cities and regions. These wider impacts may not always be positive.

Reflecting this, the three examples reported above have not only been judged as successes. They have also been subject to sustained criticism by citizens and lobby groups concerned about the social, design and environmental qualities of their cities and locales within them. Such criticism had significant effects on design and development in each case. The critique helped to keep in play attention to the public realm and the wider concerns of a diverse citizenry. Yet such big projects cannot proceed without complex work to draw together different actors, assemble sites and building capacity, organise finance and maintain a focus on development co-ordination and design quality. Throughout, achieving major projects requires careful management and continual attention to political legitimacy if such risky ventures are to succeed and later be judged as valuable for the long-term public realm benefits for the many, rather than just short-term returns for key actors. What activities does such work involve?

Although there have been many attempts at providing guidelines or 'best-practice' advice on how to go about major urban reconfiguration projects, every situation is different and what works in one place may not work in another. The three cases illustrate different ways of going about development. Nevertheless, a number of activities need to happen for such a project to come about, although they do not necessarily occur in any particular order (see Figure 6.7). One involves recognising an opportunity to create some new qualities in a locale. In the 1980s in the UK, the myth was cultivated that it was only private-sector developers, with entrepreneurial flair, who were capable of such recognition. Civil society activists could have an important role in highlighting new potentials, as in Boston. James Rouse fitted this archetype and Godfrey Bradman of Rosehaugh seemed to have these iconic qualities too. However, the three cases show a rather different story. James Rouse was sought out by a determined local architect-developer who used his networks to connect to and get Rouse interested in a project that had started with a heritage conservation concept. Barcelona's political-design nexus wanted to reverse the exploitation of its waterfront by capitalists and reclaim it for citizens. In Birmingham, civil society groups busy with canal restoration slowly created an asset that met up with the City Council's initiative in redesigning the city's public spaces. In all the cases, there were also locational advantages (near city centres, near waterfronts, potentially accessible by multiple transport modes) to

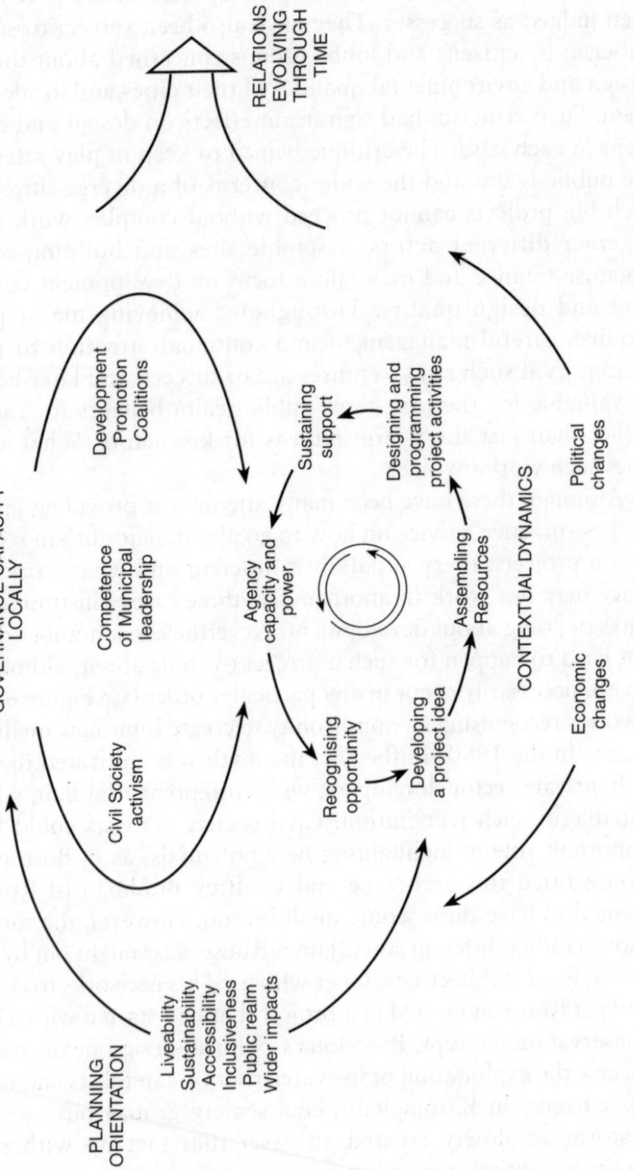

Figure 6.7 *Achieving a planning orientation in major development projects*

RELATIONS EVOLVING THROUGH TIME

Development Promotion Coalitions

GOVERNANCE CAPACITY LOCALLY

Competence of Municipal leadership

Civil Society activism

Sustaining support

Agency capacity and power

Designing and programming project activities

Assembling Resources

CONTEXTUAL DYNAMICS

Political changes

Economic changes

Recognising opportunity

Developing a project idea

PLANNING ORIENTATION

Liveability
Sustainability
Accessibility
Inclusiveness
Public realm
Wider impacts

be exploited for new projects if sites could be made suitable for new activities.

Recognising opportunity is thus not only about the presence of strategic imagination and flair. Nor are these qualities that are only to be found in the private sector. Altshuler and Luberoff (2003), in their review of major projects, identify the important role of public-sector 'entrepreneurs', clearly evident in the Barcelona and Birmingham cases (see also the cases in Diaz and Fainstein 2008). The capacity to recognise opportunity is as much to do with a mixture of persistent campaigning, or the coming together of activities and perceptions and of a kind of conjunction or serendipity. The critical spark that turns a mixture of perceptions, campaigns and initiatives into significant action lies in recognising that there is such a conjunction and that this can be converted into a moment of opportunity in which political and economic attention can become focused around a project. Major projects come to fruition when those who recognise an opportunity are able to mobilise significant attention to turn an idea into a realised project.

A second activity involves developing a project idea. It is often imagined that such projects are outlined in some kind of master plan, which guides what subsequently happens. Such plans, often publicised in the press with attractive three-dimensional graphics, suggest that this design is what will be built. Yet this is rarely the case. Some initial idea may be valuable to challenge negative perceptions or mobilise attention, but the preliminary concept may have little relation to what is finally produced. Contextual conditions may change. Development problems may emerge as ground conditions and building structures are investigated more closely. Different actors may become involved with new ideas about potentialities. New synergies may appear as other developments get underway in neighbouring areas. The Newcastle quayside (Box 6.1) shows how a new location was slowly formed through the conjunction of several projects. In Faneuil Hall Marketplace, what began as a heritage project ended up as a drinking and dining locale and tourist venue. In Barcelona, opening up the waterfront for citizens evolved into the creation of a major tourist destination. In Birmingham, a 'back space' behind major public projects became a new urban quarter.

It is often assumed that project ideas are generated by specialists – planners, urban designers, architects and others, who translate their clients' aspirations into built form, economic opportunities and a particular ambience. Sometimes a competition is organised to seek out developers attracted by a major development opportunity.

However, few projects are actually built as specified in a winning entry. The Faneuil Hall Marketplace and Brindleyplace cases show that changes in project design were often needed as contextual conditions shift and unexpected challenges arise during the long periods of project development. Some projects that are later judged to create significant value for users, developers, investors and the public realm are often the product of intense contestation with critical neighbours and other stakeholders. The resultant struggles may delay a project for many years. A high-profile example from the King's Cross station area in London illustrates what can happen when well-informed and sustained community activism confronts major property development interests (see Box 6.6). After decades of dispute, involving some of the same developers as at Brindleyplace, a high-quality design scheme was negotiated that gave significant attention to the social, environmental and public realm benefits. Activists for the community nevertheless thought that even more could have been squeezed out from the returns of the projects.

Assembling resources often goes hand in hand with evolving a project idea. This activity is not merely some abstract exercise in accountancy. It involves seeking out those stakeholders with key resources, which often means moulding aspects of projects to meet their interests. In the cases described earlier, such stakeholders included a range of public-sector agencies, such as higher tiers of government, land and property owners (who could also be public-sector agencies), infrastructure providers, companies specialising in construction and in property development, investors prepared to put up funds for the development period and to take over management and maintenance in the long term, and specialists of different kinds. It may often mean working with lobby groups interested in the project for various reasons, and communities and businesses in and around the project area, as in the King's Cross case. The latter were important both as stakeholders likely to experience disruption costs as development proceeded and as potential critics, whose voices could challenge the legitimacy of a project.

In all the cases, the projects would not have proceeded without careful attention to the relationships between politicians, key technical experts, key funders and those actually doing the development. To some extent in Barcelona the situation was simplified by the dominating role of the public sector and the use of a prestigious event to focus attention. In Boston, an imaginative developer exercised great persuasive power backed by a keen sense of social responsibility. In Birmingham, however, a great deal depended on the skilled negotiating of a few professionals who acted, within their own organisations, as persistent project champions. Major projects need such skilled champions, to do the work of continual troubleshooting, co-ordinating, finding ways through tricky disputes, keeping key principles in play and negotiating good deals (Frieden and Sagalyn 1991).

This complex work of obtaining, co-ordinating and continually managing the resource flows and interactions necessary for a project to proceed has enormous potential to undermine initial ideas of what the new 'piece of city' could be and to reduce attention to achieving quality in all dimensions of a project. Many projects fail as belief sags when the difficulties of assembling resources pile up. Others proceed through short cuts that undermine the long-term value and sustainability of the built product and social ambience produced. In Boston, Barcelona and Birmingham, those involved were lucky that contextual conditions helped them survive through some of the more difficult moments. Land-assembly costs turned out to be low in all the cases. In Boston and Barcelona, the land was already largely in public ownership. In Birmingham, Argent acquired the site at a very low price from the receivers. All three were fortunate in having some stable political support over a long development period. But throughout, key actors gave careful attention to project details and were prepared to engage in tough negotiations as they sought to acquire and combine resources through the design and programming of project activities. For such projects have to be broken up into sections and stages to proceed in real time.

It is here that strategic conceptions take concrete form. Initial design ideas get fixed into actual alignments for streets, infrastructure lines and plots/parcels for specific projects, such as an apartment complex, a stadium, a conservation project or a park (Askew 1996). In Barcelona, this was done in the City Planning Office, which also acted as guardian of the design aspirations of the overall waterfront reclamation project. The office then worked with infrastructure agencies to deliver what was required and either developed the plots themselves or sought private enterprises or some kind of partnership arrangement for specific plots, within the context of development specifications arising from the overall design scheme. In Birmingham, the development of the design scheme proceeded in a much less linear way. Some plots had already been developed before a general design strategy was drawn up. While plots were given development briefs, these were continually renegotiated in the light

Box 6.6   Community versus capital in inner London

The area around King's Cross station on the northern margin of central London is a nodal transport point on rail, road and underground transport systems, but has always been a poor district. There are many heritage buildings in the area, along with railway and freight facilities and some remaining industries. The area, long blighted by the lack of any attention to its future, has significant potential for commercial activity if redeveloped to a high standard, but is also a locale where there has been a long tradition of working-class housing for rent and cheap accommodation for small business outfits. During the 1970s and 1980s, proposals for redevelopment for commercial purposes were repeatedly contested by activists who sought to retain the working-class mix of the area. By the later 1980s, the then British Rail enterprise, anticipating both privatisation and also the location of the Channel Tunnel Rail Link (CTRL) terminal at King's Cross, was keen to redevelop its holdings in the area. The property boom of the late 1980s provided developer interest, which was attracted by the commercial prospects of the site. British Rail hoped to cross-subsidise some of the CTRL terminal works through the profits from commercial redevelopment. To pursue these ideas, it built a partnership of interests, the London Regeneration Consortium (LRC), which included developer Rosehaugh Stanhope, with whom it had worked at Liverpool Street station.

In the meantime, however, the municipal council, the London Borough of Camden (LBC), had responded to activist campaigns seeking more social, environmental and conservation benefits in the area. The prevailing development plan argued against more speculative office development in the area. Influenced in part by a community

→

of changing ideas about the public realm context and property market conditions. These differences partly reflected differences in the way political and resource power was concentrated. In Barcelona, until the later 1990s, the municipality could assume strong political and economic power, denied to Birmingham City Council. Barcelona also used the impetus of an event to which key politicians and levels of government were committed to drive forward a co-ordinated effort to achieve a significant completion by a set date. However, such event-led programming could also produce stresses and strains that compromised quality.[17]

As all this complex work proceeds, its proponents need to sustain support for the project among several key groups. These include

$\rightarrow$

activist group, Kings Cross Railway Lands Group (KXRLG), a development brief for the area was produced in 1988. This argued for a comprehensive approach to the development of the area, attention to the industrial and railway heritage and to the adverse impacts that might be experienced by local people in and around the area. There followed a decade of conflict and uncertainty, as the LRC largely ignored the contents of the brief. Meanwhile, development conditions turned from boom to bust, and no decision was made about where the CTRL rail terminal would be sited.

By 1997, however, the wider political landscape had also changed, with a new national Labour (social-democratic) government and a new independent but left-leaning Mayor of London (Ken Livingstone). This helped to strengthen the community's hand in arguing for much more social and environmental benefits from any scheme. In the late 1990s the site for the CTRL terminal was determined, and the LRC appointed developers Argent plc to take on the site, following its successful mixed-use Brindleyplace project. Finally, LBC felt able to give approval for Argent's scheme in 2007, as the terminal was completed, and construction started on site in 2008. Community activists were still concerned that the balance of the project tipped too far to commercial interests, but there is little doubt that their sustained and well-informed activism helped greatly to improve the quality of the final scheme. However, contextual conditions had again changed by the late 2000s, and it remains to be seen how the project will survive the financial and property bust of 2008 and the resultant economic recession.

Sources: Askew 1996, Edwards 1992, 2009, www.argentgroup.plc.

other actors in the political sphere, future occupiers and investors, and the wider community who judge the development efforts and influence both politicians and future stakeholders. Emerging new urban locales need to be repositioned in the mental maps of such actual and potential stakeholders. Design sketches, computer visualisations of a future ambience and marketing texts about major projects are widely used to promote such a repositioning. Project developers may also have to respond to all kinds of criticism as a project evolves. In all three cases discussed in this chapter, there were critical community groups, design professionals and other intellectuals, continually challenging the way a project was proceeding. Yet most of the time, most citizens are likely to be unaware of what is in

progress, apart from seeing 'cranes on the skyline' and finding familiar landmarks and routes disrupted by development effort.

Project proponents therefore need to make choices about when to
create publicity about their work. This may often happen at the start
of a project, with a fanfare of design ideas and claims about future
benefits. The danger here is that citizens and other stakeholders may
hold project proponents to account for the project as described in
the fanfare, and expect a rapid realisation of the new project.
Another strategy is to wait until a demonstrable product is achieved
in at least some part of the project. For Barcelona, the Olympic
event proved an outstanding success in terms of positioning the city
in the eyes of visitors and future investors, and also making citizens
feel proud of their city and its achievements. It proved more difficult
to use this strategy again in the Cultural Forum 2004 project.
Inspired by Barcelona and Boston, many project developers have
used smaller-scale street events to let citizens know about a new
locale in their cities. However, such marketing cannot by itself
produce a valued new locale. Instead, the places now recognised as
valuable were shaped by people who devoted a great deal of belief,
energy and skill to will a new locale into a physical form and a social
ambience. If sufficient attention to quality and local resonance is
achieved, if a location continues to be favourably positioned in
urban flows, and if the political and economic context remains positive, then their efforts are likely to accumulate all kinds of value and
meaning in the urban landscape.

All these activities demand substantial energy or power to act.
While individuals in specific organisational positions (the 'mayor',
the 'developer', the 'planner') may play important roles, what is critical is the way in which different actors are linked together in a
common venture. It is this that creates the agency power that
enables a project to be realised. It is sometimes thought that such
power can be ensured by the creation of a special organisation, such
as a development company, a public–private partnership or a special
task unit in a municipal authority. James Rouse formed a company
specifically for the Faneuil Hall Marketplace project. Similarly, a
special-purpose company at arm's length from the main development company was created for Brindleyplace in the late 1980s. (This
mechanism helps protect the specific development company from
the collapse of the main company and vice versa.) In the UK,
regional and national development agencies sometimes act as the
development agency, absorbing the risks and providing the expertise
that poorly resourced municipalities may be unable to mobilise. The

value of creating such an agency is that, depending on the powers accorded to it and the legal system prevailing, it can engage as a party to a contract, act as a land-use regulator, manage financial resources and make flexible decisions to cross-subsidise from one part of a project to another, offering incentives and bridging funding gaps. It thus can have powers to act flexibly and respond to particular challenges arising on a day-to-day basis.

However, the cases discussed in this chapter show that it was not these special organisational arrangements that generated and sustained the commitment to the projects. Nor was it the existence of a masterplan or a formal contract that held a project focus together, though both were useful. The energy that kept project momentum going lay in the nexus of relations between a few key people in different organisational positions, who acted as champions for the project, nurturing it through all kinds of tangled relationships to get access to the resources and agreements necessary to proceed. It was in this nexus that the values of the planning project had to lodge in the end. Helping to keep this nexus of relations in place were two other factors. One was reasonable political stability and commitment to the projects, backed by political recognition of their technical complexity. The other was considerable continuity among the key personnel involved, even when they changed their organisational positions.[18] Without sustained political leadership and some continuity in key personnel, such projects are very vulnerable to failure.

Safeguarding the public realm in major projects

In this chapter I have argued that major projects can achieve substantial new urban locales, which enhance the qualities and opportunities of the cities in which they are located. They create, in effect, new heritage for future generations. However, they are not easy to achieve and are fragile, vulnerable accomplishments. They displace what was there before. They disrupt environmental flows and habitats, unsettle all kinds of human activities and values and, by drawing in all kinds of materials and resources, consume energy in their creative work. They may be only partially achieved, or be subject to design faults, or cost huge amounts that could have been better spent on other things. And because they are so complex to achieve and so full of risk, the potential is high that they will leave behind an inheritance of an unfinished white elephant or a permanently damaged urban environment, rather than a valued new locale. Projects that destroy too much and create too little are often publicised in the literature on planning as 'disasters' (Hall 1982, Flyvbjerg et al. 2003).

But a disaster can occur not only when a project is left unfinished or goes massively over budget. Disasters can also occur where a project focus is too strongly centred on short-term profitability or on extracting short-term political visibility. Or the emphasis may be on creating an enclave for the few, perhaps a domain for corporate business or an affluent residential district, sometimes deliberately cut off from the areas around it. Or the project area may be considered in too introverted a way, with little attention to its links to the areas around. The quality of the public spaces may also get neglected, in terms of how they flow, how they are experienced, how they are maintained and the potential for all kinds of people to find their way there and enjoy the experience. Where heritage restoration is a theme, there are dangers of a place becoming a kind of static museum in the urban fabric. Where new retail and entertainment locales are created, as in Boston, Barcelona and Birmingham, there are dangers of attracting so much attention that residents' enjoyment is crowded out.

Yet, as the cases in this chapter have shown, it is possible to reconfigure locales without disaster. Although examples can be found to support all the criticisms noted at the start – that major projects display the excesses of rampant capitalism, that they are narrowly focused on a reductive agenda of economic competitiveness, that they displace the poor, that they are merely displays of architectural flamboyance or political ambition, that their funding could be better used elsewhere and that they are typically badly managed sinkholes into which taxpayers' money is poured – these do not have to be the outcomes of a major development project. Nevertheless, the fear of such outcomes may create a climate in which another kind of 'disaster' can arise, that of persistent neglect of part of a city where all kinds of value is steadily draining away, leaving too many barriers to recolonisation except by wildlife.

In summary, the cases and discussion in this chapter underline that three capacities make a real difference to whether major projects are infused with the values of the planning project and achieve long-term public realm qualities for their cities as places to live, work, do business and visit, for the many and not just the few. The first is an energetic agency of some kind, able to combine a holistic approach to how the parts of a project relate to its overall shape, direction and wider relations, with courage, imagination and a leadership capacity to act flexibly and sensitively. A proactive governance mode is essential in this work (see Chapter 3). The second is a team of very skilled and committed people, who can combine management capacity, design and technical capability, financial understanding, a grasp of property market dynamics and of political-institutional dynamics, with a continual reference back to overall project philosophy and the search for quality in all aspects of their work. It is these teams who do the management work needed to steer major projects from initiation to completion. Such teams are often drawn from various agencies and form some kind of nexus or 'community of practice' (Wenger 1998) within which technical skill and an ethical orientation are combined (see Chapter 8). The third capacity is located within the wider political community in which a project is situated, and centres on the active monitoring of its on-going development. This implies a critical civil society as well as the mechanisms of a formally accountable municipal government.

There is a further way in which a planning orientation within major projects can be held in place. This is through a clear strategic view of how a such a project relates to the wider urban complex in which it is located. In all three cases, there was a political sense that such projects needed to be balanced with attention to neighbourhoods. In Birmingham, a city centre design strategy evolved in which the Brindleyplace project could be located. In Barcelona, there was a citywide spatial strategy that articulated key ideas about what waterfront regeneration should achieve. But how are such strategic orientations arrived at and sustained? And how do they get connected to the work of major projects and the more routine work of place management? This is the focus of the next chapter.

Suggested further reading

Most of the material listed below is already mentioned in the text or footnotes of this chapter. Particularly useful for the US experience are:

Frieden, B. J. and Sagalyn, L. B. (1991) *Downtown Inc.: How America Rebuilds Cities*, MIT Press, Boston, MA.

Altshuler, A. and Luberoff, D. (2003) *Mega-Projects: The Changing Role of Urban Public Investment*, Brookings Institution, Washington, DC.

For European experiences, see:

Moulaert, F., with Delladetsima, P., Delvainquiere, J. C., Demaziere, C., Rodriguez, A., Vicari, S. and Martinez, M. (2000) *Globalisation and Integrated Area Development in European Cities*, Oxford University Press, Oxford.

Salet, W. and Gualini, E. (eds) (2007) *Framing Strategic Urban Projects: Learning from Current Experiences in European Urban Regions*, Routledge, London.

Smyth, H. (1994) *Marketing the City: The role of Flagship Developments in Urban Regeneration*, E&FN Spon, London.

For wider comparisons, see:

Fainstein, S. (2001) *The City Builders: Property Development in New York and London 1980–2000*, University of Kansas Press, Kansas.

Diaz Orueta, F. and Fainstein, S. (2008) The new mega-projects: Genesis and impacts, *International Journal of Urban and Regional Research*, 32, 759–67.

Chapter 7

Producing Place-Development Strategies

Development management, major projects and place-development strategies

In this chapter I shift the focus of attention from the neighbourhood and the major urban project to the wider places, or localities, in which both are situated. This presents challenges to the imagination, as the 'place' of the city or urban region or sprawling megalopolis is not easy to grasp as an 'entity' or whole (see Chapter 2). For some, it is symbolised by the pathways through it. For others, the place is embodied in key buildings, or facilities, or the ambience of particular locales, such as the city centre. It may often seem an overly abstract exercise to focus policy attention on the evolving dynamics and qualities of such amorphous and ungraspable large areas. Yet as the previous chapters have shown, the more concrete activities of development management and the reconfiguration of large parts of the urban fabric have often raised issues about the relation between neighbourhoods, key urban locales and the wider urban complex. Sometimes arguments for place-development strategies are justified merely in terms of the need for better co-ordination between project initiatives, or between development management activities and major projects (see Hopkins 2001). But there are also strong arguments for such strategic attention deriving from the ambition of promoting the liveability and sustainability of the locales of daily life in large urban complexes. Place-governance initiatives also have to justify how and why particular neighbourhoods and locales are selected for concentrated action.

Making place-development strategies is often thought of as the core concern of urban planning and regional development. Such strategy-making work centres on developing an idea of a city or larger territory and imagining possibilities for its future. But what are urban areas and regional territories, and what does it mean to consider how to plan and develop them? In the mid-twentieth century the answer seemed clear. Places were imagined as existing in some kind of nested hierarchy: neighbourhoods in districts, districts in urban areas, situated in regions, within nation states (see Chapter 2). Each level of the hierarchy could or should, it was thought, be encapsulated in a formalised political jurisdiction, which could become the appropriate institutional arena for undertaking a place-development strategy for each level. This strategy would set key principles and define a spatial 'structure' within which specific developments and policies at lower levels could be set. Such a spatial strategy was best expressed, it was then imagined, in a formal document – a 'development plan', 'comprehensive plan' or city 'master plan'. In this conception, such a plan was the main instrument for pursuing a planning orientation in place-governance. A typical example has already been encountered in Barcelona's General Metropolitan Plan (see Chapter 6).

However, the cases discussed in Chapters 4, 5 and 6 show that the relations that form an urban area overflow such physical and administrative boundaries. Politicians and officials in Barcelona and Birmingham, both strongly asserting their municipalities' significance in a wider urban region, vigorously positioned their cities in a European and international geography, deliberately jumping over their national territories. The private development interests brought in to work on projects in Boston, Barcelona and Birmingham were not local to the city or region. In Boston they came from other US cities. Barcelona and Birmingham looked to the US in search of private investment, only to find, in Birmingham's case, that this tied the fate of a major project to the timing of a development scheme in Sydney, Australia. The capital for many private development projects in Vancouver came from East Asian sources. In many developing countries, international aid agencies have shaped neighbourhood improvement projects (see Simon and Narman 1999, Cooke and Kothari 2001). The energy of large numbers of young people across Japan poured into Kobe to help in post-earthquake recovery, ignoring the hierarchical levels of government bureaucracy. And if we explored the relations of the families and firms in all these areas, poor and rich, large and small, we would be sure to find many for whom the city and region were only one of many places to which they related. As discussed in Chapter 2, these days we live in worlds in which places that are near us are not necessarily the most important to us.

Yet wider strategic ideas about a city and a region were important in the cases presented in the previous chapters, sometimes causing problems but often producing benefits. In Vancouver and Barcelona, politicians and officials held to key strategic ideas that they had articulated in political struggles in the 1960s and 1970s. These shaped how they identified investment priorities, selected key projects and, in Vancouver's case, entered into discussions with neighbourhoods. In Kobe, in Birmingham, and later in Barcelona and Boston, in contrast, civil society groups and academics felt that they had to challenge this municipal nexus to assert the needs of less powerful groups – the elderly, poorer people, those from minority groups. They challenged strong pro-growth coalitions oriented to attracting international investment. What emerged as priorities in such cases came as much from the resultant struggles and the balance of power between groups as from a clear urban strategy. In Vancouver and Omaha, politicians and officials sought a different way to link the plurality of different material needs and ideas about urban qualities and priorities together. Through complex, interactive processes, people were encouraged to connect their concerns about their neighbourhood environments to the wider urban context and the impact they had on other people and places in the overall urban area. This then helped to shape what became consolidated as an urban strategy. In Birmingham, the negotiation around major development projects interacted with an evolving city centre urban design strategy that focused on linkages between projects from the point of view of many different kinds of city centre users.

However, a strategy that is lodged in the minds of key actors may be difficult to keep in play as major projects are brought into existence and the routine work of development management proceeds. If a strategic orientation fades away or is never articulated, it can easily happen that projects undermine each other through destructive competition for the same kind of market or funding. An effective place-development strategy works by creating synergies and potentials, by mobilising attention to some opportunities and not others, a kind of highlighting and lowlighting effect. It connects parts to some larger whole, even if both are continuously evolving. It helps to stabilise the development scene, so that developers and investors have some idea about assets that may emerge in the future and about conditions in the market for which they develop. It helps politically too, so that citizens can take part in, and find some justification for, establishing the agenda of major investments and key regulations that shape their city and their experience of it.

Put simply, strategies for urban areas and regions become useful by providing a wider referent to help those involved in place-development activities position what they are doing. They set out a wider context in which to situate major projects and on-going development-management activity. Strategies become valuable for those promoting a broad policy, such as a socially and environmentally sustainable city, when the policy needs to become operationalised into projects and programmes. It reminds actors about the impacts and synergies their projects may have and highlights responsibilities to the wider public realm they may be called on to attend to. A strategy helps in setting priorities, in co-ordinating actions and in justifying choices made, especially when there is public demand for action in very many areas and not all can be satisfied in the short term. A place-development strategy thus becomes a key piece of institutional infrastructure in efforts to promote urban development trajectories that could lead to more liveable and sustainable conditions for future generations.

This assumes that a strategy is capable of performing some kind of strategic work. In other words, it is not merely a rhetorical invocation or a dusty document, but exists as a set of ideas or a 'frame' that is actually used as a referent by those involved in more operational work. It mobilises regulations and investments, through creating orienting ideas that come to command legitimacy (see Chapter 3). A strategy that accumulates the power to do such governance work becomes the basis for selecting investment priorities. This points up a contrast between strategies that have such power, and those that are merely produced to satisfy some formal requirement for accessing a funding stream or legitimating a bundle of regulatory norms and standards.[1]

Rhetorical invocations and formal documents called strategies should not therefore be equated with the strategic orientation I discuss here, although expressing a strategy in formal documents and in political or professional rhetoric may be valuable adjuncts to such an orientation. A strategy that comes to shape future actions may be primarily lodged in the hearts and minds of key actors, such as the politicians and officials in Vancouver and Barcelona, or the urban design planners in Birmingham. But it sometimes helps to lodge a strategy into a document, to give it textual expression in words, maps, pictures and diagrams. This expression is especially valuable where strategies for the place development of an urban area are concerned. Through words and images, what is understood as the urban area, taken as a whole, can be conjured up and linked to recognisable features of an urban landscape. In the Barcelona case, for example, opening up the waterfront was continually linked by politicians and officials to creating more facilities in the periphery, providing more green spaces throughout the crowded residential neighbourhoods and improving accessibility across the city generally. A visual expression of a strategy also helps to show how parts and connections relate to the imagined whole. Figure 7.1 provides images from two influential strategies for London's development, one from British planner Patrick Abercrombie's Plan for Greater London 1944, the other from the 2004 London Plan.

In the great days of mid-twentieth century city planning, the planning idea focused on this visual and diagrammatic expression of a city development strategy. The 'plan' was expected to express a strategic idea of a city, translated into a detailed physical morphology. This was linked into specific proposals for the development of major infrastructures and zones of key new development activity, with norms and standards for development to guide change in areas of existing development. Thus the powers of capital investment and of land-use regulation were tied into the overall strategy, as in the Barcelona General Metropolitan Plan. The expectation was that the city would evolve in line with the drawing-board plan. And in some cases, this actually happened. Barcelona in the late nineteenth century was laid out following Cerda's plan. Amsterdam in the twentieth century unfolded physically to a large extent in line with a sequence of development plans. In such cases, a strategic spatial plan really did act as a major tool for pursuing place-governance with a planning orientation.

However, in most cases events did not work out like this. Those making the plans typically over-estimated their power to control land and property development markets, to influence the spending of other public-sector bodies, to keep politicians in line with the plans and, in many developing-country contexts, to control informal development that went on outside the parameters of the plan (as at Besters Camp, see Chapter 5). Plan makers also over-estimated their power to predict future demands and needs, and to relate wholes to parts. As a result, many neighbourhoods, as in Kobe, found themselves tied into formal planning requirements that bore little relation to conditions and needs on the ground. The city as expressed in how people and businesses lived in, moved around in and imagined it kept running away from the planners' plans. In the 1980s, researchers Brian McLoughlin and Margo Huxley carried out a major study of how far urban growth in the city of Melbourne, Australia had conformed to the land-use allocations and infrastructure investment

Figure 7.1   *Visualising London*

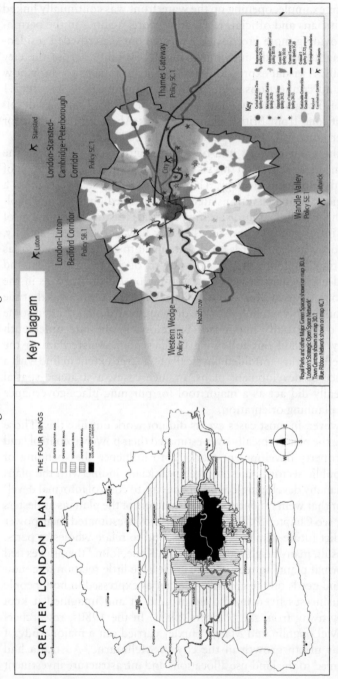

(a) The Greater London Plan 1944: rings of expansion contained by a greenbelt (see horizontal shading)   (b) The 2004 London Plan: expansion along 'corridors'

Sources: 7.2a: Stephen Ward; 7.2b: The Greater London Authority

proposals contained in prevailing plans (McLoughlin 1992). They found very great disparities. Such conclusions could be repeated from many other parts of the world, especially in rapidly developing urban areas in Asia, Latin America and Africa. This capacity for the city to run away from the plan was especially serious where the formal plan conveyed land and property-development rights or was used to establish land values. In the developing world, such plans, referred to as part of a 'master-planning' approach, are much criticised for imposing a bureaucratic land-development regime, largely irrelevant to rapidly expanding urban complexes. One consequence in such situations is that much development activity in such cities was treated as informal or illegal (UN-Habitat 2009).

These experiences led to a strong criticism of urban planning activity, vigorously voiced in North America and Western Europe from the 1960s. The planning community, both practitioners and academics, responded by evolving new ideas about plans and strategies. An important development was to emphasise the difference between an orienting strategy, and a specific statement of regulatory norms and standards to guide detailed land-use change. In the UK, the legal tool of a 'development plan' was divided into a 'structure' (strategic) plan and a 'local' plan. In countries where zoning plans give development rights, strategic plans were separated from zoning plans.[2] Planners often argued that spatial strategies needed to be linked to other city development strategies, such as for economic development, transport investment, housing improvement and development, and the expansion of green spaces. However, the effort to integrate different strategies continually encountered difficulties where government activity was divided into separate functional domains (see Chapter 3). Discussion within planning circles also emphasised the importance of linking broad strategic conceptions that might shape how a city evolved to where the resources would come from to implement the strategic idea, emphasising the role of strategic plans in co-ordinating development activity (Hopkins 2001). Instead of conformance with a physical layout, this newer thinking emphasised that strategies should be judged by their performance in shaping policy programmes, the form and location of investment projects and key regulatory principles (Mastop and Faludi 1997).

But these considerations implied that a strategy that could accumulate the power to shape future investments and smaller-scale changes to how cities evolved was not just a planner's technical tool, but a major political and organisational enterprise. It needed to be lodged in the 'hearts and minds' of the actors who commanded the key resources and ideas that shaped development trajectories. This is what the Barcelona politicians and officials understood so well. They came to argue that a strategy was best expressed through strategic projects, rather than in general morphological plans for a whole urban area. In contrast, in countries where national political attitudes turned against the public shaping of market opportunities, the idea of having a place-development strategy was seen as irrelevant. In the UK in the late 1980s, the value of city-wide strategies was continually attacked by a national political regime that advocated market initiative as the most effective way to produce urban areas. The activity of planning was deliberately reduced to a kind of land-use regulation practice, guided by development plans oriented primarily to providing justifications for land-use regulation decisions. This regulatory emphasis was set in the context of disparate national planning principles and legal judgments about what was a legitimate limitation of private development rights (Thornley 1991). Local authorities, such as Birmingham, had to work against the grain of such a political climate to keep some idea of wider strategic questions alive (Vigar et al. 2000).

By the 1990s, however, the costs of the neglect of a strategic orientation were becoming clearer. In Europe, there was a strong revival of interest in strategic spatial planning.[3] This influenced planning ideas in other parts of the world, including Durban in South Africa (see Chapter 5). Even in the US, as the social and economic costs of ever-expanding suburbia and hollowed-out city cores became increasingly evident, there was a renewed interest in urban strategies (Wheeler 2002, 2004). But if the political climate for strategic planning had become more positive, the challenges of responding to it were substantial. Those promoting such initiatives had to consider what area to focus on and what political jurisdictions it related to. They needed to think about what place qualities to highlight in a strategy and whose values about urban life and opportunities to promote. They had to consider the work a strategy could perform, the institutional arenas that could be used to prepare it, and who among the many potential stakeholders should get to have a voice in its content and form. These issues raise difficult political and organisational challenges of institutional design and governance practice for urban polities. Some governance contexts have proved more accommodating to a strategic planning approach than others. Yet the effort to develop a strategic approach may itself help to create a more accommodating context. In other words, effective strategy-making work may help to build governance capacities and, more widely, urban polities, just as it draws on those capacities and governance cultures.

In this chapter, I now present two experiences. One is from the Netherlands, in Europe, where the city of Amsterdam has had nearly a century of experience of combining aims of social justice, economic expansion and environmental sustainability. It has developed a tradition of strategic planning that is continually reviewed and adjusted in relation to changing urban realities. My second example is from the US, where the city of Portland, Oregon, became a paradigmatic case in the late twentieth century of a strategic approach to sustainable urban development that has produced many benefits for residents and other stakeholders. This case provides an example, as with Vancouver and Barcelona, where activists struggled to transform a governance culture into one with the strategic capacity to pursue such an agenda. Through these two cases, I explore what it takes to create a strategic framework that keeps attention to the relations and connections of a large urban area in play as development activity unfolds. I consider how and how far such strategies contribute to keeping the values associated with the planning project alive through the unfolding of events, and how to arrive at strategic frameworks that are broad and rich enough to allow for the inevitable changes in contextual conditions.

A century of planned development: Amsterdam, Netherlands[4]

Amsterdam is the capital and commercial centre of the Netherlands, a rich and very densely urbanised north west European country on the low-lying plain where the great Rhine–Maas river system reaches the sea. The Netherlands is a commercial nation, with a long-standing political culture committed to seeking agreement between different segments of a country where the potential for violent conflict between religious groups was once a real threat. In 2000, the municipality had an expanding population of over 730,000 people, within a wider metropolitan area of over 1.5 million. Amsterdam itself is situated in a delta landscape, evident in its old urban core and rings of canals that are so attractive to residents and tourists alike, expanding onto a landscape of flatlands and networks of waterways, much of it reclaimed from the sea. Managing this environment, whether for farming or for urban development, has always required careful and sustained collective action, and will continue to do so, as climate change raises sea levels. Partly because of this physical context, it is widely accepted in the Netherlands that national and local government should have a major role in how the territory is developed. The national level has key roles in water management, in selecting locations and providing funding for urban development, in infrastructure investment and in funding social infrastructures. Through its land reclamation work, the public sector came to own substantial land resources. Amsterdam City Council not only owns considerable areas of land, it is also the freeholder for most of the city area. So Amsterdam is both a place and, in its embodiment as a municipality, a very active agent in the development of its area.

The Netherlands is a unitary state, not a federation, as in the US. Under the umbrella of the national state are provinces and municipalities. In contrast to the heavily centralised UK, however, Dutch government works in a less hierarchical way, with the different levels collaborating more or less as equals, especially where big cities such as Amsterdam are concerned. The three levels continually negotiate to arrive at agreement on development locations and priority investments. These negotiations are typically dominated by elected politicians and government officials, experts in different areas of government work. Some major business interests, such as those involved in the logistics industry and the development of Schiphol airport, have sometimes been included in these negotiations. Amsterdam also experienced energetic protests against urban redevelopment in the late 1960s. Since then, including citizens' voices in discussing and developing place-development policy and projects has become 'normal practice'. Within this governance context, 'spatial planning' (*ruimtelijke ordening*) has for many years been a key government activity, both at national and municipal levels. This activity is not only visible in the country's clearly ordered landscape, it is also valued by citizens.

Amsterdam as a city has often been praised for the quality of its place-management and development work. But it also attracts attention for the liveability of its diverse neighbourhoods (see Box 2.2 in Chapter 2) and its continual attention to an inclusive sense of social justice. Urbanist and planner Susan Fainstein considers Amsterdam as an exemplar of the qualities of an egalitarian and just city (1997, 2001b). As in Vancouver, there can be no doubt in Amsterdam that the qualities that now make the city an attractive place to live, work and do business in, as well as more inclusive and environmentally sustainable than many other cities, are in part the result of sustained, planning-oriented, place-governance effort. What is interesting about the Amsterdam case is that this effort has persisted through several generations of development experience.

Amsterdam as an urban area was initially centred within the municipal jurisdiction, which expanded from time to time onto reclaimed land and neighbouring municipalities as the city grew in the first part of the twentieth century. People were crowded into an old urban structure of three to four storeys, with poorer people often living in single rooms in tenements. Workplaces were concentrated in the city centre and the industrial zone along the harbour frontage on the northern banks of the city, which opened onto river channels to the sea. Early twentieth century planning initiatives sought to provide space for better housing and living environments through the provision of lower-density urban extensions and green spaces. By this time, the City Council had a strongly social-democratic orientation, reflecting the strength and activism of the area's working classes. The role of the City Council was to provide and service the land, act as area developer, and often to do the actual building work for properties that would then be provided for rent. The Buitenveldert project in the tour in Chapter 2 was developed in the 1950s in this way. However, the practice of master-planned urban extension was challenged in the 1920s by a new generation of planners influenced by the emerging modern movement in architecture and planning. Cornelius van Eesteren, an important figure in this movement, became head of the Amsterdam planning office and insisted on a more strategic approach to the city's development. He was particularly concerned to connect development locations to transport investment. His efforts resulted in a strategic plan for the city (see Figure 7.2). The material realisation of this plan can be seen in much of the way Amsterdam subsequently developed, strongly contrasting with McLoughlin's conclusions from Melbourne. The strategy expressed an idea of a relatively compact city, centred on its city centre (downtown) and the major harbour industrial areas, surrounded by neighbourhoods and green spaces, articulated by transport routes that were provided with a relatively dense tram network.

Until the 1970s, the city planning office and its real estate department were core agencies promoting and to a large extent realising development activity in the city. Even today, the promotion of major development projects, the making of development strategies and the provision of a research and intelligence function about

Figure 7.2   *Amsterdam: The 1935 General Extension Plan*

Source: Adapted from versions provided by Amsterdam City Council. To see the originals please visit: www.palgrave.com/builtenvironment/healey

urban development in the city remain important areas of the City Council's activity. Working closely with politicians, and in continual active discussion with the National Spatial Planning Department[5] as well as other government departments, especially those concerned with water management and transport infrastructures, ideas about development locations and infrastructure investments were intensively discussed, with final agreements being confirmed in formal development plans (*structuurplannen*) and the investment programmes of the relevant government departments. The National Spatial Planning Department produced regular Statements (*Nota*) about the spatial development of the whole country, to give a context and justification for particular projects, some of which crossed municipal boundaries. This activity, both nationally and in Amsterdam, was for many years highly regarded by politicians, other government departments and important stakeholders working with government (Faludi and Van der Valk 1994).

Spatial development strategies, in such a context, carried sufficient power to shape emerging physical development patterns, though strategies were incrementally adjusted to accommodate the stresses and strains that built up as new realities challenged the planning conceptions. So in the early years after World War II, Amsterdam's plans were revised to focus on the redevelopment of bombed and other run-down areas in the city centre and to open up better access for road transport and expand the city's underground metro system. However, the disruption to inner-city neighbourhoods caused by this redevelopment work fuelled vigorous citizen protest in the 1960s, as in Vancouver, Boston and, as we shall see, Portland. In the Amsterdam case, younger-generation radicals of the late 1960s linked their local protest to wider social movements in Europe that advocated different approaches to urban renewal and more participative democratic practices. New people entered the City Council, carrying these ideas. Established politicians, in the context of the Dutch political culture of collaborative negotiation of public policy, agreed to give much more attention to attending to the social consequences of redevelopment and to providing broad and deep channels to allow citizens' voices to shape development policy. This led to an expanded role for neighbourhood organisations and tenants' associations in all areas of place-governance work. The effect was to prevent further redevelopment of city-centre neighbourhoods for commercial activities.

Meanwhile, de-industrialisation and shifts in port activities towards much larger and deeper ports such as Rotterdam undermined the importance of the city's industrialised waterfront. In contrast, the area around Schiphol airport in the neighbouring Harlemmermeer municipality, which was emerging as one of Europe's major hub airports (see Box 2.3), was rapidly developing into a new urban node in the Amsterdam region, while the new town of Almere, across the river Ij to the east, was expanding into a major residential and industrial area. The image of Amsterdam as a city revolving around its central core was thus increasingly challenged, as the urban linkages of Amsterdam became more metropolitan in spatial spread and more multicentred, or 'polycentric', to use the planning vocabulary that became fashionable in European spatial planning circles a decade later (Davoudi 2003). By the 1980s, the spatial development strategy in Amsterdam was in need of a radical rethink.

This culminated in the 1980s, with the preparation of a new

structuurplan, approved in 1985 (see Figure 7.3). Although produced through elaborate consultation with different stakeholder groups, the strategy embedded in this plan was deeply structured by the dominant ideas current within the Dutch professional planning community. This emphasised a strong environmental agenda of conserving open land, making cities more compact by raising densities, and encouraging greater use of public transport and bicycles.[6] The strategy of compact development was particularly relevant to Amsterdam City Council, which by this time was feeling boxed in as regards greenfield development opportunities. Neighbouring municipalities resisted annexation, while stronger regulations limiting development around airports because of noise were now in place. So Amsterdam could only expand in area by reclaiming more waterfront land, which was expensive. The 1985 Amsterdam *structuurplan* is often presented as the high point of the 'compact city' approach. The urban area was still seen as centred around the old core, but expansion space for commercial activity was to be provided by redevelopment and land reclamation of the waterfronts and in subcentres on the road/rail transport ring created following van Eesteren's pre-war plan. Higher-density residential development was encouraged in the existing urban core. This strategy thus reflected an attempt to resist, by shaping the pattern of physical development and transport investments, the tendencies to sprawling metropolitanisation and emerging polycentricity.

However, containing such pressures proved to be beyond the powers of the city planners. The costs of developing and reclaiming areas along the northern waterfront were substantial and very contentious within the city. Nationally, funds for reclamation and redevelopment were being more carefully prioritised as the financial crises facing welfare states in Europe began to bite. Further, commercial interests were not greatly attracted to such locations. Large corporate businesses preferred the peripheral subcentres, particularly those near Schiphol airport. Slowly, a new development axis was emerging along road and rail routes in the city's southern periphery, where the value of commercial property was rapidly rising relative to the city centre and the northern waterfronts, most notably at what came to be called *Zuidas* (southern axis). In this context, both politicians and planners came to realise that a new approach was needed that accepted the reality that the Amsterdam urban area, measured in terms of the way people moved around in daily and weekly flows, was now much wider than the municipal area. It also contained not one central node but potentially several.

Figure 7.3 *Amsterdam: The 1985* structuurplan

A first initiative, strongly promoted by Amsterdam politicians, was an attempt to expand the city into a larger metropolitan unit. After much discussion with neighbouring municipalities about what this would involve in terms of resource distribution and the prioritisation of projects, a proposal was eventually put to the citizens of Amsterdam. Citizens, however, voted down the proposal in 1995, because they feared the loss of identity and the access they felt they had to the City Council as it was. Somewhat bruised by this setback, the politicians turned away from strategic planning for a while, focusing instead on the ongoing major projects, including a shift to more residential development along the waterfront. This has since led to the creation of new and attractive neighbourhoods in the city. But the city's planning office believed that attention was still needed to the way in which urban realities in the Amsterdam area were evolving. They were also aware of new ideas

Box 7.1   From a 'compact city' to a 'network city': Imagining an emerging metropolis in Amsterdam

In the mid-1990s, city planning staff encouraged discussion and debate on urban futures in various arenas in Amsterdam and listened carefully to discussions ongoing in civil society and among academics about the city and how to understand what cities are and could be.[7] Although the idea of a formal metropolitan agency had fallen through, the city planners worked hard to maintain less formal arenas for discussion about urban futures among politicians and officials in neighbouring municipalities. Through these informal arenas, ideas and agreements about development locations and investment priorities began to emerge, in parallel to debates at the national level. By the later 1990s at the national level, general urban development funding programmes had been reduced and passed down to the provincial level, apart from major projects identified as in the national interest, such as the location of high-speed rail routes and the expansion of Schiphol airport. One factor bringing neighbouring municipalities together was the need to find a new way of prioritising projects in this rather different resourcing climate.

In this context, and with the renewed support of politicians, Amsterdam produced a new *structuurplan*, which the city planners understood as firmly located in the context of a metropolitan strategy. This focused on concepts of development corridors, linking the southern axis of Amsterdam city's development to that in Schiphol and also to Almere in the east, and to the rest of the Dutch economic heartland, in recognition of the complex cross-movements of people and goods within the region. No longer was the city understood by the city's planners as revolving around its old urban core. Instead, the urban area was imagined as the site of an array of complex, partially interlinked networks. Its special character, in the metropolitan context and in the wider context of the Netherlands and neighbouring countries, was its particular cosmopolitan 'urbanity'. So the role of the city's development strategy was to cultivate this quality, while sustaining liveable neighbourhoods, facilitating development along major regional 'corridors' and generally improving accessibility options across the wider urban area (see Figure 7.4).

$\rightarrow$

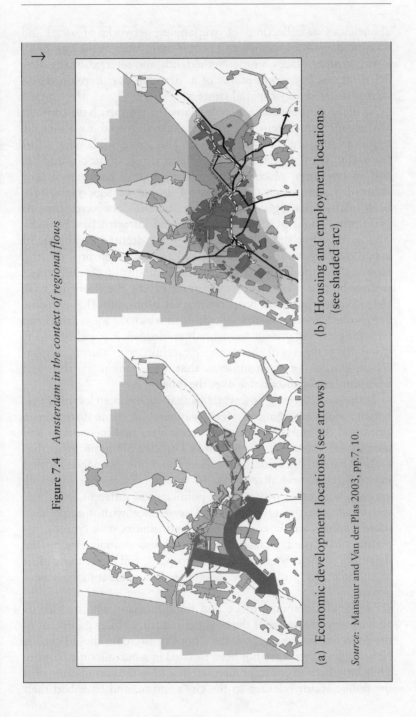

Figure 7.4 *Amsterdam in the context of regional flows*

(a) Economic development locations (see arrows)

(b) Housing and employment locations (see shaded arc)

Source: Mansuur and Van der Plas 2003, pp.7, 10.

about cities as collections of overlapping networks of social and economic relations, connecting people and places in the city to all kinds of other places, in the Netherlands and internationally. Box 7.1 describes how conceptions of a 'network city' developed and were translated into a spatial strategy.

So in the Amsterdam case, politicians and planners have continually encouraged citizens and other stakeholders to think about the city as a whole and its wider linkages. This strategic planning effort has had a major impact on the physical structure of the city and has had an important place in Amsterdam's overall governance. The arenas for articulating the content of formal strategic plans have been institutional spaces where key stakeholders have come to agreements about major development and infrastructure projects. This in turn has shaped substantial public-sector investments in urban development, encouraging linkages between projects and ensuring that performance criteria of liveability, accessibility and sustainability are kept in play. To some extent, the strategies have shaped urban land and property market behaviour. This outcome has resulted from a governance culture in which the ideas associated with the planning project are strongly embedded. It is widely understood that places should be managed carefully, with a strong emphasis on producing environments that will remain liveable and environmentally sustainable over the long term.

In the past 20 years, however, this shaping has been less effective, with tensions emerging between planners' ideals about compact cities and the emerging realities of complex, multinetworked and multinodal urban agglomerations. The city planning office has worked hard to open out to new ideas about how to understand and manage these new directions. In intense discussion with one another, with other officials and politicians at different levels and sectors of government, with urban academics, with multiple civil society groups and in consultation opportunities with citizens, the planners have tried to create new ways of understanding the spatial dynamics of their dynamic urban metropolis, and to use these ideas to shape major projects and on-going development-management activity.

So the city planning office and the politicians who oversee its activity acted for most of the twentieth century as key guardians of the collective interest in how the city of Amsterdam should evolve. Nevertheless, they have not been isolated in a bureaucratic bastion. They have been in constant interaction within the various arenas of the public sector relevant to the city's future, and have had their listening and learning antennae tuned to a wider range of different forms of knowledge about the city. They are continually criticised by an active civil society culture, but are themselves part of this culture, drawing inspiration and critical evaluation for their own work in shaping development activity. It is this rich civil society, with its capacity to maintain an idea of Amsterdam as a place in need of continual and careful public attention, that in the end has sustained the governance capacity for co-ordinated urban development in the service of a complex urban society. This is combined with a positive view of the role of a strong public sector oriented to public welfare. Amsterdam's qualities as a 'good', 'just' and 'liveable' city are the product of this nexus, as much as of the public planning work that the governance culture supports.

A polity that developed a planning culture: Portland, Oregon[8]

Portland (see Figure 7.5) is on America's Pacific west coast, situated where the river Willamette joins the great Columbia river on the final lap of its journey from the Rocky Mountains to the sea. Settled by former Europeans only since the mid-nineteenth century, for many years, like Vancouver and Seattle further north, its economy was centred on commerce and manufacture related to primary products: forestry, furs, fishing and farming. Settlers and their descendants valued the open green landscapes of rolling hills, wide rivers and varied forests, with the backdrop of snow-capped Mount Hood in the near distance. Until the mid-twentieth century the city of Portland grew steadily, shaped in part by the ideas of American planner Frederick Law Olmsted, who emphasised the importance of parks and green spaces. By 1950, the city of Portland itself had only around 375,000 people, and the wider area a maximum of 750,000. But since then, it has expanded into one of the US's second division of metropolitan areas, with a population of nearly two million spreading across an area of 80 kilometres (50 miles) in diameter, with growth speeding up at the end of the century. The area's economy has shifted from an emphasis on processing and trading primary resources to a strong development of knowledge-intensive industries. It is home to some very successful firms of the later twentieth century, including Nike, Intel, Adidas America and Tektronix (Mayer and Provo 2004). By the 1990s, it had also acquired a reputation as one of the most liveable cities in the US and, not unrelated,

Figure 7.5   *Portland city centre*

Source: City of Portland, Oregon Bureau of Planning and Sustainability.

as a city where land-use planning powers, with their strong restrictions on private actions, are considered 'a legitimate expression of the public interest' (Abbott 2001:6).[9] This is a striking achievement in the US, and particularly in the areas of settler expansion in the west, where the freedom to own and develop property without restriction is valued as a cornerstone of political liberty.

Until the 1960s, the city of Portland, and the state of Oregon in which it is administratively situated, was a rather sleepy backwater, with less of a violent frontier history than California to the south. In the 1960s, the young 'hippie' generation discovered its landscapes, which were by this time becoming obviously threatened by deforestation from logging activity, while its rivers were increasingly polluted by agriculture and manufacturing in the Willamette and Columbia river catchment areas. Meanwhile, Portland itself was expanding, beginning to sprawl in large urban plots across neighbouring farmland. Local political leaders sought to service this growth with major highway projects, which drove through older areas of the inner urban fabric. These not only disrupted neighbourhoods, as in so many other cities at this time, but, in Portland's case, turned the central city waterfront in the 1940s into an arterial highway, as in Boston. It was these experiences, and the pressure from incomers, that woke the city up politically. Concern about urban growth and its threat to the state's traditional landscape was also shared by those involved in farming and fishing, and by recent migrants from the US east coast who valued the peaceful outback. The result was a collective movement by a new generation of activists who sought ways to combine the urbanisation needed to accommodate economic growth and improvements in urban qualities with safeguarding rural and natural landscapes from the kind of sprawling urbanisation turning up elsewhere in the US, and particularly in California. As Carl Abbott (2001:174) describes, these activists and the political culture that grew under their influence summoned up an idea of the city of Portland as a contrast to Los Angeles' apparently inchoate urban form and the nearby rapidly expanding manufacturing nexus of Seattle to the north.

The activists and other key actors of the 1960s became the politicians and the planners of the next decades, taking the governorship of the state (Tom MacCall, who had been an investigative journalist) and the position of Mayor of Portland (Neil Goldschmidt) for sustained periods from the early 1970s. It was this group and their alliances, as in Vancouver and Barcelona, who carried key strategic ideas about both the substance of urban development strategy and the processes through which it should be articulated. Advisers to Neil Goldschmidt, who became Mayor in 1972, had already 'sketched out an integrated strategy involving co-ordination of land use and transport' (Abbott 2001:142). These strategic ideas were thus lodged in their heads, as well as in their manifestoes and the plans produced. Critical to this strategy were actions at three organisational levels. The State of Oregon passed into law in 1973 a requirement that every municipality had to prepare a comprehensive land-use plan that regulated where development could occur. (States in the US have the power to devise and adopt land-use planning measures. The Oregon system emphasises increasing densities and providing urban growth boundaries.) Municipalities were encouraged to increase urban densities and set urban growth boundaries in order to avoid further sprawl and safeguard farmland and natural landscapes. They were also required to make provision for affordable housing. Social and environmental concerns were thus combined with the recognition of different kinds of economic interest.

In the Portland area, given that development had already spread beyond the boundaries of Portland municipality itself, a metropolitan agency was created in 1970. This became an elected authority in 1978 and is now known as Metro, with powers to deliver collective services and engage in urban planning (Abbott 2001). It became the channel for distributing federal funds for urban improvement and was also the organisation with the power to define the Portland area's urban growth boundary. This boundary was formally approved in 1980.[10] The politicians and their advisers in Portland produced their own formal 'comprehensive land-use plan' in 1979 in this context. Until then, they had put more emphasis on downtown improvements and revitalising neighbourhoods. A first initiative had been the production of a Downtown Plan, approved in 1972 (see Box 7.2).

An Office of Neighbourhood Associations was established in 1974, to provide resources for the various voluntary neighbourhood associations that had grown up during the 1960s and since. This

---

Box 7.2   The Downtown (city centre) Plan

'Preservation of a user-friendly downtown was the strategy's cornerstone. Business worries about suburban competition and parking problems coincided at the end of the 1960s with public disgust over a blighted riverfront. [This] public concern ... fired imaginations about radical responses to other downtown problems. [A consultant and a city official] introduced the idea of a comprehensive rethinking of downtown. They helped to organise a process by which the younger generation of technically sophisticated citizen activists worked with city officials, downtown retailers, property owners, neighbourhood groups, and civic organisations to treat the interrelations of previously isolated issues, such as parking, bus services, housing and retailing ...

The Downtown Plan of 1972 offered integrated solutions to a long list of problems that Portlanders had approached piecemeal for two generations. It was technically sound because the proposals were based on improvements in access and transportation. It was politically viable because it prescribed tradeoffs among different interests as part of a coherent strategy. Specifics included new parks and plazas, high density retail and office corridors crossing in the center of downtown, better transit and new parking garages to serve the corridors, districts for special housing incentives, and pedestrian oriented design' (Abbott 2001:144–5). Key to much of this was the reorganisation of public and private transport routes. The riverfront highway was reduced in scale and redesigned to produce a large riverfront park. A bus transit mall was created as a spine running through the downtown, which is free within the downtown area. Investments have been made in improving bus transit across the metropolitan area, and developing a light rail transit system. One result between 1987 and 1997 was a stabilisation of levels of car commuting and a big increase in public transit passengers (Abbott 2001:150).

distributed funds made available by the city, as well as US federal government funding, which was channelled through Metro. The office had a political purpose as well as a developmental purpose. It helped to strengthen the political base for municipal government, and to limit the activist confrontations that had occurred over highway projects in the 1960s.

The 1979 comprehensive plan developed the emphasis in state and Metro strategies on more compact forms of urban development and provided mechanisms to promote increased urban densities and sustain a stock of affordable housing for rent.[11] In addition, the Portland strategy sought, first, to shift transport investment priorities from highways to public transport in order to improve air quality, enhance the accessibility of older urban neighbourhoods and encourage workers and shoppers to use the downtown. Secondly, the strategy sought to revitalise neighbourhoods, through improving housing, providing amenities and increasing densities. Thirdly, the importance of focusing on the quality of the downtown area was underlined, as a vital business centre and an attractive place to visit, both to sustain downtown businesses and as a way to increase the attractiveness of inner-area neighbourhoods. Thus Portland in the early 1970s set out on a path that other cities sought to follow in the 1980s and 1990s, particularly those promoting visions of a 'sustainable city' (see Satterthwaite 1999, Williams et al. 2000, Wheeler 2004).

By 1988–9, Portland was winning accolades in the US for the quality and liveability of its downtown. By 2000, the population of the city itself had grown to over half a million. Through careful neighbourhood planning, the connections between downtown and surrounding residential areas flowed more easily. In 1988, the plan was updated into the Central City Plan, which included some of these neighbourhoods. The development of Portland's Neighborhood Association programme has attracted widespread attention in the US. Commentators note the lively energy of citizen engagement with planning and public realm issues, as in Amsterdam, and how such engagement has contributed to producing the liveability of urban life (see Johnson 2004, Witt 2004). However, the success of the downtown strategy brought its own costs, as gentrification set in and housing costs rose. The city negotiates with developers to include affordable housing for rent in schemes, but this is not always easy to obtain. Municipalities elsewhere in the wider metropolitan area compete to attract retail and business projects.

This strategy, expressed in various planning documents and

political manifestoes at various times, has lasted for three decades.[12] It centres on the idea of a compact city, revolving around a strong city centre, articulated through transport investments that maximise accessibility without leading to excessive congestion and pollution. It works by shaping investment priorities and locations, and by influencing regulatory norms pursued through the powerful land-use controls available via the Oregon State land-use planning system. It has been sustained by the work of politicians, planning officials and academics, in city councils and in the Metro agency. This work includes providing information about and promoting the idea of Portland's special qualities. However, it is not only politicians and specialist planners who have been guardians of the strategy. Portland has a rich array of civil society organisations promoting various aspects of the strategy. Key elements have been regularly tested in referenda, and citizens until recently gave their support. This in part reflects the attention given in Portland to developing inclusive planning processes. The political ambition has been to develop a political community. This combines citizen and stakeholder energy with political representatives, their officials and other advisers, in which a particular idea of Portland could become embedded and out of which specific strategic interventions could gather support. In developing a shared idea of the city, it helped that Portlanders could compare themselves and the liveability of their city with other, more sprawling urban places in the US. A key quality of this political culture has been that neighbourhood-level discussion has been interlinked with debates about strategic investments in an interactive way, relating the parts of the urban complex to consideration of a wider whole, in terms of geography and politics. People are continually encouraged to think of themselves as citizens of Portland and of Oregon State, rather than merely as people with specific individual or group interests. This continues into the late 2000s with vigorous on-going discussions about a new strategic plan for the city.[13]

However, as commentators are careful to point out, there are weaknesses and vulnerabilities in this success story of strategic planning for an urban area. As key stakeholders have come to play the land-use regulation game at state level, tensions have broken out. The house-building firms continually demand that a sufficient supply of housing land is made available to accommodate predicted growth within the urban growth boundary. Such practices have led to a focus on the amount of housing built rather than on the design and quality of residential development.[14] The urban growth boundary is criticised as too rigid, although in the Portland area it has been expanded several times and has become, just like Britain's green belts, an iconic expression of the region's distinctive planning approach (Abbott and Margheim 2008).[15] And despite the emphasis in the Portland Planning Department, the Metro agency and Oregon State on being inclusive, there are some interests that are excluded and some groups who feel distant from the political consensus. Abbott (2001) notes that those in search of large residential lots are squeezed out and move to more accommodating municipalities. There are also questions about how inclusive the Portland development strategy has been. There are a variety of ethnic groups in the Portland area. Those who do not conform to the majority group standards have found themselves squeezed out of opportunities, leading to some socio-spatial segregation. A new generation of incomers from other parts of the US and from more Latino areas is less aware of the political culture that has built up, and less interested in sustaining it. So, as the strategy ages, its future is called into question.

There is no doubt that Portland, Oregon, has successfully used an urban development strategy to shape a city along sustainable, liveable and inclusive lines and, in parallel, has helped to create a political community that values the environment that has been created. It is a place of lively debate about urban and environmental issues. It attracts people from many other parts of the US not merely because of economic opportunity but because of the liveability created through strategic initiatives. The guardianship of Portland's qualities is now shared not only among civic leaders, officials and active pressure groups, but with citizens quite broadly, as in Vancouver. It has built governance capacity in which a planning orientation is strongly embedded. But it remains to be seen how far this political culture can sustain itself.

Making place-development strategies

In both Amsterdam and Portland, strategic ideas about place qualities and place futures became key elements of the governance infrastructure of their urban areas. Strategies provided a reference point for arguments about what needed to be done to sustain qualities of liveability and environmental sustainability when challenged by narrowly economic interests, or by the threat of sprawling development. However, the power of these strategies did not lie in their existence in a plan or other document. Such statements were but one mode of their expression. Nor did their power derive purely from the quality of the analyses that helped to support them, although such technical work made an important contribution. Their power lay in their roots in local political and developmental realities, articulated through citizen activism that was able to lodge itself in formal government arenas. The strategies also had resonance with what citizens and other stakeholders recognised as important in the flow of their lives.

These resonances did not develop overnight but grew slowly, through struggles and conflicts and through the evolution of understandings of place qualities. Many times, initiatives in spatial strategy making fail because there is no fertile ground in which they can take root. If there is no wider social movement supporting a strategy that will promote daily life liveability and longer-term sustainability as key priorities, then it will be hard for a strategy embodying these values to survive. In Portland, politicians and planners knew they had to expand the base of support for such a strategic orientation. In some contexts, it is much more difficult to develop such support. Yet even in less fertile contexts, some strategic ideas may live on to shape future possibilities. One famous example is the 1909 Burnham Plan for Chicago, which promoted conserving an open waterfront, though its social dimensions were soon forgotten (see Ward 2002, Smith 2006).

This underlines that evolving a strategic approach to place development needs active work to bring strategic ideas to public attention, to encourage debate and to form a public around the issues, the debates and the need for a place-development strategy. In Portland, the public that politicians and planners helped to form and to inform grew in size and spread out among citizens and stakeholders. Something similar happened in Vancouver (see Chapter 4). In Amsterdam, such a public had been formed in the working-class struggles for improvements in living and working conditions in the early twentieth century. Later generations of planning staff and politicians then continually sustained attention on the value of a strategic orientation in maintaining the city's qualities as a liveable and sustainable place.

Strategy making in the planning field requires complex imaginative, intellectual and technical work, involving a wide range of sources of understanding and imaginative power. The challenge for the planning project as introduced in Chapter 1 is to mobilise this power and focus it in the service of promoting liveability and sustainability, and contributing to the public realm of an urban area, taken as a whole. Two key activities are central to achieving such spatial strategies. The first centres on the formation and mobilisation of conceptions of an urban area, which can act as key integrative devices through which the whole in question is called into consciousness and comes to do real, material work. The second centres on the processes through which such conceptions are developed and sustained, and what needs to be in place to prevent critical public realm dimensions from being sliced off or shifted to the background by powerful interests that seek to slip out of the constraints a powerful strategy may impose on them.

As discussed in Chapter 2, developing an idea of the 'place' of a large urban area is not straightforward. It involves summoning up into imaginative consciousness some conception of a whole urban complex, which can express important qualities about an area and which can hold within itself in significant ways the various parts, groups and dimensions that constitute it. Creating such a conception also generates a sense of an entity that can then be positioned in relation to a wider landscape of evolving places. Such an idea needs to be persuasive enough to get used in public policy and become a part of the infrastructure of the public realm. The challenge in generating such a conception is to make it broad and rich enough to encompass a plurality of experiences and ways of thinking about a place, strong enough to do real work in shaping future development investment projects and regulatory criteria, but yet flexible enough to be relevant to the different situations of particular groups and areas within the whole as these change over time. As noted at the start of this chapter, planners and urbanists have tended to express their ideas about such conceptions in a spatial imagery, which describes the 'structure' of an urban area. (Hence the term 'structure' plans, which came into use in north-west Europe in the 1970s; see for example Amsterdam's *structuurplan*.) Cities have typically been presented in such imagery as having nodes (city centres and subcentres), networks (transport hubs, spokes, grids and corridors) and neighbourhoods. As in the London Plan of 2004, Amsterdam and Portland used such imagery.

But while the strategy makers originally focused on the concept of a compact, hierarchically organised city, they had to adjust to a reality where the nodes of economic and social activity were no longer clearly focused on the city centre, but diffused across a sprawling urban fabric. The need for alternative spatial conceptions has become even more urgent in the giant megalopolises appearing in many parts of the world. Within Europe, the Milanese urban region (with over nine million people) provides an important example, where there has been much work analysing and representing its qualities. Milan has a traditional urban centre, with a sense of itself very like a traditional Greek 'polis'. But it sprawls out to encompass the vigorous small industries of the affluent La Brianza area, where close family ties in the locality combine with all kinds of trading links worldwide. It stretches northwards in its commuting range across the western Italian Lakes into Switzerland, as well as towards Turin in the west and Venice to the east. The movement of people and firms across this megalopolis are complex, with all kinds of patterns of nodes and networks layered across each other. The formal government arenas are also very complex, with place-governance responsibilities spread among the region (Lombardy), the core province of Milan and the core municipality of Milan. In the mid-2000s, the province sought to encourage greater comprehension among its constituent municipalities (all 189 of them) about the way different parts of the complex related to each other and to many other, wider sets of relationships. The ambition was to provide the basis for more co-ordinated action over common infrastructure issues, and also to encourage greater attention to the liveability of the different parts of the urban complex. As a way to start, they encouraged all kinds of groups to contribute innovative ideas about improving conditions and about ways of representing the polycentric complexity of the area. The initiative as a whole was called 'the City of Cities' (*CittadiCitta*) and the team of planning experts contributed their own visual representation to get people thinking. This shows the urban region as a complex scatter of smaller towns expanding and merging with each other, as farmland between them is steadily eaten up by development (see Balducci 2008 and www.palgrave.com/builtenvironment/healey).

In this Milan example, the urban whole that the planning group sought to draw to public attention is a vast, amorphous sprawl, with all kinds of neighbourhoods and other nodal points and with a diversity of groups, each with its own particular connections within the Milan area and beyond it. On the one hand, this sprawling complex is an expression of a culturally and economically dynamic nexus in one of Western Europe's most affluent areas. On the other, it creates enormous challenges in articulating improvements in major infrastructures and public facilities, and in reducing environmental stress. In this fluid and formless reality, social distress often accumulates unnoticed. Older locales deteriorate unheeded until serious problems capture public attention. If, spatially, the challenge is to find a way of expressing the relations between nodes, networks and neighbourhoods, socially the challenge is to keep in mind the diversity of social relations and the experiences of different social groups. It is these challenges and the moral concerns these raise that, in the Milan area, animate efforts by those with a planning orientation to draw attention to the 'whole' of an area.

In Amsterdam, those involved in metropolitan region planning initiatives had also tried to express a polycentric, multinetworked urban reality in spatial imagery (see the figure in Box 7.1). But the result, while illustrative, is not easy to grasp as an inspirational image. A more spatially specific expression might create all kinds of political tensions between municipalities across an urban area that maybe cannot agree in advance on what projects should have priority. For this reason, some planning teams have resorted either to general statements about qualities to be prioritised or to an iconic representation of an area (see Figure 2.3). In a term that combines a religious sense of an inspirational mission and a visual sense of a future to be glimpsed, these have come to be called 'vision' statements, a term borrowed from the business management field (Shipley 2002).

Such vision statements and images may provide a more flexible way of imagining an urban area. If developed with sensitivity and rich intelligence, such statements may be better suited to keep at the forefront of policy attention the diversity of social groups and the tensions between the forces shaping economic, social and environmental futures as these play out in an urban area. An iconic imagery may help in persuading an area's residents and key stakeholders to notice particular qualities about the wider area in which they are located. This was a major ambition in Milan's *CittadiCitta* initiative. The challenge is then to connect the vision to its implications for the diverse parts encompassed within the whole. A strategy gets to carry structuring power if it succeeds in articulating a conception of the whole of the place, and connect this to parts recognised in different ways: as physical locales with particular ambiences, as overlapping networks of people, groups and their interconnections, and as different dimensions of existence. It can provide an integrative force, a way of keeping at the forefront of attention a sensibility to the multiplicity of forces and relations that affect the future of an urban area, and to the complex ways in which people's lives are and could be affected by how the future unfolds. Such conceptions, and their translation into action programmes, are not easily arrived at, as the Portland example shows. It is all too easy for contentious or less vocally represented aspects to slip out of attention as time goes by.

This raises important questions about how strategic conceptions are arrived at and to whom they belong. In the 1960s, many planners thought that an objective specification of an urban system could be arrived at through analysis. Developing a good, systematised knowledge base, supported by relevant information, is certainly a valuable resource for strategic planning work, as was appreciated in both Amsterdam and Portland. However, building up a strategic conception of a place by calculated aggregation proved unable to capture a resonating sense of place with integrative power. There are just too many dimensions to analyse and too many variables to relate to each other. Instead, analysis has come to be used to test hypotheses and assumptions and to help select between one project and another. Similarly, an overall conception of a place and its development possibilities cannot be arrived at by adding together conceptions of 'bits of a city' – neighbourhoods, centres, special zones and so on. Instead, a place-development conception needs to articulate an integrative idea and fill it with meaning, in a way that has the power to carry key values and priorities through time and across a complex governance landscape. Strategies can thus themselves become nodal points, drawing together many different ideas and relationships critical to place futures (see Healey 2007, Salet and Thornley 2007). Arriving at strategies that become persuasive because of the meanings and resonances they express requires imaginative work and a kind of strategic judgement that draws on, but does not become dominated by, all kinds of analyses, experiences and interactions between the on-going flow of work on development management and major projects. A lively, broad-based political culture and strong local leadership of politicians, experts and other activists are key resources in creating and sustaining broad and rich place-development visions that come to make a difference. Strategy making of this kind works through skilful combinations of analytical, deliberative and proactive modes of governance (see Chapter 3). It gets to achieve effects by developing a governance capacity to combine inspirational appeal with the ability to be selective in identifying critical actions with the potential to promote desirable future possibilities (Albrechts 2004).

Who, then, does and should take the initiative in preparing such strategies? In the mid-twentieth century, it seemed obvious that municipalities should have a planning office that acted as the critical arena for articulating place-development strategies and that local politicians and planning officials should take the lead in preparing them. In both Amsterdam and Portland, it was staff in municipal planning offices and, in the case of Portland, in Metro who played key roles in developing and detailing spatial strategies. But by the end of the twentieth century, this allocation of responsibility was no longer so dominant. The capacity and legitimacy of formal municipal government and trained experts came under serious challenge. Although political parties still provide an important co-ordinative force between levels of government and between state, economy and civil society, as in Barcelona and Porto Alegre for example, in many other areas they no longer attract respect or even much attention. Finding an institutional locus that could command sufficient attention and respect over the long term was a major challenge for the planners in Durban, South Africa, when in the 2000s they came to prepare an 'integrated area development strategy' (Breetzke 2009). In the Milan *CittadiCitta* initiative, the planning team was drawn from the academic community, and the work on a spatial strategy for the region of Flanders in Belgium in the 1990s was similarly led by an academic (Albrechts 1998, 2001). In England, 'local strategic partnerships', operating tangentially to municipalities, were encouraged in the 2000s to take a leading role in developing municipal spatial strategies (Nadin 2007). In the context of more diffused, fragmented governance landscapes (see Chapter 3), it is often not clear where the arenas and initiatives for engaging in place-development strategy making could and should lie, while the challenges of legitimating strategies and of co-ordinating the actions that they prioritise are often acute (Salet and Thornley 2007). Yet, despite all the criticisms of local government capacity, municipalities remain key agencies in both creating place-development strategies and acting to put them into effect. Not only are they answerable to a constituency related to all residents within their jurisdiction.[16] They are also multifunctional agencies, with the potential, if not always realised, of linking different activities together. The increasing emphasis in Europe and internationally on devolving more power to the municipal level is a reflection of this recognition (see Chapter 3).

The challenge for municipalities in the twenty-first century who engage in spatial strategy making is to recognise, first, that they are only one agency among several that hold the future of an area in their hands. Secondly, they are often too small to be able to act as autonomous units. Performing their tasks effectively, whether in relation to managing health, education and welfare services, taking care of local environments or taking business development initiatives and improving infrastructure provision, involves forms of collaboration and partnership with neighbouring agencies and other service providers, both public and private. This recognition has led to all kinds of initiatives to create new agencies, arenas and networks focused on some aspect of a wide locality. In some instances, strategy-making initiatives may arise through the formation of development coalitions initially outside the arenas of formal government (see Healey 2007, Briggs 2008).

Such initiatives and partnerships, of course, do not just happen. They result from active work in developing networks, creating arenas and organising processes through which the voices of the 'parts' can somehow find expression and help to create a 'whole' out of the fragments of a governance landscape. This active work in turn helps to generate the energy and commitment to carry forward strategic ideas in ways that can have a real influence. Inevitably, such processes take time to get initiated, to gather momentum and arrive at a strategic focus. The advantage of Amsterdam and Portland is that there already existed a capacity for self-reflection among those engaged in governance, combined with a wider polity with traditions of vigorous active critique. Discussing issues to do with the changing character of the urban area in ways that reached out to this wider polity also raised awareness among the key stakeholders whose actions a strategy affected most directly. So although such rich democratic practice takes time and continual engagement, this time may be recouped in the long term through greater understanding and firmer legitimacy for strategic actions. How far this is possible, however, will depend on contextual conditions. In the Milan area, the challenge of creating and sustaining governance attention to the dynamics of place development and their emerging consequences was much harder, because the Milan City Council itself did not wish to act to promote debate in a wider metropolitan arena.

Where such a political culture does not already exist, the example of Portland shows that it can slowly form. Here, a 'public' was created around the idea of a liveable and sustainable city, in a similar way to that which formed in Vancouver. In these cases, as in Barcelona, the initiatives started from the political mobilisation in protest at insensitive urban redevelopment policies. These generated political leaders as well as new planning officials, who played a key role in shaping the evolution of a new political culture in their cities. In US cities in the past, it has often been business lobby groups with land and property-development interests that have mobilised strategic planning initiatives (see Fainstein and Fainstein 1986, Logan and Molotch 1987, Briggs 2008). In contemporary Europe, environmental groups have been active in mobilising for changes in policy and practice in urban areas. Recent research also suggests that transport companies and agencies operating regional and subregional networks have also been important actors in promoting attention to the 'whole' of a locality (see Salet and Thornley 2007).

However, protest movements, lobby groups and specific agencies do not necessarily have a focus on liveability and sustainability. They may be more concerned with specific interests rather than with the many who dwell or have a stake in an urban area. They may have only limited awareness of the complex interdependences and interconnections that link the parts, projects and groups that are at the forefront of their attention with others with a stake in an urban area. A critical challenge for all these efforts in place-development strategy making is how to avoid a narrowing of focus to merely the interests of the most powerful activists. Some initiatives try to engage in widespread citizen participation, such as that developed in Porto Alegre's budgeting process (see Box 3.1). This has the great advantage of mobilising all kinds of knowledge and imagination to help focus attention on what may really make a difference to how a place develops in the future. But inevitably, not everyone can be included as a direct voice in a process related to the future of a large area of hundreds of thousands or millions of inhabitants. Even knowledgeable and skilled expert teams, committed to promoting the values of the planning project, can easily let their focus narrow down under the pressures of time, political challenge and their own enthusiasms. This underlines the key message from the Amsterdam and Portland cases that, in developing spatial strategies, the guardianship of the public realm is not so much located in any one person or agency, but in the interaction between key actors, their networks and the wider political culture. This helps to sustain the 'comprehensive consciousness' (Hoch 2007) or 'enlarged intelligence' (Dewey 1927/1991) that holds in place the breadth and depth needed to ensure that conceptions of the wholes and parts of an urban area are as pluralistic and dynamic as possible.

The place-development strategies in Amsterdam and Portland evolved in contexts in which such an enlarged intelligence was available, resonating with the particular history and geography of each locality. Both governance contexts provided conditions favourable to the emergence of place-governance with a planning orientation, which in turn helped to enlarge and sustain such contextual conditions. A key aspect in both cases in the later twentieth century was the emergence of collaborative modes of governance as normal practice, in which many could participate in discussing and shaping strategic ideas and their translation into specific projects, programmes and regulatory actions. This did not mean that such collaborative efforts were an alternative to having effective bureaucracies and clear goals or ideological principles. Instead, it meant that a combination of periodic active engagement, along with an attentive and assertive public, came to drive the valuable bureaucratic work needed to deliver services and the various project and programme initiatives undertaken by specific agencies. In this way, a place-development strategy became a kind of localised structural driving force. It was not merely an ideological manifesto or set of goals, but a locally specific orientation, which spread around the governance culture and development activity within a locality.

Such governance capacities often do not exist. In these cases, as several examples in this book illustrate, activists may campaign to generate attention to one or more place quality issues and eventually attract political attention. Technical experts, including those who consider themselves as planners, may provide information about changing conditions, to alert people quietly to challenges and threats that lie ahead. In Portland, early initiatives in the 1970s started in this way. The important issue for those considering elaborating a place-development strategy with a planning orientation is to understand the governance culture within which a strategy needs to take root if it is to have a long-term shaping effect on urban development, and to assess the potential for it to shape how that governance culture itself evolves.

In summary, strategies that succeed work by creating a whole, in a geographical and in a political sense, with which many parties with a stake in a place come to identify. They create a language about 'our place' with which actions can be justified and arguments grounded. Effective development management can make a real and positive difference to those who live in the neighbourhoods and nodal parts of a locality. Major development projects reconfigure some parts of a locality, to recreate ambiences and reposition them in a locality's changing geography. Major infrastructure projects shift patterns of accessibility to bundles of opportunity. Such projects may have substantial impacts on urban geographies and the liveability and sustainability of urban areas, overall and in the experiences of their parts and groups. The effort of producing and sustaining place-development strategies that acquire the power to shape on-going development management, and to focus choices about the location and form of major projects, may potentially have even greater transformative effects, especially where strategic ideas become embedded in a governance culture and in governance practices. Though many such strategy-making initiatives fail to acquire sufficient power to perform in this way, they are major political projects.

Many so-called place-development strategies are not efforts in such transformative work. They may be undertaken because they are formally required under some procedure related to development-management practices, or because of the demands of an external funder. Despite such demands, a transformative place-development strategy may not be needed in a particular instance. Yet the cases throughout this book have shown that, without a broader strategic conception of an evolving urban area, it is difficult to keep an eye on the complex interconnections between one area and another, and the experience of one group and of others. Place-development strategies that get to make a difference, in contrast, help to sustain a 'comprehensive consciousness', even as they are selective in focusing attention on particular areas, groups and actions. They get to achieve this because they convey an understanding of a shared if diverse public realm within which the many co-exist, in which strangers find themselves neighbours, to use Sandercock's metaphors (2000).

The making and monitoring of a place-development strategy, as presented in this chapter, becomes a project that is jointly produced by key stakeholders such as politicians, technical experts and key agencies and activists, but that depends for its power on its resonance with the wider political community and governance culture. It is an activity that is awash with complex and inter-related political and technical judgements. Those with a commitment to the planning project and trained in planning work often play key roles in orchestrating such efforts and making sure that strategic ideas are kept alive through time and across many governance arenas, as the cases of Amsterdam and Portland show. But without a connection to the momentum of the wider socio-economic and political landscape, such efforts may have only limited, or even perverse, effects. Spatial strategies for place development with a planning orientation succeed by becoming part of the governance infrastructure of a political community. They belong to these communities, not to a particular group of trained experts. Yet expertise is important in their production. In the next chapter, I consider the challenges faced by those who contribute such expertise and the roles and positions through which such work is done.

Suggested further reading

There is an expanding literature on strategic spatial planning and spatial strategy making (in the US, sometimes known as a 'new regionalism'). The following provide helpful introductions:

Albrechts, L., Healey, P. and Kunzmann, K. (2003) Strategic spatial planning and regional governance in Europe, *Journal of the American Planning Association*, **69**, 113–29.

Healey, P. (2007) *Urban Complexity and Spatial Strategies: Towards a Relational Planning for our Times*, Routledge, London.

Hopkins, L. (2001) *Urban Development: The Logic of Making Plans*, Island Press, Washington, DC.

Salet, W., Thornley, A. and Kreukels, A. (eds) (2003) *Metropolitan Governance and Spatial Planning: Comparative Studies of European City-Regions*, E&FN Spon, London.

Wheeler, S. M. (2004) *Planning for Sustainability: Creating Livable, Equitable and Ecological Communities*, Routledge, London.

Chapter 8

Doing Planning Work

Who does 'planning' work?

At the start of this book, I presented planning activity as seen from the outside, from the perspective of residents, critical of the wider systems that they felt ignored them, and of academics, critical of the way well-meaning government intentions opened up complex social tensions. Then, in the chapters on the different fields of place-governance work, I showed how active, committed people interacted with and enlarged moments of opportunity within which the promise of the planning project could be realised. In this chapter, I look more closely at the demands made of those who do place-governance work with a planning orientation, and especially the contribution of those trained as 'planners'.

It is often assumed that place-governance – that is, deliberate place-management and development work – is the special responsibility of trained planners: planning experts. Many such people were involved in the cases discussed in the previous chapters. As noted in Chapter 1, they are presented in popular culture in conflicting imagery. They are characterised as defenders of the collective interest in shaping how places develop, and as tiresome regulators of our individual initiatives. Stereotypical images of 'the planner' stalk the iconography of the media, as well as much social science writing about planning and planners. The planner is portrayed as an opinionated bureaucrat, with a rather weak foundation in knowledge and expertise, who lays claim to expert status and professional position. This character joins the many other specialist groups that emerged with the expansion of government activity in the twentieth century, such as social workers, healthcare specialists and environmental health experts, whose members sought to join the specialists of earlier eras: the doctor, the lawyer, the architect and the engineer (see Johnson 1972, Healey 1985). These days, such specialists are viewed with an ambiguous attitude. We are dependent and beholden to them, as they provide knowledge and expertise that we lack. We are irritated by them, as they are often gatekeepers to realising our aspirations and regulators of our behaviour.

Yet, as the previous chapters show, many people, including many kinds of specialists, get involved in place-governance activity with a planning orientation: citizens, politicians, development companies, architects, engineers, consultancies, community development workers. And although there were many people trained as planners who make significant contributions to improving place qualities, some of these other people also play an important part in keeping a planning orientation at the forefront of attention. What, then, is the particular contribution of those trained as experts in the planning field and employed to make a planning-oriented contribution to place-governance work? How far is such expertise really needed? Could it not be provided by any of us, as part of our ordinary experience? Is not much of what planners do really an activity that politicians, our 'representatives', should do?

The importance of expert knowledge and trained judgement emerges in all the areas of place-governance work discussed in this book. Such experts were located in different situations – as consultants, as academic expert advisers, as staff in development companies, and in particular in municipal planning offices. A cadre of trained people working in municipal planning offices or agencies with a development planning remit proved a valuable resource in the cases referred to in the previous chapters. Such people not only provided expertise, they also acted as guardians both of the ambition of the planning project and, related to this, of attention to collective concerns. This meant a practical respect for the diversity of specific interests, needs and values, and an ethical commitment to the health of the public realm available to present and future generations. The previous chapters also show that such work was challenging, requiring considerable grasp in understanding and skill in performance. For example, in Amsterdam the strategic planners needed to know about how changing economic dynamics and environmental relations were affecting the spatial geography of the wider Amsterdam area, and what the impacts were of shifts in priorities for infrastructure provision and the potential location of future urban development. They also needed to work out how best to present the knowledge they arrived at to different constituencies within the area and how to help frame the practical judgements that politicians and others would from time to time have to make. As others have shown in detailed accounts of planning work (Hoch 1994,

Kitchen 1997, Forester 1999), they needed skill in connecting analytical and political work. But doing analysis is just one activity that people trained as planning experts get involved in. They may play many roles. In South Tyneside, they acted as considerate regulators. In Besters Camp, they were community development workers. In Birmingham, they were careful and committed negotiators, and in Barcelona, vigorous shapers of future possibilities. In Vancouver and Portland, they both facilitated neighbourhood plan making and advocated attention to wider social and environmental issues.

Clearly, then, in the examples of effective planning activity presented here, these people were not value-neutral objective scientists. Nor were they merely administrators of bureaucratic protocols. They were focused, through a mix of personal commitment, specialist training and professional identification, on promoting, in one way or another, the values of the planning project. They were committed to enhancing the liveability and sustainability of places for people taking account of wider connections, now and with future generations in mind, in knowledgeable and transparent ways. In this way, they acted as guardians of the public realm of place qualities. This implied that, in whatever role and position they found themselves, they had a responsibility to think of many sides to an issue, not only one, and to consider many constituencies, not just a narrow range or a dominant voice. They needed a pluralist attitude.[1] This is no easy challenge, pitching those contributing expertise to place-governance work 'into the middle', faced with balancing and integrating many claims for attention. In addition to grasp and skill, this difficult work therefore also demands continual attention to the moral and ethical dimensions of doing planning work (Forester 1999).

In this chapter, I look more closely at what is involved in this work. I consider first the content of the expertise needed to accomplish place-governance work with a planning orientation. I then look at the different arenas where such planning work is done, the various roles that emerge to do this work, and the ethical challenges that arise. Through this discussion, I focus on what helps to keep a planning orientation at the forefront of attention as place-governance work is done, on the roles and relationships that develop between experts trained as planners and others, and on the interaction between doing place-governance work with a planning orientation and the wider governance culture in which such activity is situated.

Planning expertise

A century ago, those advocating the planning project tended to think of it as combining the knowledge of the analyst of urban and regional dynamics with the imaginative capacity of the designer in integrating multiple considerations into a design synthesis that expressed a future for a place. One of the heroes of modern planning, Patrick Geddes, provided ideas about the range of knowledge needed and the kind of 'survey' work that was needed to acquire it (Geddes 1915/1968). Architects and engineers provided 'theories' about possible designs (Keeble 1952). Since Geddes' day, the knowledge he considered important has become split up among an array of different social and natural sciences, while the design professionals have been challenged by both scientific analysts of 'systems' and by creative artists in terms of skills in imaginative synthesis. The potential sources of formalised knowledge and of design skill that have a potential to contribute to planning work are therefore much wider and more diffuse than earlier promoters of the planning project imagined.

However these days, it is recognised that it is not just the systematised knowledge of experts that is important in planning work. As the health campaigners in Brooklyn, New York understood (see Chapter 1), experiential knowledge is also important. People living in an area observe, in the flow of daily life, complex relations between effects and causes, and may know a great deal more than experts whose analyses are too coarse grained to pick up locally specific detail. Place-governance work with a planning orientation demands such engagement with locally specific detail. It is for this reason that much more attention is now given to tapping into the knowledge of what Fischer (2000) has called 'citizen experts' in getting to know about place qualities and potentialities. Encouraging public participation and civic engagement in place-governance work has for this reason moved beyond a general ideological commitment, or a desire to improve democratic accountability. Engaging with citizens and other stakeholders helps to improve the richness of the knowledge base for planning work, through drawing on what is often called local knowledge.[2] Larry Beasley, who played a key role in Vancouver's City Planning Department for 30 years, argues for a 'deep and continuous level of engagement with citizens' to generate a planning practice grounded in people's experiential appreciation of their urban environment (Grant 2009:364).

Nevertheless, local knowledge by itself is not enough for planning work. It is often difficult for local communities to grasp the wider dynamics in which they are situated. In the Kobe case in Chapter 4, local activists developing *machizukuri* (community development) practices knew that they needed more specialist advice. They found it initially through informal links with local universities. But their need for expert help was recognised more systemically in the mechanism of an 'expert despatch system', through which government funding was supplied to enable local communities to be put in touch with expert advisers. The *Planning Aid* system in the UK performs a somewhat similar function.[3] The challenge is to combine technical expertise and experiential knowledge in productive, interactive ways.

A century ago, promoters of the planning project such as Patrick Geddes emphasised a holistic understanding of urban and regional dynamics as the basis for developing planning expertise. But since his time, systematic knowledge development has become fragmented among the different professions and academic disciplines. In addition to geography, sociology and biology, place-governance work with a planning orientation demands a shrewd grasp of governance landscapes and their dynamics, the knowledge field of the political scientist or the policy analyst. In the US, planning is often presented as a kind of policy analysis (see Fischer and Forester 1993, Hoch 1994). Such an understanding is not just some kind of objective analysis of political parties and factions. Nor is it a journalistic account of fights and struggles between key individuals. Instead, what those doing place-governance work with a planning orientation need to appreciate is the complex relation between the shifting forces that shape the evolving political, socio-economic and environmental dynamics that are to be found in a locality. They need to know how this affects the projects and strategies of the various groups and factions to be found there and, in turn, how this moulds specific arguments and claims about place qualities and connectivities. It is such understanding that those experienced in the social movements of the 1960s brought to planning work in Vancouver, Portland and Barcelona in the 1970s. Such a sensitivity infuses former Manchester Chief Planning Officer Ted Kitchen's book on planning skills (Kitchen 2007) and accounts by Larry Beasley of his work in Vancouver (Grant 2009) and by Norm Krumholze of his experience as planning director in Cleveland, Ohio (Krumholz and Forester 1990).

This understanding encourages attention not merely to the

surface manifestation of conflicts and relations between actors, although it is very important to be aware of these. It also involves awareness of how shifting political, economic and socio-cultural forces both shape these conflicts and relations, and provide moments of opportunity for new relations and attitudes to develop. Such attention to shifts in political cultures and values helps to suggest opportunities for transforming current practices into new forms and to develop the values of the culture of a polity as a whole. It was this 'grasp' that shaped how the planners in Portland set out to change their governance culture in the 1970s. Such an understanding involves a capacity to see broad relations in fine details and the specific implications of more general forces. This is sometimes referred to as the ability to relate to the 'whole picture' when focusing on a part.[4] The critical challenge for planning work, which always relates to specific situations and contexts, is to maintain the relation, so that the uniqueness of parts is not lost as attention to wider issues is kept in play. Hoch (2007:277) refers to this as maintaining a comprehensive outlook or consciousness.

Place-governance with a planning orientation thus demands an expertise that draws on a wide range of sources of specific knowledge and integrates them as they relate to the specificities of a particular problem or issue (Kitchen 2007). It is much more than analysis, though a key value for those doing analytical work in a planning context is to make the knowledge and reasoning behind conclusions and judgements as transparent as possible. It is also more than balancing competing claims in the way that lawyers and judges are encouraged to do, weighing one claim against another, although it is often helpful to make clear the various claims that are 'in play', if only to prevent valid claims from being excluded from consideration. Such integrative skill provides a basis for arriving at 'synthetic judgements', those creative leaps of consolidation that lead to recognising what really matters and what is at stake in a specific situation. The core of planning expertise is the ability to make such practical judgements with respect to the challenges and dilemmas of place-governance. All capable experts, managers and politicians need this capacity for informed practical judgement. For those doing place-governance work with a planning orientation, this capacity is linked to substantive knowledge about the social, economic, environmental and political dynamics shaping particular places and the opportunities for human flourishing there.

The grasp and capacity for judgement needed for planning work are therefore broad and complex. The planning literature is full of proposals for methods and protocols that offer systematic steps to remove some of the uncertainty and riskiness from doing such work. In the mid-twentieth century, those trained as planners were taught that they should prepare plans by conducting a survey, doing an analysis and then arriving at a plan. In the 1960s, an alternative protocol was suggested that started with the goals set by politicians, followed by analysis and the production and evaluation of options to achieve goals, with the judgement about which option package to choose being left to politicians. These days, there are all kinds of ideas about how to do impact analyses and appraisals, and how to generate and explore ideas about future options. Formal planning systems may create procedural protocols to follow in making regulatory decisions that aim to create greater certainty and reliability in the difficult work of making judgements (see for example the South Tyneside case in Chapter 5). Such systematisations may provide helpful reminders when scoping a situation or designing a process. However, if taken too far they remove the expertise from planning work, and turn the staff of a planning office into conformance-checking administrators rather than creative experts. This leaves such offices bereft of the capacity to do strategic planning work. All too often, it exacerbates the conflicts among neighbours that are so common in the work of development management.

Experienced planners emphasise the importance of seeing a situation as an 'entity', in a holistic way. Arie Rahaminoff, an architect-planner, talks about getting people in an old Arab city on the Israeli coast to see it not merely as a locale for various tourist projects:

> So ... we had to convince the government to see the Old City as a whole. To do that, first of all we had to make it clear that there are no 'tourist-only' services: there is no pavement for tourists which is separate from the pavements for residents; there is no infrastructure just for tourists, and no infrastructure just for residents. We have to see the holistic qualities of the city. (Forester 1999:67)

Geoff Wright, reflecting on his experience in Birmingham City Council when involved in the Brindleyplace project, talks of distilling down multiple considerations into what became the City Council's specific objectives for the project (see Chapter 6). Ted Kitchen, the Manchester Chief Planning Officer referred to above, emphasises the importance of the skill of seeing the strategic dimension even in the fine-grain details of regulatory work. For him, this involves a capacity not only to 'make sense out of a range of perspectives' on the issue in hand and to 'integrate' them. It also involves a 'synoptic' sense, by which he means linking understanding to a sense of direction and purpose (Kitchen 2007:193). Louis Albrechts, a Belgian academic who was asked in the 1990s to make a major contribution to developing a new 'structure plan' for the region of Flanders, expands on the importance of this synoptic sense in helping politicians and citizens imagine new possibilities for the future of their places (see Box 8.1). Such work requires knowledge about place dynamics, but also insight, imagination and the capacity for judgement as to what matters and what is at stake.

Where can such expertise be found and how can it be acquired? As noted above and in the cases in previous chapters, expertise in place-governance exists among many groups: citizens, other experts, academics, politicians, government officials, special agencies and pressure groups. Such people are often focused by an orientation to the values of the planning project. But, as with other specialist experts, it is experience in the craft that counts. Many experienced planners talk about bosses and role models who showed them the craft in action. This 'craft' experience is partly about becoming socialised into a work group, a 'community of practice' (Wenger 1998). Nicholson (1991) describes his 'socialisation' into a British development control team, after an early experience in the very different work practices of a planning academic. Such socialisation has both positive and negative potentials, depending on the culture of the work group. It shapes the way in which, in the course of daily activity, practical judgements are made about what knowledge to search out, how to acquire it, how to interact with others, and how and when to offer what kind of advice, to whom and in what form (Hoch 1994).

In addition to experience and on-the-job training, most of those hired for their planning expertise now have an academic education in the planning field.[6] Planning education programmes come in many forms. Some are undergraduate, some postgraduate. Some build on a design background, in engineering and architecture schools. Others develop from business management or public policy schools. Increasingly, in the late twentieth century, planning programmes dominated by a broad social science perspective. This reflected the importance of knowledge about societies in interaction with environments, of urban and regional dynamics, and of politics, institutions and governance dynamics. Students are also typically

Box 8.1   Reflections of a strategic planner

'My whole life I had a clear focus on structural issues and argued for transformative practices ... For me it is unthinkable that planners would refrain from playing a role in the construction of visions/images and act as mere neutral observers. Planners are necessarily involved with and instrumental in substantiating/formulating and implementing images/visions ... A lot of my time went into convincing citizens, politicians and other planners that they can have meaningful choices and will not have to be a complete prisoner of circumstances, to make them aware that they are interdependent, that they share the same physical space and may therefore face similar problems, and that there are some problems that they cannot solve on their own, that they may lose if they do not cooperate. In my experience visioning helps to think more broadly about the future and its driving forces and to realize that one's own actions may move a place towards a particular kind of future. It allows people to step away from entrenched positions and identify positive futures that people can work towards creating. For me, the real test was never whether we had fully achieved the "conceived" future, but rather whether anyone has changed his or her behavior because he or she saw the future differently. All of these factors, of course, have an impact on the role, the position and the skills of strategic planners. My experience is that you sometimes act as catalyst, as counterweight, as initiator of change. You mobilize and build alliances. You present real political opportunities, learning from action not only what works but also what matters. You substantiate change and refuse to function smoothly as a neutral means to given and presumably well-defined ends. Hence, the need to challenge "mental models" about places and lift the blinkers" that limit creativity so planners' resourcefulness can be used as a building block for designing and formulating structurally new concepts and discourses.'[5]

taught about the history of planning activity and about the field of ideas on the nature, purpose and method of planning (planning theory). It is hoped in this way to cultivate a critical reflexivity, to help planning experts in later life recognise when familiar dilemmas face them in practice. The academics who teach on planning programmes are also these days encouraged to engage in active research around place-governance issues, and are also often involved in doing place-governance with a planning orientation in some capacity or other. In this way, the experience of planning education raises awareness of the scope and content of place-governance work, of examples of how it is undertaken in various places, and provides some initial ideas about what the craft of the expertise involves. It provides practitioner novices with a critical eye with which to observe the practice situations in which they find themselves. Many go back to the academy later, for further formal education or to seek advice from their former tutors. However, formal education can be no substitute for experience in the craft.[7]

The expertise needed for place-governance with a planning orientation thus involves combining often diffuse sources and forms of knowledge into creative practical judgements, sensitive to the specificities of the problems that people face in a particular place-governance situation. No one person is able to 'know' everything needed for this work. In the past, and still today, planning offices and consultancies build work groups that combine within them a range of contributions to create a capacity for planning work (Krumholz and Forester 1990, Pell 1991). But even more important these days is the recognition that the knowledge needed for effective place-governance with a planning orientation is spread among a wide range of people, from local residents and businesses, to special agencies and interest groups, and various departments and levels of government. So those trained as planners are not merely expert advisers to a client. They are positioned in a complex institutional landscape, with a particular political culture and several agencies undertaking governance work. A key activity for those promoting planning-oriented place-governance may involve the creation of institutional sites where interaction between these various parties can take place. In this way, such work has come to involve the design of settings and staging that can release the energy among those involved to think about place-management and development issues.

Institutional sites, roles and positions

Planner experts working for municipal governments are often portrayed by outsiders as sitting in their planning offices, either surveying their territory with a possessive and controlling eye or bent over their plans and procedures, checking conformance with formal norms and standards. Yet the cases described in this book suggest that place-governance with a planning orientation is undertaken in all kinds of locations, not only the office, and that people trained as planners are commonly out and about, in meetings, on the street and among communities of various kinds. Nor are these locations necessarily ones chosen by planning officials and experts.

Civil society groups, as in Kobe, Japan, may ask municipal planning staff to come to *their* meetings. In South Tyneside, development control staff were often on the streets in the locality, noticing developments and talking to residents, shopkeepers and businesses.

Whether in an office, at a meeting or on the street, those contributing trained expertise to place-governance work carry with them not only strands of knowledge that will come together into some kind of expert judgement, but an awareness of key institutional sites where conflicts will be played out, the parameters of decisions shaped and judgements made. Sometimes these are pre-given – the council meeting, a public hearing or inquiry, a session of a special planning board or a legal court. Or the key site may be the board meeting of a special development company, or a regular neighbourhood meeting. In other situations, a special arrangement may have been created, such as a community forum to discuss issues that everyone is concerned about. Or a partnership body of some kind may have been formed to deal with a specific challenge.

Which institutional sites and what social practices evolve in and around them may vary with the kind of place-governance work being done. In Table 8.1, I link the different tasks generated by the activities discussed in the previous chapters to three kinds of governance work. The first (forums) refers to situations where the challenge is to work out what the issues are and what is at stake. The second (arenas) centres on developing specific policies and programmes of action to address the issues identified. The third (courts) deals with problems arising where parties remain in intense conflict over what has been decided.[8]

These different kinds of governance work are often intertwined (Bryson and Crosby 1992). The experience of repeated and expensive recourse to legal courts when policies are challenged may encourage more open discussion before policies and project parameters get fixed, to avoid the time and cost involved. The 2004 reforms to the English planning system sought to encourage such a shift, 'front loading' policy debate in an attempt to reduce the conflicts that arise after decisions have been made.[9] The potential for such conflict arises because issue agendas and perspectives are progressively narrowed as wider discussion gets fleshed out into the specifics of a regulatory decision, a development brief for a project or an agreed strategy.

The significance of these different kinds of institutional site lies not merely in their settings and rules of performance. Getting access to them is variable too. Forums are likely to be more inclusive than

Table 8.1 Institutional sites and planning work

Task/institutional site	Forums (the communication of meaning)	Arenas (policy making and implementation)	Courts (normative regulation of conduct)
Development management			
– Routine regulatory work	Discussions between planning officers and applicants	Planning Office Council Chamber	Semi-judicial inquiries Legal courts
– Neighbourhood guidelines	Discussions between planners, developers and residents	Planning Office Council Chamber Residents' committee	The above, but as a last resort
– Community development	Discussions between planners/ community workers and residents	Residents' groups Special Community Development Agencies	The above occasionally used, often with the 'experts' supporting residents' groups
Major projects	Discussions between politicians and planning staff Discussions led by advocacy groups Discussions promoted by developers	Project teams (in planning offices, in special partnerships) Council Chambers and developer or partnership board rooms	Inquiry processes and courts, if conflicts cannot be resolved by negotiation
Spatial strategy making	Public debate Discussions between politicians, planning staff and other government departments Public discussion with citizens, advocacy groups, key stakeholders etc.	Council Chambers A spatial strategy team or partnership A higher-tier authority	Inquiry processes Courts – for challenges to authority and procedure

arenas, but courts may also be able to reinforce rights of access to an influence on decision making.[10] Institutional sites also vary in the basis of their legitimacy. Forums rest on the legitimacy of democratic participation, popular voice and the quality of reasoning developed within the forum. The legitimacy of arenas may rest on the formal authority of the agency that provides their location – the Council Chamber, a partnership board, or a committee chair.[11]

These different institutional sites also vary in the roles that those trained in planning-oriented place-governance get to play (Hoch 1994, Forester 1999). Depending on who has set them up, such experts may act as chairs of forums, lead speakers, facilitators for the voices of many people or note takers and record keepers. Sometimes they are advocates of a particular position or vigorous critics, relying on their expertise alone. Or they may carry forward what has been discussed in a forum into an arena, where issues may get more focused. In arenas, planning-oriented experts may be the primary decision maker, though more usually they are advisers to those with formal decision roles, such as mayors or committee chairs or board chairs. Or they may act as providers of consultancy advice in an arena. In some instances, they may merely be an information processor and provider. In courts, they are called on as expert witnesses, sometimes acting for their client, who could be a municipality or a developer, or as an independent expert witness. Many planning-oriented experts are continually having to 'switch hats' and play different roles in different contexts. Hoch (1994) gives an example of 'Tom', who saw himself as a professional expert and advocate of urban design quality and the provision of affordable housing, but eventually lost the trust of the municipal board for which he worked, which was dominated by the idea of outcompeting a neighbouring municipality in attracting firms to locate in its area.

The problem for planning-oriented experts is that many people with whom they interact know that they play different roles (see Box 8.2). So, for example, in a forum with residents they may not be trusted to be fair and impartial chairs and facilitators. Many a planner has got flustered when attempting both to put a case and to chair a public meeting. John Forester (2007) has drawn attention to the mistakes planners can make if they try to combine the role of negotiator with a developer with that of mediating a dispute between the same developer and the planning authority.

Yet roles are often combined. Geoff Wright, in discussing his work on the Brindleyplace project in Birmingham, recalls that sometimes

---

Box 8.2   Roles that those trained as planning-oriented experts may play

'Agonistic' critic	Manager of projects and
Advocate	processes
Analyst	Mediator
Applier of regulatory rules	Process designer
Chair	Project promoter
Critical friend	Provider of expert judgement
Envisioner of futures	Provider of information
Facilitator	Provider of systematised
Guardian of the public realm	knowledge
Judgement shaper and maker	Synthesiser of multiple
Leader	viewpoints

---

he acted as a 'hard-ball' negotiator, firmly laying down the City Council's position. At other times, he worked on building relationships between key actors to smooth the co-ordination needed for such a complex project to proceed.[12] Forester (1989) notes that planners often engage in such shuttle diplomacy, which, he argues, demands a particular sensitivity from planners to the positions they occupy and the roles they play. The BBC TV series *The Planners Are Coming* gave a human face to shuttle diplomacy at street level, as planners involved in regulatory work tried to find constructive solutions to bothersome neighbourhood disputes.[13] Erik van Rijn, strategic planner in the municipality of Haarlemmermeer in which Amsterdam's Schiphol airport is located (see Box 2.3), describes another kind of role for planners. He identifies himself with the project of his council and aldermen, which emphasises the need to promote the development of the airport, but also the liveability of local neighbourhoods. He comments:

> In the current decision-making process [about the future development of the airport] in which every actor is involved, we realise that both our goals ... should be pursued. But being aware of the presence of powerful advocates for economic development, I am able to put more emphasis on the quality of life, liveability and measures to diminish noise-nuisance ... Even though the aviation actors have shown an increased concern for the interests of the regions and the environment, when the economic core values are at stake, especially in times of rising oil

prices and economic standstill, we [the regions and residents] are largely left alone with our social ambitions.[14]

The implication is that part of the craft of planning-oriented expertise involves routinely thinking about what role is called into play in which situation and bearing in mind the challenges and ethical demands associated with that role. Donald Schon (1983) has called this the skill of the 'reflective practitioner'. This practice does not just mean periodically standing back and assessing one's performance. It requires continual attention. Perhaps this is where the politicians and planners of Barcelona eventually began to lose their effectiveness. They moved from being advocates and 'agonistic' critics (that is, providing a critical voice for what was ignored and adversely affected by the dominant planning strategies of the time[15]) in the 1960s, to being leaders from the 1970s to the 1990s. But then came demands for a more interactive relation with diverse stakeholders, which demanded a more facilitative and negotiative role, which was not part of the work culture they had built up. In contrast, in Vancouver and Portland the planners may have started off as critics and advocates, but their power base initially was far too fragile to play a strong leadership role. So they played all kinds of roles, as they slowly built up a new, participative governance culture for managing development change in their cities.

Of course, people who become planning-oriented experts vary in their commitments and abilities. Some prefer interactive work, building relationships and accumulating knowledge from diverse sources. Others make a more backstage contribution. Hoch (1994) introduces a planner, 'Nancy', who talks about her preference for doing well-grounded but yet persuasive research and analysis. An agency with a planning remit may contain within it individual planners with different but complementary skills. In Vancouver, it was the way individual contributions were welded into the team culture of the City Council planners that was important, enduring over decades (Sandercock 2005). Norm Krumholz and John Forester, in their account of Krumholz's experience as planning director in Cleveland, Ohio, underline this point:

A successful planning practice depends on the committed and cooperative efforts of many people, not just the planning director, however central he or she may be. (Krumholz and Forester 1990:xviii)

Krumholz later describes how he appreciated his own limitations in community development work and was appreciative of the sensitivities and skills of his colleague, Janice Cogger, in this field.

The significance of group culture is particularly important in relation to the roles that planning-oriented experts play with respect to guardianship of the public realm. The importance of this role in promoting liveable and sustainable places for the diverse many is underlined in the cases in the previous chapters. Such a role is sustained by personal commitment that brings people to the field in the first place, by education and often by membership of a planning professional body that demands such a focus. This commitment is not easy to sustain when all the pressures are for different priorities. A development company may hire planners or a planning consultancy to 'get' a planning permit for them. A mayor or leading politician may seek to engage primarily in the politics of patronage or, even more narrowly, use planning powers merely to line their own nests or those of friends. A city council may take a narrow focus, perhaps on 'growth at all costs', neglecting the complex interrelation with issues of environmental sustainability, social justice or the welfare of future generations. Then the advice of planning-oriented staff and consultancies may be ignored, or staff may be subverted to work for these narrow or corrupted agendas, or, if they can, they leave.

It is for this reason that planning-oriented experts need to have a politically shrewd grasp of the institutional landscape in which they are positioned. They may be in the planning department of a municipality or some other form of local planning authority. They may work for a consultancy, with client bases with different profiles. They may work for a property development company, or for the development arm of a company that has a major infrastructure interest or need for land for its activities. They may work for specialist advisory agencies, or for pressure groups and lobby groups. They may work in research agencies or universities. Each position carries with it some authority, some responsibilities to others and some form of accountability. Sometimes, planning-oriented experts find it hard to explain the conflicts that have to be faced in their work when different claims clash.

The planning official in the Ditchling story (see Chapter 1) had difficulty in this situation. When called on to explain why the replacement of the valued local pub in the village by flats and houses could not be resisted, the planner in Luke Holland's television programme looks uncomfortable and embarrassed as he explains that there are no formal grounds to refuse a development permit and, if refused, the council would be liable for the costs of an appeal if the applicant challenged the decision. 'Tom', in the case cited earlier in this chapter, is taken aback when his political masters fire him for disagreeing with them. Erik van Rijn, in Haarlemmermeer, felt more comfortable in aligning himself with local residents and their political representatives, in their struggles to maintain attention to the liveability of the area around Schiphol airport. Ted Kitchen (2007), in his reflections on planners' skills, underlines the importance of providing clear explanations for the claims and arguments that planning-oriented experts put forward. This provides transparency in argument even when clashes arise. Some years earlier, he commented that the hardest relationship in his experience was that between planning staff and the politicians who employ them (Kitchen 1991). Another Chief Planning Officer, from a London borough, has described how such transparency in argument in the end built trust between council politicians strongly associated with a right-wing political mission, and a planning staff strongly committed to the values of the planning project (Crawley 1991).[16]

So how is it possible to maintain attention to what planning-oriented expertise shows to be important in a situation, and to struggle to keep public realm issues in play, when the surrounding politics seeks to ignore such issues? And where anyway do such experts get the legitimacy for voicing such issues when their advice is being sidelined? How can they be both experts serving a client and advocates for the planning project? What does it take to do potentially transformative work as an insider expert and how can such activity be justified?

Practical ethics in planning work

All social encounters involve an ethics. When we interact with others, we have to think about how to behave and what expectations others may have of us. Ethics in the public service, whether specifically as an employee or contractor to a public agency or as a commitment arising from expertise and professional identification, adds more layers to these ethical demands. Different roles and different positions generate different expectations and demand attention to what is appropriate behaviour. In addition to this ethics of conduct, those who are committed to the focus and values of the planning project, as proposed in this book, also have to attend to an ethics of purposes. This demands that they maintain a focus on enhancing inclusive liveability and sustainability as places develop, keep in view future possibilities as well as present challenges, and promote knowledgeable interventions, respectful of diverse modes of life, in ways that make the arguments for actions as transparent as possible. These values in turn give added emphasis to how planning work is performed, the ethics of conduct (Forester 1999). A commitment to inclusive consideration goes with a conduct of respect and fair treatment for all those with whom planners interact. A commitment to creating a political culture in which the complex issues of 'sharing space while living differently' can be openly debated and decided requires that planners provide reasons and arguments for the advice they give and that they explain their position in a governance system. And they have to be able to do this not only behind closed doors but in the open – when talking to aggrieved residents, at meetings, to stakeholders of all kinds and in reports and studies. As Kitchen states, what matters in such public life is not just what planners do, but what they are *seen* to do (Kitchen 1991:142).

These two dimensions of ethics – the ethics of conduct and the ethics of attention to specific values – arise in all areas of place-governance work with a planning orientation. Planning officials in Vancouver from the 1970s to the 2000s built a practice culture that supported their commitment to maintaining attention to public realm quality and to improving the situation of the least well off, in the complex, on-going and often conflictual work of developing neighbourhood development guidelines. In the difficult environment of the neighbourhood squatter upgrading project in Besters Camp, Durban, community development staff quietly worked away to try to make sure that resources really went, in transparent and trustable ways, to those who needed replacement housing. Erik van Rijn talks about the importance of balancing different considerations, but also about taking a stand if the powerful airport stakeholders tip priorities too much against considerations of liveability. Ted Kitchen had to deal with an incident where a telephone call from an aggrieved applicant highlighted procedural neglect in the planning office. In an instant, he had to weigh up whether to cover up or apologise. He took the latter path, worked out a way of proceeding to correct the neglect, and then went to sort out the whys and wherefores of what happened and what must now be done (see Healey 1992; Ted Kitchen was deputy Chief Planning Officer at the time of this 'day' in his 'life' as a senior planner).

Such ethical dilemmas are routinely present in development-management work, in many forms. In major development projects, they are often presented more as a clash between ideological stances, a struggle between titans, the interests of big capital versus community and the interests of future generations. The foghorns of academic critique and media publicity often construct moral issues at stake in this way (Diaz and Fainstein 2008). But the cases in Chapter 6 show that determining what is at stake for the collective interest and the public realm is a continuous challenge, as conditions change and agencies and stakeholders come and go in their involvement with a project. And the role of guardian of the values associated with the planning project may be found in some unexpected places, such as the sense of social responsibility of some private developers.

In spatial strategy making, ethical issues arise not just in relation to the content of a strategy (does the strategy pay sufficient attention to the plurality of social groups in an area, to the spread of impacts of a strategy within and beyond an area, to how well it will stand the test of time and retain support through time?), but to the ways in which a strategy is arrived at. Strategy makers in Portland thought carefully about how to develop the ground for a recognition of the value of a spatial strategy for the city (see Chapter 7). This underlines the point often made in debates in planning theory that issues of process are intertwined with the substantive content of the issues to be addressed and the institutional context in which they are dealt with (Forester 1999, Campbell 2006, Healey 2007).

These experiences underline that engaging in place-governance work with a planning orientation work, especially for those with a commitment to the planning project, involves navigating through an institutional landscape strewn with ethical minefields (Campbell and Marshall 2000, Campbell 2006). In situations where serving the public and a sense of social responsibility are given little attention by political elites, it is all too easy, even for those with a planning-oriented education, to let the prevailing culture take over. There are many examples from rapidly urbanising countries where local administrations have few powers and limited resources. Often, the regulatory tools of a planning system, intended to produce a minimum quality in built environments, get used and abused in the struggle between those with power over land and property resources seeking to maximise land-value returns as urbanisation proceeds (UN-Habitat 2009).

Elsewhere, planning-oriented experts may be pulled in different

---

Box 8.3   The 'clients' or 'customers' of a UK municipal planning service

1. Applicants for planning permission
2. Local residents affected by applications in an area
3. The wider general public in an area
4. The business community
5. Interest or pressure groups in the community
6. Other agencies whose actions impinge on the development process
7. Other departments of the local authority
8. The elected members of the council
9. The formal control mechanisms of local government
10. Purchasers of planning services

Source: Kitchen 2007:105, Box 5.1.

---

directions by their various roles and positions. Some have focused on the tensions between the different client constituencies to which such experts have a responsibility. The American sociologist Herbert Gans argued in a famous essay that planners should always put first their commitment to the public at large, and particularly the disadvantaged, before their responsibility to their employers (Gans 1969).[17] This is what 'Tom', referred to above, did. Ted Kitchen in Manchester found this dualistic formulation too limited a way of expressing the clients or customers to whom he felt he should pay attention, and came up with the list in Box 8.3. In his accounts of his practice, he is acutely aware of the ethical challenges he faced in carrying awareness of all these clients with him in the flow of his work (Kitchen 1997, 2007).

Another way of thinking about the tensions experienced by planning-oriented experts is to consider sources of legitimacy for their work. As Box 8.4 shows, these too are various, reflecting the political and technical dimensions of contributing expertise to planning-focused place-governance. Legitimacy could be derived from the goals of an employer. Many planners search out employers who have a commitment at least to public service. But, as Gans highlighted, they often do not. In such a situation, 'Tom', in Hoch's study, steadily worked away to make sure that attention was given to affordable housing issues, even though local politicians persistently ignored them. Norm Krumholz, in Cleveland, took a more radical position, creating in his planning department a vigorous advocacy for attention

> **Box 8.4   Sources of legitimacy for planning work**
>
> Employer
> The public, especially the systematically disadvantaged
> The public at large
> A specific moral principle or principles
> Professional commitment
> Systematised knowledge and 'evidence'
> Higher tiers of government authority
> Legal authority
> Specific technical expertise

to social justice and the needs of the disadvantaged. Both Tom and Norm base the legitimacy of their stance on a mixture of professional commitment and personal commitment to a specific moral principle, concern for social justice. Other planning-oriented experts may have as strong a commitment to environmental sustainability, or historic conservation, or the quality of urban design. Sometimes, planning-oriented experts can face tests that threaten their whole future. In Newcastle in the late 1980s, urban design consultants were forced to accept the then Tyne and Wear Urban Development Corporation's view that a riverside site should be used for a large hotel, blocking the development prospects for the area behind (Davoudi and Healey 1990). In the early days of post-war reconstruction in the Russian sector of Berlin, planner-designers were told to abandon 'modernist' designs in favour of the 'socialist realism' style advocated by the Russian leader, Stalin (Strobel 2003).

Yet what is at issue is rarely so clear-cut. What exactly fills out conceptions of the 'public' being served, the 'public interest' and the 'public realm' is open to many interpretations and contestations. Planning work is continually at the centre of such constructions and conflicts, reflecting the complex balancing of multiple claims that is at the centre of efforts to shape place development for collective benefits over time (Campbell 2006). Nevertheless, if it is done skilfully and with a strong moral commitment, much can be achieved. As Norm Krumholz and John Forester note:

> Caught between ... [idealism ...], their professional mission, and the constraints and corruption of city politics, the Cleveland planners amassed a record, in fits and starts, wins and losses,

that suggests the real limits, but also the real possibilities, of public-serving city planning practice. (Krumholz and Forester 1990:xxiii)

Another resource is to fall back on 'science' and 'evidence'. This strategy seeks legitimacy through systematised knowledge and inquiry, so-called objective knowledge. However, such knowledge too is open to challenge. Scientific communities are themselves always debating their own arguments and evidence, and each community has its particular biases. In the search of some secure basis for judgements about place-management and development issues, planning-oriented experts may also turn to government protocols and policy statements as their authority, or to legal decisions and interpretations. However, overuse of such sources of legitimacy can have a corrupting effect, turning experts into conformance-checking administrators rather than giving creative attention to balancing complex claims and integrating a range of issues into a form that makes a positive contribution to a specific situation.

For, in the end, skilled planning-oriented experts gain respect through the quality of their practical judgements, through the exercise of their craft. They do complex 'in between' work, whether in relation to the details of managing local environments, or making major projects move from conception to completion, or producing strategic ideas to frame how different parties may contribute to the future shaping of the locality in which they have some kind of stake. In such work, such experts are continually exposed to critique of one kind or another. Those involved in such work need to find ways to listen and learn from such critique. Planning-oriented experts who get to be admired by their colleagues are not known for the quality of their specific solutions to problems. Mostly these are the outcome of complex interactions between many contributors. Nor are they renowned for their particular discoveries. They are known instead for their interactive capabilities, their expansive approach to acquiring knowledge, their commitment to the values of the planning project and the quality of their judgement. They display confidence without being arrogant; they are humble about the limitations of what they know, but prepared to bring to attention the knowledge they have; able to listen and learn from all kinds of sources, but also able to sift through material to identify what and who is 'at stake'; prepared to stand up for values they care about, but seeking to avoid polarising positions and debates; prepared to make judgements, but acknowledging that there is always a risk of being wrong; acting with honesty and integrity, but accepting criticism, even if unfair.

Planning work and governance cultures

In this chapter, I have argued that the work needed to progress the planning project, as understood in this book, in addition to a sensibility to multiple forms of knowledge, involves the exercise of technical skill, shrewd institutional grasp and ethical conduct. It also requires an attitude that understands the value of creating public realm resources that allow people to get on with realising their lives and livelihoods, while spreading the chances for those with least and paying attention to the quality and sustainability of facilities and spaces held 'in common', available to all. The work is complex and often presents difficult challenges, and the contribution of individuals may not easily be recognised. Nevertheless, practitioners often talk of the satisfaction they get from walking and talking around the areas where they have worked, and being able to say: 'yes, we got that one right', 'it's a good thing we stopped that proposal, what has happened now is much better' and 'the developers all seem to be clustering here, as we had hoped; the strategy seems really to be working'.

It has always been understood that planning work contributes to place qualities through managing and enhancing the physical fabric and public realm of material qualities, connectivities and opportunities. This fabric not only provides material goods. It also gives aesthetic pleasures, offers stimulation to the formation of meanings about places and provides a setting for the development of a social ambience. But I have also argued that how place-governance work is done contributes to the qualities of the governance culture of urban areas. If the tools of urban design and city remodelling are used to serve the purposes of imposing a colonial order on a conquered population or the grand designs of an ambitious dictator, as in Berlin in the mid-twentieth century, then such practices may serve to reinforce an oppressive governance culture. This is not the ambition of the planning project as outlined in this book. The project as understood here is to promote the liveability and sustainability of the daily life environments of the diverse people who co-exist in a place. However experienced, skilled, knowledgeable and shrewd they may be, planning-oriented experts cannot do such work on their own. They need not only to blend their contributions with the efforts of citizens, politicians and other stakeholders in a place. They also need to recognise the importance of cultivating a place sensitivity and a planning orientation within the relevant political community. Sometimes, no openings seem available through which to develop such an orientation. Then those experts committed to the planning project may have to move elsewhere or bide their time, leaving seeds around to grow if and when the governance situation improves. However, in many cases shrewd promotion of the planning project can help to expand understanding of the value of a focus on the place qualities emphasised through the planning project. In this way, place-governance with a planning orientation can contribute to the public realm through enriching the issues that attract public attention, encouraging active participation in debates about the conditions and futures of places, and showing by example what it means to serve the public (see Forester 1999:Afterword, du Gay 2000, Sager 2009). By making such a contribution, those trained with a planning orientation help to shape the evolving political culture in which they find themselves.

However, no political community should leave it to one group of experts or other special role to monitor itself. People who do place-governance work with a planning orientation are just like everyone else: they have flaws, make mistakes, get the balance between personal and professional roles wrong, lose perspective by being over-passionate about a specific issue, find being accepted by the strongest more attractive than struggling to open opportunities for alternative futures. And planning-oriented experts may often be too idealistic not just for their own good, but for the good of the political communities they aim to serve. Political communities with an open and richly discursive governance culture help to keep experts in sympathy with the planning project, as well as making their contribution easier and more rewarding to engage in. Those who act as planning-oriented experts should not therefore complain about being surrounded by critical voices. These serve to remind them of the issues at stake and the multiple claims to which they have to pay attention. Further, those committed to place governance with a planning orientation can themselves contribute to cultivating a critical climate of multiple claims and arguments. They are well advised to resist attempts to smooth conflicts away or crowd them out by an overly dominant attitude or leadership. Accepting the position of being 'inbetween', but dedicated to 'public service' with respect to place development (du Gay 2000), is what makes for quality planning-oriented expert work. Through their skill and commitment, those doing such work can, over time, contribute to enlarging the governance capacity of an area and its ability to shape and challenge the wider structuring forces that affect future outcomes.

Suggested further reading

The material given below has already been introduced in the text. While the work of Schon and Sandercock is quite widely known, the rest tends to be known only to those within the planning field. Almost all of the experiences referred to are from the US or the UK. The material is listed in chronological order.

Schon, D. (1983) *The Reflective Practitioner*, Basic Books, New York.

Krumholz, N. and Forester, J. (1990) *Making Equity Planning Work*, Temple University Press, Philadelphia.

Hoch, C. (1994) *What Planners Do*, Planners Press, Chicago.

Forester, J. (1999) *The Deliberative Practitioner: Encouraging Participatory Planning Processes*, MIT Press, London.

Campbell, H. and Marshall, R. (2000) Moral obligation, planning and the public interest: A commentary on current British practice, *Environment and Planning B: Planning and Design*, 27, 297–312.

Sandercock, L. (2003) *Mongrel Cities: Cosmopolis 11*, Continuum, London.

Kitchen, T. (2007) *Skills for Planning Practice*, Palgrave, Basingstoke.

Chapter 9

Making Better Places

Towards more liveable and sustainable places

The previous chapters have taken readers on a journey through different types of deliberate place-management and development work, which I have identified as the core action arena of the 'planning project'. This project, as I have presented it, approaches such work with the ambition of improving liveability and sustainability, and in creating places that have enriched the public realm of urban life. Through the chapters, I have tried to show how such activities are accomplished. The cases, selected because they were later judged as valuable places that made significant contributions to people's quality of life, highlight the challenges that those involved in such work faced, and the skills and moral commitments they brought to the work. They also show that place-governance with a planning orientation involves a complex mixture of political activity, of technical expertise and moral sensibility. It is political in the sense that such work arises from the challenges of living with diverse neighbours in urban environments and deals with collective concerns about place qualities and relationships arising within a political community. It is political in another sense, in that political communities have to decide how to go about such management. It is also political in that there are often intense struggles between different groups over whose concerns should take precedence, frequently underpinned by deeper tensions generated by wider economic, political, socio-cultural and environmental forces. Planning work also demands the mobilisation of technical expertise, such as knowledge about urban dynamics, about formal law and procedure, about real-estate markets and about easy-to-use accounting systems. This technical work intertwines with the political work and cannot neatly be compartmentalised into a separate sphere of 'planning work'. Those doing place-governance work with a planning orientation find that they have to walk the boards of public life, explaining what they are doing and why in response to all kinds of challenges and objections.

And this politico-technical work is infused by moral questions about what actually does and should contribute to advancing the collective interest of a political community, and which political community is in play in a situation.

The cases show that place-governance work is not a simple task of identifying what needs to be done and then implementing it. Its immediate products are strategies, frameworks, management practices, development projects, policy principles and regulatory norms that inter-relate with one another and with urban development dynamics in complex ways. Arriving at such products is not merely a matter of translating design ideas into physical form, or of scientific analysis into policy criteria and action programmes. Instead, it arises from complex back-and-forth processes of discussion, experimentation and challenge. Through these processes, actors and wider political communities learn about what is at stake and what can be done. In Vancouver, citizens and other stakeholders got to recognise that what happened in one neighbourhood affected neighbourhoods across the city. Through civil society activism in Kobe and elsewhere, local and national government administrations in Japan gradually realised that they needed to listen to and respond to citizens' concerns about their local environments. By focusing attention on place qualities and what citizens were concerned about, those involved got to consider place qualities as more than mere material assets. They came to understand the political and moral implications of what was at stake. Those faced with making critical judgements, about future directions, about the allocation of resources between competing projects and about whether to accept or challenge a norm or requirement imposed by a higher authority, not only had to balance competing claims from particular groups. They also kept in mind the way different spheres of society and different fields of concern inter-relate as places evolve. Place-governance undertaken with a planning orientation required not only linking the spheres of political life, socio-cultural life and economic life (see Chapter 2) as these influence how people make use of and value places. It also involved considering how social, environmental and economic relations intertwine to produce or undermine present and future possibilities for liveable and sustainable places. It demanded an integrative, holistic imagination, centred on people's experience of living 'in places'.

This work sometimes seems so difficult that those undertaking it, for example as officials working within the institutions of formal planning systems, turn to other authorities to justify their actions. These external authorities may be higher tiers of government, or external consultants, or the authority of scientific analysis. Another way to simplify the challenge is to identify a single criterion that can be used to trump all others, such as the promotion of equity, the reduction of carbon emissions, increasing the numbers of dwellings produced or attracting new businesses to an area. Or officials may simply undertake the tasks formally required of them as routines, without considering whether the way they perform these tasks and the outcomes that result advance what the wider political community is concerned about or the values of the planning project. In situations where there are few checks and balances on politicians, experts and officials, the result may be prolonged neglect of attention to the quality of places and to the promotion of liveable and sustainable neighbourhoods, communities and urban complexes. In such situations, formal planning institutions may fall into disrepute.

It is to challenge such neglect that the orientation of the planning project, as I have identified it, needs to be affirmed loud and clear. In this book, I underline the focus of this socio-political project as centred on improving the conditions of life for people, in all our diversity and in our commitments to future as well as present generations, especially in urbanising contexts (see Chapter 1). It is not only about creating better opportunities and chances for individual people, or particular social groups, or people in a particular place, or even just the human species as a whole. It is about how we relate to all others who inhabit the world with us and to the broader natural forces that shape our planetary existence. Such a project demands that we try, in thinking about and acting with respect to place management and development, to see the larger issues in small actions and the little implications of greater endeavours. I have often referred to this in previous chapters as the ability to relate parts to wholes and wholes to parts. However, to address the complexities of twenty-first century urban life, it is important to move away from conceiving such relations as a kind of nested hierarchy of systems, each one tiered above the other until you get to the planet, and then, maybe, the solar system and the universe. Instead, systems are better imagined as overlapping, loosely bounded and 'loosely coupled' sets of relations. Especially in our lives today, it is important to recognise that people and other species often live in several places during a year and a lifetime, and that in any one life we may have several identities at once (see Chapter 2). As people, we also attach importance to all kinds of places, near and far, as well as the ones in which we currently live and/or work. So those who engage in place-governance with a planning orientation need to think of a plurality of wholes in which people in particular places may participate, while the 'wholes' we value may link together people with a plurality of identities. This demands a pluralistic sensibility and the encouragement of pluralistic forms of political community (see Chapter 3).

Learning from situated experiences

The cases in this book were chosen because they achieved considerable improvements in the qualities of specific places and, in several, to the wider public realm of their cities and societies. Those who worked to bring about such outcomes were committed to most or all of the philosophy expressed in the planning project as I have identified it. They struggled to achieve place quality, for the many and not just the few, for present generations and future ones. Across the world, there are many who also struggle for these values. But the case stories also show how very different are the contexts in which such struggles are positioned. Each place is situated in one or more larger places. Each neighbourhood and each city has its own story of such conjunctions and its own future possibilities. Layered over these particularities are differences in national systems of law and politics, and in cultural attitudes to how to conduct political, social and economic life and how to relate to wider environmental forces. These differences shape how people express their concerns about place qualities, the way they engage in political action and address issues of collective concern, and the kind of knowledge that is privileged. Such differences infuse the political, technical and moral work that is mobilised in place-management and development activity.

This means that great caution is needed when learning from experiences in other places. All too often, an apparently 'successful' exemplar is used as a template in another situation. James Rouse's work in Boston and Baltimore, and the 'Barcelona' model (see Chapter 6), have come to be used in this way, as has the Porto Alegre experiment in participatory budgeting (see Chapter 3). Vancouver has become an icon of high-quality inclusive place development (see Chapter 4). Nevertheless, the cases show that the success of such exemplars is rooted in local conditions that are not easily replicated. From Vancouver, we can learn that a participatory neighbourhood management practice can evolve, but an important precondition was the extent of autonomy enjoyed by the City Council. The release of energy and broad-based support for the City Council in the post-dictator period was a key factor in shaping the Barcelona story. In Porto Alegre, political organising through a workers' party in a post-dictator situation lay behind the achievement of a participatory budgeting approach.

However, to assert that history, or what regional economic geographers have come to call 'path dependency', shapes futures is not to deny the capacity to change direction (Briggs 2008). Persistent local action without favourable preconditions can in the end make a difference, as the sustained citizens' initiative in Kobe shows. Such actions can be of many kinds, from design and development ideas, such as the idea of a leisure and conservation-focused retail mall in Boston, to the use of new techniques, such as the neighbourhood participation processes in Vancouver. It could involve developing new instruments, such as simple accounting systems, as in the Besters Camp/INK project in Durban (see Chapter 5) or the land readjustment process in Japan (see Chapter 4). Yet each such innovation is locked into complex socio-cultural and political practices that created moments of opportunity within which new practices could take shape.

This situatedness of the specifics of place-governance practices does not mean that we cannot learn from the experience of other places. Instead, it means that those seeking to learn what it means to develop the planning project in specific situations need to give careful attention to the contexts in which particular practices have evolved. They need to be prepared to go beyond 'best-practice' guides and look at the political, technical and cultural forces and understandings that were in play. They also need to pay attention to the often long timescales involved in creating place qualities that future generations come to appreciate. Approached in this way, as much can be learned from failures as from successes, and there are plenty of examples of such failures. But there are also many successes, small and large, achieved by ongoing, committed and skilled actors. Their achievements are often unsung and unnoticed. Yet, as we go about our daily lives, even those who are knowledgeable about planning matters and know what to look for may fail to register that, behind the scenes, backstage, attention is being given to the qualities of the places we live in, work in and visit. To return to the questions raised at the end of Chapter 3, what does it take to achieve the planning project, in all kinds of different contexts and situations? How far can the project have transformative effects, on material conditions, on how we think about the places we care about, and on the cultures of our political communities?

Realising the planning project

In this book, I have illustrated the wide range of activities involved in deliberate place management and development. These are performed in many different ways and make use of a range of different kinds of instrument. Similarly, planning-oriented place-governance cannot be reduced to the use of a particular instrument, such as a formal development plan. Nor does its contribution lie in a specific task, such as strategy making for shaping the future of an urban complex. Nor does such an approach necessarily imply the adoption of a particular mode of governance. Planning-oriented work often involves a combination of modes (see Box 3.2). Barcelona combined an ideological focus with proactive flair. In Vancouver, vigorous participation at neighbourhood level was combined with a transparent bureaucratic practice of land-use regulation, with the overall approach infused by a commitment to inclusive opportunities for the plurality of citizens in the city. In South Tyneside, regulatory work was undertaken with a human face, while a similar sensibility was fostered in the Besters Camp project, combined with a commitment to transparent resource allocation. How these combinations take place depends in part on the development task, on whether the emphasis is on the fine-grain management of changes in the urban environment, on creating new or reconfigured development nodes or on providing city-wide development frameworks.

What makes such work an expression of the planning project lies in the orientation that focuses how activities are performed and connected. This orientation emphasises attention to future impacts and possibilities, to conditions that foster liveability for the many in the context of seeking out more sustainable relations between people and the wider world within which we exist. It emphasises interdependencies and interconnections along multiple dimensions. It calls for the cultivation of an informed intelligence as a basis for collective place-governance actions and for governance practices that strive for openness and transparency (see Chapter 1). But, as I argue in Chapter 8, place-governance with a planning orientation focuses on achieving these qualities and values through drawing together, or synthesising, concepts of how the qualities of particular places could develop. It involves finding ways to connect what could happen in these places to larger dynamics and to the fine grain of daily life in places. It demands a continual effort in balancing multiple claims, the concerns of multiple groups and many different places, as these affect particular options and decisions faced in a particular place at a particular time. Deliberate place-development and management work thus involves mobilising a particular type of imagination, one that 'sees' places and spatial interconnections and recognises the complex dynamics through which we experience place qualities as we and they evolve.

Such planning work cannot easily be guided by generalised and abstract intellectual or ideological principles. Declaring the ambition of achieving social justice, or greater equity, or environmental sustainability, or poverty reduction, or liveability and sustainability, may help to create a climate of thinking in which the planning project can make a contribution. But the challenge for the planning project is to work out what such a principle might mean with respect to the experience of a particular neighbourhood, or an area of empty buildings abandoned when an industrial or commercial nexus collapsed, or the development budget of a specific city or urban area. It it also likely to mean accommodating a newly highlighted principle with all kinds of other claims, some just as legitimate, some less legitimate but backed by powerful forces, reworking the balancing and integrating what had been going on before. In north-west Europe, for example, newly articulated concerns about climate change involve working out how the implications of rising sea levels and more frequent episodes of violent storms affect not only the management of sea defences and river system management, but also the location of development and the content of building codes. This awesome challenge now has to co-exist with the need to respond to the aftershocks and disruptions caused by the latest major collapse in the systems of capitalist financial accumulation and investment.

Place-governance work with a planning orientation thus rarely involves a smooth translation from 'policy' to 'action' (Barrett and Fudge 1981) or from declarations of general policy principles by politicians in parliaments to programme delivery. Instead, it involves sustained struggle in the various arenas where place-management activity is performed, or major development projects nurtured from initiation to completion, or strategies converted into specific action programmes. In these institutional sites, the values of the planning project, and of politicians, professionals and social movements committed to improving place qualities, can all too easily be subverted without the commitment of key insiders and the continuous monitoring and challenge of the wider polity. Realising liveable and sustainable places cannot therefore just be left to committed politicians and to training a cadre of experts imbued with the values of the planning project. Without continual pressure for openness and transparency from the wider political community, well-meaning policy initiatives are readily captured by special interests. Place-governance work, focused by the planning project as I have described it, benefits especially from fostering general public attention to place qualities and spatial connectivities, and the role of the public realm as a physical and political resource. Such a project needs the engagement of an active political community. Transforming place-management and development practices to achieve more liveable and sustainable places where a plurality of people can co-exist and flourish implies developing such a community around the qualities of places, as well as achieving material improvements. But what if there is no such active political community or socio-political momentum to foster attention to place qualities? Does the opportunity for achieving the planning project depend entirely on contextual conditions, or the configuration of structuring forces, as many argue (see Chapter 2)?

Context matters

Through the cases, I have tried to show how political, socio-cultural, economic and environmental forces have helped to create the particular conditions that shaped what happened. The Vancouver neighbourhood management practice benefited from substantial municipal autonomy over its resources and regulations. In Barcelona, the city council that emerged after the fall of the Franco dictatorship carried the hopes and trust of a citizenry urgently seeking to emerge into a new democratic future. In Birmingham, the Brindleyplace project had room to manoeuvre as a real-estate project creating public realm benefits because of its specific timing in relation to multinational boom/bust cycles in property values and investment patterns. Amsterdam has had a long history as a social democratic city. The turbulent political environment in Durban and South Africa limited the impact of the Besters Camp initiative, while in South Tyneside what could be achieved was limited by the context of a heavy, centralised state.

Context in part shapes how place-governance has evolved and the emphasis given to the values of the planning project. Ward (2002) argues that the fortunes of urban planning in the twentieth century had a much more favourable context in continental north-west Europe than in the US or Britain. Other academic commentators argue that place-management and development practices in the later twentieth century in the West were captured by a narrow, neo-liberal emphasis on promoting the economic competitiveness of places in the context of the globalising strategies of multinational capitalist companies. Such practices were turned from a broader welfare focus to serve the purposes of 'entrepreneurial' states (see Chapter 3). This suggests that place-governance with a planning orientation will always be shaped by dominant forces that structure social, political and economic relationships. Social theories of structural dynamics often suggest that activities such as deliberate place-development and management work are inherently 'creatures' of dominant structuring forces (see Chapter 2).

However, the case narratives in previous chapters demonstrate much more varied situations. They show on-going struggles to maintain broader agendas and to change the focus of collective action. This struggle is very clearly identified in the municipality of Harlemmermeer, faced with an international airport on its doorstep, a key hub in global economic relations. In Vancouver and Portland, the struggle in the 1960s was to challenge a nexus of political and business elites interested in large infrastructure projects and, in Vancouver, to re-orient the efforts of affluent established residents to hold on to their privileged living environments as the city grew and changed around them. In Besters Camp, the challenge was to create an opportunity for the very poorest to have a say in finding ways to improve their housing situation in a context dominated not simply by a history of racial oppression but by a kind of tribal warlordism that had evolved to challenge that oppression. So, while broad generalisations about contexts and critical social theories provide valuable ideas about how to understand structuring dynamics and what to look for in specific situations, they are no substitute for a careful analysis of the politico-institutional dynamics of particular contexts. Few 'contexts' are rigidly fixed. Through such an analysis, those seeking to challenge established governance practices in order to promote improved place qualities are better able to identify cracks in established ways of doing things, which create moments of opportunity, some smaller, some larger, for moving forward with the agenda promoted by the planning project and for resisting its capture by narrowly focused agendas and the forces promoting these. Big cracks through which a new politics can break through, as in Barcelona, are only occasionally available. Nevertheless, this does not mean that efforts at slowly opening up smaller institutional cracks should be neglected. Transformative activity demands continual commitment to achieving alternative futures, both in large and small ways.

For much of the twentieth century, the struggle in western countries was to generate and sustain a focus on quality of life for people in places, against the forces associated with rampant capitalist exploitation and self-serving administrative regimes created by expanding states. Through this struggle, political communities emerged that have become ever more vocal in asserting their concerns. Such communities have helped to create the climate in which attention to place quality, to the politics of place, has become more important. There is widespread support for the idea that wealth and opportunity should be spread in ways that are not too unjust, and that development should happen in ways that do not damage present and future environmental conditions too much. The financial crisis of the late 2000s has made it very clear that unfettered capitalist entrepreneurialism can lead to collective disaster, enlarging the understanding that economic markets are themselves structured by collective action. As even pro-market advocates argued in the mid-twentieth century, market processes need some institutional ground rules, such as exclusive property rights and a legal system for dispute resolution (Hayek 1944). Property developers look to planning strategies and development regulations to help reduce the uncertainty and instability of markets prone to boom and bust. Where physical urban development depends on private investment, carefully constructed spatial strategies and development management practices can shape property market opportunities through ground rules demanding contributions to achieving liveability and sustainability in places over the long term. Just as financial policy is now turning to ways of creating the conditions in which the resources needed for manufacture, trade and consumption activity can flow once again, so the planning project offers a way of thinking about how to structure land and property markets in ways that can achieve wider community objectives. This way of thinking then itself becomes a public realm asset. As the Vancouver case shows, this does not mean that the public sector does all the development work. It means creating a climate in which development industry actors structure their projects and expectations within a context of these wider objectives. Place-governance work with a planning orientation, and the tools and practices of planning systems, can thus have an important role in regulating and shaping land and property-development markets.

The opportunity for pursuing the planning project is therefore not just dependent on context. It actively contributes to shaping that context. Its practices, developed over time as in places like Vancouver, Portland and Amsterdam, succeed through their structuring effects. Structuring dynamics get changed as people act to will into being different futures than might otherwise happen. This recognition is not merely the wishful thinking of idealists, who live in an illusory world far from the messy machinations of political and institutional life.[1] The planning project, as I have identified it, enters into these messy machinations as an active force. This can take the form of the urban social movements of the 1970s, but also of the determined efforts of officials in South Tyneside and community development workers in Besters Camp to focus on quality of life and place, in work contexts where all kinds of other pressures were in play. Backstage in Birmingham, middle-level managers in a city council and a development company struggled successfully to maintain development momentum and public realm quality at Brindleyplace, despite the crisis of a property bust.

Over millennia, energetic actors and groups have promoted changes to the physical landscape of their cities, seeking to express the values and visibility of a new regime or a new geo-political position. They have willed into being a new physical landscape, the remains of which we can often still witness. Such projects continue into our present age, especially where newly wealthy regimes are rapidly urbanising, as in places such as Shanghai in China and Dubai in the United Arab Emirates. The planning project, as it had evolved by the end of the twentieth century, has a different flavour to most of these. It is infused by a sensitivity to the everyday, to the experiences of ordinary people and to easing the accomplishment of our everyday lives and aspirations. This focus is a product of a democratisation of politics, in which responsiveness to the concerns of ordinary citizens becomes a measure of the health of a political community. Among these concerns, as noted above, are not merely considerations of fairness and equitable treatment for all community members. They also include consideration of the impacts and responsibilities that people in one community have for conditions elsewhere and for the overall health of the wider planetary environment, both in its fine grain and in its broad movements. We are these days much more aware that our accumulated actions may destroy the conditions for our lives and for environmental relations more generally. It is for this reason that, at the end of the century, many became sceptical of grand narratives, grandiose projects and ambitious rhetoric. Instead, the political demand is increasingly for attention to details, to the quality of life in neighbourhoods and to the ease of accessibility across complex urban structures. Citizens, increasingly knowledgeable about urban life and about governance processes, ask how collective action initiatives actually work out, what they deliver, to whom and where. The moment of opportunity for the planning project is to respond to and to enlarge these concerns, to help deliver, in all kinds of different situations, places that afford more liveable and sustainable conditions.

Agency can make a difference

Transforming place qualities and enlarging the capacity to achieve such transformation demands the active work of many people. As many social theorists now argue, just as what people think and do is shaped by wider forces, so these forces are themselves the product of how people have thought and acted. This interplay of structure and agency (see Chapter 2) may often be masked because those who shaped the forces we now experience are distanced, in time and place, from ourselves. However, the planning teams that worked to create the spatial strategies in Amsterdam and Portland in the 1970s and 1980s helped to structure the political climate in which place management and development now goes on in these cities. In Vancouver, citizens, politicians and planning experts worked together to produce a development culture and a political community that are now experienced as a significant 'structuring force' in the city. Even in a situation where it was very difficult to make any difference to the wider political community, community development workers in Besters Camp/INK worked hard to provide transparent and trustable governance processes through which they allocated opportunities for improvements to housing conditions for those in extreme poverty. In this way, they helped to create a microclimate of aspirations and expectations around the project.

The promotion of the planning project, as I have identified it in this book, thus places large demands on the energy, knowledge, skill and above all the commitment of its advocates. Where contextual conditions are very unfavourable to the values of the project, perhaps because of a narrow political focus, where local action is restricted by overly centralised and remote national governments, or where the formal machinery of government is taken over by self-serving and corruptible elites, it may be very difficult to sustain such a commitment. Countries such as the UK have had a long and apparently strong planning tradition. However, when the so-called planning function of local authorities was narrowed down during the 1980s and 1990s to delivering land-use regulation under a regime of targets that emphasised crude measures of speed over quality (see Chapter 5), many of those who entered planning work full of commitment to 'making the world a better place' became demoralised by the restricted parameters in which they were expected to work. Those who remained in post were assailed in the mid-2000s by demands that they 'change their culture'.[2] A positive attitude to work, let alone to the values of the planning project as articulated here, is hard to maintain after such experiences.

However, the national-level attempts to reform the planning system in the UK in the mid-2000s have enlarged the institutional space for the planning project, and there has been a renewal of energy and commitment to planning, as the political climate has changed to give much more attention to the quality of life in places, to the quality of the public realm and to attending to environmental dynamics and consequences. Despite the acute experience of economic crisis at the end of the 2000s, such attention is unlikely to fade away. There are many pressure groups energetically maintaining attention to the role of place quality in promoting social welfare and enhancing environmental sustainability. These concerns continue to be actively present in political party agendas. The planning profession is also energetically advocating a version of the values of the planning project. In such a context, the energy, skills and commitment of individuals can expand the scope and force of those promoting the values of the planning project, and join with others seeking ways of reconfiguring the heavy national state system inherited from an imperial past. There has thus been in Britain a moment of opportunity in the 2000s to push for greater attention to place qualities. The challenge for the 2010s is to prevent a narrowing down of this momentum in response to the severe economic recession and crises in public finance.

But place-management and development work that advances the liveability and sustainability of the many, now and in the future, in intelligent, open and transparent ways, is not just the result of the aggregate activities of lots of individuals. Nor is it the product of the vision of a 'great planner'. The range of expertise that needs to be mobilised is too great for any one person to encompass. Place-governance with a planning orientation is almost always done in teams of one kind or another. Even in regulatory work, a planning officer usually needs to co-ordinate with many others. The energy,

skills and commitments of individuals are enlarged (or reduced) by
the qualities of work groups and the cultures that build up in
communities of practice (see Chapter 3). As in the South Tyneside
case in Chapter 5, this implies that team leaders and managers have
a particular responsibility for sustaining the orientation of their
work groups, drawing in the energy and imagination of individuals,
but enlarging it through group interaction. The cases in Chapter 6
show extraordinary energy devoted to achieving major projects
among groups of people working within and across formal organisational boundaries. The power of agency in the planning field is
thus that generated by individuals working together in some form of
group or co-ordinated action.

Nor are those doing this work only people trained as planning
experts. As noted above, some people, once trained as planners, may
themselves lose track of the project or be subverted from it. Instead,
the energy, knowledge, skills and commitment of those promoting
attention to place qualities and the public realm, to liveability and
sustainability, may be diffused among a political community. Such
people may be spread among an activist movement or a group of key
stakeholders. They may be scattered around the organisations of the
public sector, or in informal networks and coalitions that cut across
the boundaries between government, businesses and civil society
organisations. What holds them together, and maintains a focus on
seeking ways of realising the planning project, is a commitment to a
task that is larger than their own self-advancement. For some, what
counts is the commitment to a wider project of making a contribution to society, city or place, or to public service generally. For others,
it is a commitment to doing a good-quality job, to exercising a craft
in skilled ways, that gives personal satisfaction. It is people who share
such commitments who tend to gravitate towards collective action
that helps to improve place qualities for the many into the future.

The agency that is mobilised in place-governance practices with a
planning orientation is thus not defined by any particular organisation or legal arrangement, such as a city planning office or the procedures of a particular planning system. Such practices are the product
of people whose personal aspirations, commitments and identities
get drawn into and shaped by work cultures and by the experience of
working with others in all kinds of different situations. These days,
as in the cases in this book, those centrally involved typically find
themselves working across the divisions between formal government
and the rest of society, with residents, pressure groups, business
lobbies, development companies, non-profit agencies, as well as

among those within the public sector. These groupings seek out and sometimes create institutional spaces where such energy can flourish.

There is always a danger among such collaborations that those involved develop an introverted sense of what they should do and how they should do it. This can happen in activist and voluntary community groups as well as within a municipal planning office. It is here that the wider culture of the political community in which such practices are located has an important role. A background of continual critique helps to limit tendencies to introversion, providing an ongoing critical chorus. A tradition of activism helps to ensure that new activist groups challenge older ones who may now be doing place-governance work, as in Portland and Vancouver. Critical academic work, investigative journalism and formal inquiries into performance also play an important role in monitoring how place-management and development work is done. So too do efforts to promote ideas about alternative futures, through constructing utopias or building future scenarios in various ways. A political community with a lively and critical public life is a valuable, if often uncomfortable, resource for those advancing the planning project.

Yet critique that demolishes without having an agenda for change, and those who criticise without grasping just how challenging it is to do the fine-grain balancing and synthesising inherent in planning work, may undermine established ways of thinking and acting. It may help to widen cracks and create moments of opportunity. But such critique may offer few resources to those seeking to move through the cracks and advance new agendas and practices. It may destroy the very capacity needed to deliver new initiatives. As I argued in Chapter 8, it is important for the wider political community not just to criticise but also to cultivate some understanding and respect for what it takes to do place-governance work that contributes to liveability and sustainability for the many, and creates public realm resources for the future.

The planning project and its commitments

The planning project evolved during the twentieth century to address the political challenge of increasingly urbanised societies in which citizens have become more aware and demanding with respect to the quality of life and opportunities available to them. In Western countries a century ago and still in many developing countries today, the challenge was and is to secure the provision of basic needs of food, shelter and security. These days, with more and more people living in urban conditions and able to move beyond staving off starvation, citizens demand more attention to daily living conditions and to the unfolding of future opportunities for themselves and their children. Place-development and management practices have evolved under these pressures to provide for an expanding conception of needs, to curb the excesses of capitalist exuberance, and to provide ground rules for the co-existence of neighbours with diverse aspirations and socio-cultural identities. Those promoting the planning project have helped to build up skills and knowledge to contribute to such practices, focused by a moral commitment that has contributed to challenging those forces that neglect the quality of life of people in places over time.

The twenty-first century looks set to be a period in human development where the challenges of living urban lives while reducing the chances of environmental calamities will become an increasingly dominant political concern. In the currently developed world, with long experience of urbanisation, urban areas will need continual reconfiguring and maintenance, as lifestyles, technologies and economic relations change. In the developing world, an enormous agenda already exists in relation to making the huge urban complexes that have appeared so suddenly become more liveable and sustainable. In both contexts, citizens are likely to be more demanding and more knowledgeable than ever before, and the struggles over who gets what will bear down on governance initiatives with great force. Creating and sustaining governance practices for place management and development that are trusted, open and transparent, and that deliver benefits for the many and not just the few, will be a severe test of the governance capacities of political communities across the world.

The planning project, as presented in this book, is thus not simply a phenomenon of the twentieth century, to be discarded in the emerging new worlds of the new century. Instead, place-governance practices informed by the planning project are likely to be increasingly valued and sought after. However, as I have tried to show in this book, realising the project is no easy task. It demands knowledge, skills and commitment. It demands much more than the provision of a good plan or a team of technical experts, as was often imagined in the twentieth century (Ward 2002). Politicians, public officials, experts in a variety of different fields and stakeholders in place qualities need to be persuaded that these qualities matter. They need to arrive at a recognition that attention to place qualities is not a one-dimensional focus, but involves inter-relating and integrating all kinds of dimensions as they affect how people inhabit, move around in and value their living environments. They need also to come to the realisation that governance works best when it is not treated as a one-way street from the governors to the governed. A more knowledgeable approach is called for, more sensitive to particularities, where there is constructive interaction between citizens and governance interventions, both at the level of detailing how these are delivered and in their overall design. The planning project, if it is to help improve the chances of human flourishing in sustainable ways in complex and challenging urban environments, needs also to be owned not just by advocates and committed experts. Its focus and orientation need to be supported and shared by the wider political community. Without this, place-governance work is too easily captured by dominant interests and the concerns of established elites. This support from the wider society does not imply some kind of stable consensus. The only agreement may be that attention to places and their qualities is important. Beyond that, it is the arguing, monitoring and criticising within a political community that help to sustain the focus of place-governance practices on values such as those promoted through the planning project.

This planning project itself evolved during the twentieth century. It is no longer about achieving mastery over the destiny of places. Instead, it focuses on helping people with stakes in places to manage their daily co-existence and to find ways to stimulate and cope with all kinds of major changes in conditions and context, in material dynamics, ways of life and values about place qualities. Place-governance with a planning orientation needs to be well informed about the various forces affecting how the future of a place is emerging, but also inspired by imaginative concepts of alternative futures and evaluations of all kinds of impacts. It may often be useful to analyse situations, to pull apart problems, issues and conflicts, to identify what is at stake and what assumptions are being made about cause and effect, values and actions. But it is also necessary to encourage stakeholders to consider how different issues and values are inter-related in the way places and their qualities evolve, to engage in imaginative conjecture. Place-governance inspired by a planning orientation involves creative work as well as analytic capability. It involves developing holistic perspectives about a place along with an appreciation of fine-grain diversity. It demands judgement that finds a way through conflicting evidence and arguments, and preparedness to make choices even where consequences cannot be known. That is, it involves taking risks. Above all, it demands a commitment to the belief that it is worth paying attention to the quality of life of people in places, and to finding ways to improve that quality in inclusive ways, both now and with the future in mind.

Such a project has the potential to transform the material conditions of people's lives and to contribute to reducing the damage that human activity has done to the life-sustaining conditions of the wider environment. It also has transformative potential in changing the way political communities think about places and how they relate to them. These two transformations may in turn have wider effects, on socio-cultural dynamics, on economic options, on regional and global environmental sustainability and on the attitudes and practices of political communities. Such impacts may often lie unrealised or never reach their ambitions, but that does not mean that transformative effects should not be sought out in the flow of doing place-development and management work. There is always a chance – to widen a crack, to create a basis from which later, often unimagined, possibilities may grow. The planning project is thus a political project, not in the sense of a move in the game of politics, but as a contribution to the creation and active construction of the collective life of urbanised societies. As with any project of this kind, it does not happen by itself. It has to be willed into being in an active way. Through this book, I have sought to show what is involved in pursuing this project in all kinds of different situations and conditions, and thereby to illustrate what its contribution can be to human flourishing in environmentally sustainable ways.

Suggested further reading

For other books and papers arguing for the promotion of better place qualities for human flourishing, especially in contemporary urban conditions, see:

Amin, A., Massey, D. and Thrift, N. (2000) *Cities for the Many not the Few,* Policy Press, Bristol.

Amin, A. (2006) The good city, *Urban Studies,* 43, 1009–23.

Fainstein, S. (2005) Cities and diversity: Should we plan for it? Can we plan for it? *Urban Affairs Review,* 41, 3–19.

Friedmann, J. (2002) *The Prospect of Cities,* University of Minnesota Press, Minneapolis.

Sandercock, L. (2003) *Mongrel Cities: Cosmopolis 11,* Continuum, London.

Notes

Preface

1. Note that my use of 'positive' here is as opposed to 'negative'. It does not imply any adherence to 'positivism' as a philosophical position in the philosophy of science.
2. For a valuable discussion of the role of case studies in social science generally from a planning academic, see Flyvbjerg 2001. For 'thick description', Yanow and Schwartz-Shea 2006.

Chapter 1

1. This story is taken from Luke Holland's television series for the BBC, *A Very English Village* (a ZEF production for BBC Storyville, zef@mistral.co.uk, 2006).
2. A British singer who made her reputation in World War II.
3. In UK planning legislation, only applicants for planning permission have a right to request a review of a planning decision. This lack of 'third-party rights' disturbs many, including environmental groups (see Ellis 2002).
4. That is, the formal definition of poverty used in the US.
5. I use the term 'human flourishing' rather than 'well-being' to emphasise that our lives are about more than just basic needs, although the latter are of great importance. The term flourishing is one translation of the Greek term *eudaimonia*, which also sometimes gets translated as 'happiness', which again seems too narrow a meaning (see Nussbaum 2001:31, fn 23).
6. This analysis was echoed in later accounts of urban politics in the US. See Fainstein and Fainstein 1986, Logan and Molotch 1987.
7. See www.UN-Habitat.org, *Regional Overview of the Status of Urban Planning and Planning Practice in Anglophone(Sub-Saharan) African Countries*, undertaken as background material for UN-Habitat 2009.
8. The ESDP is the product of the promotion of a spatial planning perspective by advocates in member states and the European Commission, and has had some effects on the subsequent development of planning ideas and practices in EU member states and elsewhere (see Faludi and Waterhout 2002, Faludi 2003).

Chapter 2

1. See *Wonen in Amsterdam 2007: Leefbaarheid*, available from Amsterdam City Council website (www.iamsterdam.com).

2. The designer here was not the modernist van Eesteren but his colleague Ms Mulder, who had a more sensitive approach to what made housing environments liveable for ordinary families.

3. Such a layout has also allowed for changes, with some areas of 'green' converted into new apartment blocks, the shopping complex reconfigured to provide for new shopping habits, and some new uses introduced.

4. Another crucial element was not to do with the planning principles, but related to housing allocation policy at the time this neighbourhood was first occupied. Rents and prices were slightly higher than in the areas that have since experienced difficulties, so the people who came to live here initially were slightly more affluent, and suffered less from the problems brought on by acute poverty.

5. A key divide in these debates is between those who feel that there must be some transcendent principles, beyond human experience or laws of the natural world, in which the principles that guide human behaviour should be grounded, and those who feel that the only principles we can have are those that we articulate in the experience of life in particular times and places. Those who take the first perspective search outside human experience, in the metaphysical realm or the laws of nature, for the principles that should guide us. Those who take the second perspective search in critical inquiry into history, the experiences of other societies than our own and into the different and evolving 'cultural worlds' that co-evolve in the present, although many also advocate a way to overcome such a duality. I incline to the second perspective.

6. There is a substantial literature on these questions. Within the planning field, the work of Young (1990) and Castells (1997) has been particularly influential.

7. The terms 'space'/'spatiality' and 'place'/'place quality' are tricky ones to use, as are other geographical terms such as space and territory. There are different traditions of usage in different academic disciplines, and arguments within disciplines about their meanings. I use the term 'spatiality' to refer to the 'whereness' of things and relations, the consequences of the co-location of things and the relations that link them together. See Madanipour 2003, Healey 2004b, Massey 2005, also Castells 1996.

8. Edited from text provided by Erik Van Rijn to Patsy Healey, 15.08.08.

Chapter 3

1. Of course, states varied in their power. In seventeenth-century England, the Parliament had already established its authority over the King, but neither King nor Parliament had the power to impose Christopher Wren's design scheme on the rebuilding of London after the Great Fire in 1666. Instead, land and property owners were quick to claim back and rebuild on their old sites. In contrast, in Paris in the mid-nineteenth century, it was still possible for the monarch and the national state, advised by Georges-Eugene Baron Haussman, to drive through a massive redevelopment scheme that created the great boulevards of today's city, while displacing thousands of property owners and their tenants. See Harvey 1989, Porter 2000, Madanipour 2007.

2. The sphere of government is also sometimes referred to as the 'state'. Different definitions of these terms are used by different schools of thought. I use the term 'state' to refer to an organised polity that provides rights of citizenship, as in a nation state or a region in a federal structure.

3. See Pennington 2002 for the promotion of such an agenda in the planning field. So-called regulation theorists argue that shifts in 'modes of (economic) accumulation' needed to be accompanied by shifts in 'modes of regulation', by which they meant governing processes (Harvey 1989). Bob Jessop built on this idea to introduce the concept of a shift from a social-democratic 'welfare' state to a neo-liberal 'work-fare' state (Jessop 1995). For a more general critical discussion of neo-liberal development strategies, see Leitner et al. 2007.

4. See Abers 1998, Petersen 2008, Crot 2009; for a more critical view, see Baiocchi 2003.

5. This is sometimes referred to as a 'mentality' and, by extension, 'governmentality', a term used by Foucault (see Dean 1999).

6. Briggs derives this concept from the political scientist Clarence Stone (2005). I have used the terms governance culture and institutional capacity (Healey 2004a). The concepts of governance culture, institutional capacity and civic capacity reflect similar phenomena to that in the concept of 'social capital' as used in an influential account by Putnam (1993), but are broader and richer.

7. The metaphors of drama, performance and front/back stage are developed in the policy analysis literature by Majone 1987 and Hajer 1995, 2005.

8. Clientelism refers to a form of politics in which patrons distribute the fruits of control of government to client groups. For other studies of situations where different rules for the game of politics have come into conflict, see Flyvbjerg 1998 and Watson 2003.

9. These legal schemes were not only intended to give rights to develop sites in particular ways. In countries such as Germany, they also

became the basis for establishing property values. See Sutcliffe 1981, Davies et al. 1989.

10. Such practices, associated with 'clientelistic' forms of governance, plagued the practice of planning in countries such as Italy in the second part of the twentieth century.

11. For discussions of this mode with particular relevance to the planning field, see Forester 1999, Rydin 2003, Healey 2006, Innes and Booher (2010).

12. See, for example, the case discussed by Crot 2009.

13. There are many reasons for this, from overload at national government level, to encouraging non-governmental actors to take on more of the tasks of governance, to promoting more participatory forms of active democracy. A significant argument for greater decentralisation is to promote more locally relevant and co-ordinated place development at the municipal and urban region scale.

14. For the difficulties of infrastructure co-ordination, see Graham and Marvin 2001.

15. There is a substantial literature in sociology on how to make a relation between structure and agency (see Seidman 1998). In relation to planning and land policy, see also Healey 1988.

16. The concept of 'moments of opportunity' comes from the social movement literature. See Tarrow 1994.

17. I use the vocabulary (developing/developed) adopted by UN-Habitat 2009, although this is not really adequate for the complex geopolitical world of the twenty-first century

18. For the main cases I have drawn on available accounts and, where possible, my own knowledge. I also asked 'local' experts to review my accounts, to help me reduce errors and to critique my interpretations. Sources are given in footnotes for each case.

Chapter 4

1. This account is drawn especially from Punter 2003, supplemented by Sandercock 2005, a talk by Larry Beasley, formerly Head of Planning in Vancouver, at UBC (09.06.07), a field day with Nathan Edelson, formerly of the Vancouver Planning Office (09.06.07) and Attili and Sandercock 2007. See also Grant 2009. Thanks also to André Sorensen for helpful corrective comments.

2. See Table 3.1 for zoning regulations as an instrument of place-governance.

3. This account has been constructed from the various contributions in Sorensen and Funck 2007, supplemented by Hirayama 2000, Sorensen 2002, Ishida 2007 and www.city.kobe.jp; thanks to Kayo Murakami, Maki Ryu, Carolyn Funck, André Sorensen and Shun-ichi Watanabe

for very helpful comments on my understanding of the Kobe situation. See the unpublished case study prepared for UN-Habitat 2009.

4. There is considerable discussion in Japan about the meaning of this term, but the translation that seems most appropriate is 'community making' (see Sorensen and Funck 2007).

5. Social housing is a term that has come to be used internationally to refer to housing provided for rent to those on low incomes.

6. The categories were residential, commercial and industrial, although some tolerance of mix was generally assumed.

7. This requirement grew out of practices related to the longstanding mechanism of land readjustment and urban redevelopment, where land and property owners were expected to agree, combined with social movements in the 1970s demanding a greater role for civil society in urban planning and management (Sorensen 2002).

8. At the lowest level, the formation of neighbourhood associations was encouraged to provide channels for communicating national objectives to the local population, and to mobilise populations for national projects. These were formed from heads of households (male) and came to cover almost all urban areas.

9. The Japanese economy experienced over a decade of stagnation, following the property investment collapse at the end of the 1980s.

10. The zoning ordinance as an instrument evolved in Europe and the US to manage the urban expansion process, and has spread around the world since. Sometimes it applies to small areas where significant development is expected. But it may also apply to a whole city, in the form of a city-wide regulatory general plan, as in Italy, Spain and Brazil. In the developing world, such ordinances are often referred to as 'master plans'.

Chapter 5

1. Municipalities are called local authorities in the UK. In the formal planning systems of England, Wales and Scotland (and soon in Northern Ireland), the municipal role in the planning system is usually given to the 'local planning authority', either a separate department or a section of another department.

2. See also Briggs 2008 for a case from Cape Town. I was very fortunate in the case I chose in being able to discuss the case, via email, with some of those involved.

3. This draws on documentary materials from South Tyneside Metropolitan District, particularly the *Local Development Framework* (June 2007) and the *Annual Review of the Area Planning Group* for April 2006–March 2007, both available on www.southtyneside.gov.uk, discussion with council officials, my

general knowledge of the area over 20 years, and of the British planning system and its practices. See also Booth 1996, and Kitchen 1997, 2007.

4. The term 'silos' refers to the large circular chambers used for storing grain or gas. It has come to refer to national and local government departments that operate with little reference to or co-ordination with each other.

5. The term 'customers' was introduced in the 1980s, when public agencies were encouraged to think of themselves as more like a business. Previously, terms such as citizens or residents might have been used. Kitchen (2007) discusses whether 'clients' or 'customers' is a better term.

6. Source: STMDC Annual Report 2006/7.

7. In England, a few municipalities have elected mayors with executive powers, but in most, the key figure is the council leader, and the mayor's role is largely ceremonial.

8. Source: STUDC Annual Report 2006/7. Figures are for that year.

9. In the UK, even for small changes to a building, it is usual to seek the advice of an 'agent' with experience of building materials and design, the planning system and building codes, and to present applications through an agent. These agents (who range from individual paraprofessionals to major international consultancies) are thus critical actors in the planning system.

10. Nationally, there was much discussion about the relative importance of decision 'quality' over decision 'speed'. See Cullingworth and Nadin 2001, Rydin 2003.

11. See van Horen 2000, www.durban.gov.za, eThekwini Municipality Integrated Development Plan July 2006 and Community Participation Policy Statement June 2006, and emails from Carolyn Kerr, Theresa Subban and Mike Byerley (eThekwini municipality), Phil Martin, Adrian Masson, Alison Todes and Nancy Odendaal.

12. The term 'warlords' has come into use to describe a kind of politics dominated by groups that maintain power by fear and violence.

13. Van Horen (2000), who had a participant role in this project and then came to research it, refers to conflict between Inkatha, the Zulu-based movement, and the African National Congress movement, which struggled for dominance in the early stage of South Africa's new democracy in the 1990s.

14. Roy 2005 notes how legal regularisation was actively promoted in many countries by aid agencies, with the aim of developing formal land and property markets in squatted areas, but that such regularisation did not create active property markets in places where poverty and insecurity were widespread.

15. These issues of rapid cash flow are critical in areas where people have very limited resources, in poor neighbourhoods all over the world, as

is some tolerance of informal processes. People with no money cannot wait for funders to pay them when the priority is to eat. Yet the availability of funds may also lead to pressures to siphon off money meant for development purposes for all kinds of other ends.

16. This information was provided by Phil Martin, email 12.11.07.
17. By this time, national housing policy had specified that sites-and-services schemes should provide a house space of 30 m^2 on a serviced plot.
18. See the July 2006 *Integrated Development Plan* for Durban, p.9.
19. This is a widespread finding, see Roy 2005. But see Pieterse 2006 for the potential for the present instability to produce the political energy to generate, in time, new governance forms and capacities.

Chapter 6

1. The term 'gentrification' has come to be used to describe the process whereby more affluent people move into a poorer neighbourhood once an upgrading process has started, 'gentry' being an old word for the 'middle' or 'bourgeois' classes of a society.
2. Not everyone in a coastal city can have an uninterrupted view of the sea, for example (see Harvey 1973 on the inevitable inequalities in urban spatial opportunities).
3. My sources are historical accounts and technical reports, supplemented by comments from participants and analysts interested in each case. I selected the cases because each had created an attractive locale that is now much valued and visited.
4. Sources: Frieden and Sagalyn 1991 O'Connor 1993, Altshuler and Luberoff 2003, Keifer 2006, Murray 2006. Thanks also to comments from Stan Majoor.
5. The BRA was still in existence in the mid-2000s, though less powerful than in the past.
6. The site overall is small, around 6.5 acres (2.63 hectares).
7. This, however, increased the operating costs of the complex. The costs of cleaning and security provision in particular were much higher than in suburban malls and much of this cost was passed on to tenants of the units. At one stage, the tenants banded together to object to these costs, through a 'class action' in the courts. This dispute was in the end settled out of court.
8. Sources: Busquets 2004, Marshall 2004, Benedicto and Carrasco 2007, Font 2007, Majoor 2008. Thanks to Tim Marshall, Stan Majoor and Antonio Font for very helpful comments and supplementary materials.
9. This was the *Plan Comarcal* for Barcelona and neighbouring municipalities, approved in 1953. This took the form, used in Spain and Italy, of a city-wide zoning plan, allocating sites to land uses and

building norms and standards. It was quickly overtaken by growth pressures and adjusted by 'partial plans' for specific developments (Calavita and Ferrer 2004, Font 2007).

10. What low-cost housing opportunities remain available were increasingly being taken by immigrants from outside Spain in the 2000s, resulting in a different kind of population mix in the city centre.

11. Sources: Newton 1976, Loftman and Nevin 1994, Smyth 1994, Newman and Thornley 1996, Latham and Swenarton 1999, Barber 2007. Thanks also to Tim Marshall and Geoff Wright for comments.

12. By 2001, it was estimated that 30 per cent of Birmingham's residents had what are called in the UK 'ethnic minority' backgrounds, some of whom were living in substantial poverty.

13. The funding came from EU and national government sources, as well as some municipal funding.

14. The Highbury Initiative was inspired by the experience of US cities such as Boston and Baltimore with Urban Development Action Teams (UDATs). The UK national government was particularly interested in US experience at this time. Email from Geoff Wright 22.12.08.

15. English city centres outside London were distinctive until the 1990s in their very small populations. By this time, a community planning group, *Birmingham for People*, was also arguing for a mixed-use project, with fewer offices and more public space (Latham and Swenarton 1999).

16. Argent had undertaken small schemes in Edinburgh before this.

17. It leads to surges and slumps in the demand for building materials and labour, and creates opportunities for corrupt practices, as some parties take opportunities from the rush to completion to demand pay-offs to avoid obstruction (see Leonardson 2007).

18. Alan Chatwin of Rosehaugh became involved in another company developing the 'Mailbox' project in Birmingham; Oriol Bohigas moved from the Barcelona planning department to become a consultant but stayed involved in the Olympic and other City Council projects.

Chapter 7

1. In the late twentieth century, it became fashionable among European and international development agencies to demand that all funded programmes had 'strategies', to justify what they were doing. Many times, the strategies that were prepared were merely a justification for, or even only a standardised rhetoric, surrounding a package of investment demands or regulatory requirements.

2. See for example in Europe, in the Netherlands and Switzerland.

3. See the debates in Europe in the 1980s and 1990s on the relative role of pursuing urban transformation through major strategic projects, or through city-wide strategies (Secchi 1986, Healey et al. 1997).
4. Sources: Faludi and Van der Valk 1994, Fainstein 1997, 2001b, Musterd and Salet 2003, Healey 2007:Chapter 3.
5. Known in the Netherlands as VROM, or *Ministerie van Volkhuisvesting, Ruimtelijke Ordening en Milieu*.
6. In the Netherlands, with its level topography, bicycles are widely used and are the main competitors for bus transit. Good provision for segregated bike lanes has been provided in new developments since the mid-twentieth century.
7. There is a good, constructively-critical relationship between Amsterdam City Council and academics in the city's universities; see Healey 2008.
8. Sources: Abbott 2001, Ozawa 2004, Abbott and Margheim 2008. See also www.portlandonline.com/planning. Thanks to Carl Abbott and Sy Adler for comments and corrections.
9. It earned praise from veteran urbanist Jane Jacobs, and has become a case praised by the 'new urbanist' movement (Duany et al. 2000).
10. This was a contentious process, with some activists arguing that the boundary covered too much non-urban land (email from Sy Adler, 24.09.08).
11. The State of Oregon created a planning system that combined rural and urban concerns in ways not unlike that developed in England from the 1950s, with its emphasis on green belts, compact development and rural conservation. But the English planning system has much less power to secure affordable housing and is driven from the top of the equivalent of a US state the size of California.
12. A map showing all the plans in force in Portland in 2007 can be found on www.palgrave.com/builtenvironment/healey. This shows plans for most neighbourhoods, as well as details for open, or 'natural' areas. For more on Portland's planning work, see www.portlandonline.com/planning.
13. See www.portlandonline.com.
14. There has been a similar experience in England, see Vigar et al. 2000.
15. There were complex challenges to Metro's policies in the 2000s.
16. This is likely to be so even in states without the accountability to citizens of formal democracies.

Chapter 8

1. Here, 'pluralist' is contrasted with 'monist', or a single viewpoint. See Connolly 2005 and Chapter 3.

2. This concept is taken from Geertz 1983; see also Sandercock 2003 (Chapter 3). Corburn (2005:201) argues that such knowledge is itself a form of expertise.

3. Planning Aid, now run under the umbrella of the British professional planning organisation, the RTPI, and with funds from national government, mobilises planning experts as volunteers to provide advice to those without the resources to pay for it. See www.planningaid. rtpi.org.uk.

4. See Churchman 1979. Economists discuss the relation when talking about 'macro' and 'micro' perspectives, and sociologists about the relation between the worlds of agency and that of structuring forces (see Chapter 2).

5. This is a special reflection provided by Louis Albrechts in November 2008, in response to a draft of this chapter. For his work on a spatial strategy for Flanders, in Belgium, see Albrechts 1998, 2001.

6. See UN-Habitat 2009:Chapter 10 for a recent review of planning education from a global perspective.

7. To reveal this craft, researchers such as Forester and Hoch have created a literature around planners talking about their work and how they do it; see also Krumholz and Forester 1990, Kitchen 1997, Albrechts 1998, 2001.

8. The distinctions between forums, arenas and courts is taken from Bryson and Crosby 1992. 'We call the social practice that results in the communication of meaning *the design and use of forums*; the social practice that results in policy-making and implementation *the design and use of arenas*; and the social practice that results in the normative regulation of conduct *the design and use of courts*' (Bryson and Crosby 1992:90). Bryson and Crosby draw especially on the structuration theory of sociologist Anthony Giddens (1984).

9. However, these reforms have been deeply ambiguous, seeking to engage stakeholders in strategy making early on while also speeding up the process of preparing strategies (see Nadin 2007). A key problem here has been the assumption that conflicts over place development can be smoothed away, rather than recognising that conflict has a valuable role as a check and balance on planning activity.

10. The power of legal challenge may lie in its role as a background possibility. In some countries, such as the US, however, the courts have taken on a significant role as a *de facto* policy maker (Cullingworth and Caves 2003).

11. With the increase in the creation of ad hoc arenas, there is much concern these days about the formal accountability of such institutional sites. Courts derive their legitimacy from formal administrative law and its interpretation, along with other principles that may be important in the legal system of a country. In British law, for example, principles of precedent, fairness and reasonableness, as interpreted by

judges, are allowed to modify formal administrative law. There are significant differences between the legal systems of different parts of the world, and their implications for 'planning law' have not been fully explored. See Glenn 2007 and also Alterman 1988.

12.   Email from Geoff Wright to Patsy Healey, 17.07.08.

13.   This was a series of eight episodes, broadcast between September 2008 and April 2009. Details are available on the BBC website (www.bbc.co.uk).

14.   Text with email from Erik van Rijn to Patsy Healey, 15.08.08.

15.   For the concept of 'agonism' in a planning context, see Hillier 2002:14–15 (Hillier draws on the work of Chantal Mouffe).

16.   For a valuable discussion of the relationships between planners and politicians, see Campbell 2001.

17.   Gans referred to the disadvantaged as the planners' 'indirect client', and their employers as their 'direct client'.

Chapter 9

1.   Those who argue that governance activity in capitalist societies is inherently 'structured' by dominant political and economic forces often criticise those who suggest that active agency asserted in small ways can make a difference. They argue that this reflects a naïve idealism, divorced from 'realities'. I argue instead that 'reality' is created by the continual interaction of active agency and broader structuring processes that shape and are shaped by active agency.

2.   For comment on the reforms, see Nadin 2007 and www.rtpi.org.uk.

References

Abbott, C. (2001) *Greater Portland: Urban Life and Landscape in the Pacific Northwest*, University of Pennsylvania Press, Philadelphia.

Abbott, C. and Margheim, J. (2008) Imagining Portland's urban growth boundary: Planning regulation as cultural icon, *Journal of the American Planning Association*, 74(2), 196–208.

Abers, R. (1998) Learning democratic practice: Distributing government resources through popular participation in Porto Alegre, Brazil, in Douglass, M. and Friedmann, J. (eds) *Cities for Citizens*, Wiley, London, pp. 39–66.

Albrechts, L. (1998) The Flemish diamond, *European Planning Studies*, 6, 411–24.

Albrechts, L. (2001) From traditional land use planning to strategic spatial planning: The case of Flanders, in Albrechts, L., Alden, J. and da Rosa Pires, A. (eds) *The Changing Institutional Landscape of Planning*, Ashgate, Aldershot, pp. 83–108.

Albrechts, L. (2004) Strategic (spatial) planning reexamined, *Environment and Planning B: Planning and Design*, 31, 743–58.

Albrechts, L., Healey, P. and Kunzmann, K. (2003) Strategic spatial planning and regional governance in Europe, *Journal of the American Planning Association*, 69, 113–29.

Allmendinger, P. (2009) *Planning Theory*, Palgrave Macmillan, London.

Alterman, R. (ed.) (1988) *Private Supply of Public Services: Evaluation of Real Estate Exactions, Linkage, and Alternative Land Policies*, New York University Press, New York.

Altshuler, A. and Luberoff, D. (2003) *Mega-Projects: The Changing Role of Urban Public Investment*, Brookings Institution, Washington, DC.

Amin, A. (2002) Spatialities of globalisation, *Environment and Planning A*, 34, 385–99.

Amin, A. (2006) The good city, *Urban Studies*, 43, 1009–23.

Amin, A., Massey, D. and Thrift, N. (2000) *Cities for the Many not the Few*, Policy Press, Bristol.

Amin, A. and Thrift, N. (2002) *Cities: Reimagining the Urban*, Polity/Blackwell, Oxford.

Ascher, F. (1995) *Metapolis ou L'avenir des villes*, Editions O. Jacob, Paris.

Askew, J. (1996) Case study: King's Cross, in Greed, C. (ed.) *Implementing Town Planning*, Longman, Harlow, pp. 199–214.

Attili, G. and Sandercock, L. (2007) *Where Strangers Become Neighbours: The Story of the Collingwood Neighbourhood House and the*

Integration of Immigrants in Vancouver, video, www.mongrel-stories.com, 50 minutes.

Baiocchi, G. (2003) Participation, activism and politics: The Porto Alegre experiment, in Fung, A. and Wright, E. O. (eds) *Deepening Democracy: Institutional Innovation and Empowered Participatory Governance,* Verso, London, pp. 45–76.

Balducci, A. (2008) Constructing (spatial) strategies in complex environments, In van der Broek, J., Moulaert, F. and Oosterlynck, S. (eds) *Empowering the Planning Fields: Ethics, Creativity and Action,* Acco, Leuven, pp. 79–99.

Barber, A. (2007) Planning for sustainable urbanisation: Policy challenges and city centre housing in Birmingham, *Town Planning Review,* 78, 179–202.

Barnett, J. (2003) *Redesigning Cities: Principles, Practice, Implementation,* University of Chicago Press, Chicago.

Barnett, J. (2006) Omaha by design – all of it: New prospects in urban planning and design, In Saunders, W. S. (eds.) *Urban Planning Today,* University of Minnesota Press, Minneapolis, pp. 93–105.

Barrett, S. and Fudge, C. (1981) *Policy and Action,* Methuen, London.

Benedicto, J. L. L. and Carrasco, J. V. (2007) Barcelona Universal Forum 2004: Culture as driver of urban economy, In Salet, W. and Gualini, E. (eds) *Framing Strategic Urban Projects: Learning from Current Experiences in European Urban Regions,* Routledge, London, pp. 84–114.

Booher, D. and Innes, J. (2002) Network power for collaborative planning, *Journal of Planning Education and Research,* 21, 221–36.

Booth, P. (1996) *Controlling Development: Certainty and Discretion in Europe, the USA and Hong Kong,* London, UCL Press.

Boyer, C. (1983) *Dreaming the Rational City,* MIT Press, Cambridge, MA.

Breetzke, K. (2009) *From Conceptual Frameworks to Quantititive Models: Spatial Planning in the Durban Metropolitan Area, South Africa – the Link to Housing and Infrastructure Planning,* UN-Habitat, Nairobi.

Bridge, G. and Watson, S. (eds) (2000) *A Companion to the City,* Blackwell, Oxford.

Briggs, X. d. S. (2008) *Democracy as Problem-Solving,* MIT Press, Boston, MA.

Bryson, J. and Crosby, B. (1992) *Leadership in the Common Good: Tackling Public Problems in a Shared Power World,* Jossey Bass, San Francisco.

Busquets, J. (2004) Barcelona – rethinking urbanistic projects, in El-Khoury, R. and Robbins, E. (eds) *Shaping the City – Studies in History, Theory and Urban Design,* Routledge, London, pp. 14–40.

Calavita, N. and Ferrer, A. (2004) Behind Barcelona's success story – citizen movements and planners' power, in Marshall, T. (ed.) *Transforming Barcelona,* Routledge, London, pp. 47–64.

Callon, M., Lascoumes, P. and Barthe, Y. (2009) *Acting in an Uncertain World: An Essay on Technical Democracy*, MIT Press, Cambridge, MA.

Campbell, H. (2001) Planners and politicians: The pivotal planning relationship, *Planning Theory and Practice*, 2, 83–100.

Campbell, H. (2006) Just planning: The art of situated ethical judgement, *Journal of Planning Education and Research*, 26, 92–106.

Campbell, H. and Marshall, R. (2000) Moral obligation, planning and the public Interest: A commentary on current British practice, *Environment and Planning B: Planning and Design*, 27, 297–312.

Cars, G., Healey, P., Madanipour, A. and de Magalhaes, C. (eds) (2002) *Urban Governance, Institutional Capacity and Social Milieux*, Ashgate, Aldershot.

Castells, M. (1977) *The Urban Question*, Edward Arnold, London.

Castells, M. (1983) *The City and the Grassroots*, University of California Berkeley Press, Berkeley, CA.

Castells, M. (1996) *The Rise of the Network Society*, Blackwell, Oxford.

Castells, M. (1997) *The Power of Identity*, Blackwell, Oxford.

Chambers, R. (2005) *Ideas for Development*, Earthscan, London.

Churchman, C. W. (1979) *The Systems Approach*, 2nd edn, Dell Publishing, New York.

Cockburn, C. (1977) *The Local State*, Pluto Press, London.

Committee for Spatial Development (CSD) (1999) *The European Spatial Development Perspective*, European Commission, Luxembourg.

Connolly, W. E. (1987) *Politics and Ambuguity*, University of Wisconsin Press, Madison, WI.

Connolly, W. E. (2005) *Pluralism*, Duke University Press, Durham, NC.

Cooke, B. and Kothari, U. (eds) (2001) *Participation: The New Tyranny*, Zed Books, London.

Corburn, J. (2005) *Street Science: Community Knowledge and Environmental Health Justice*, MIT Press, Cambridge, MA.

Crawley, I. (1991) Some reflections on planning and politics in Inner London, in Thomas, H. and Healey, P. (eds) *Dilemmas of Planning Practice: Ethics, Legitimacy and the Validation of Knowledge*, Avebury, Aldershot, pp. 101–14.

Crot, L. (2009) *The Characteristics and Outcomes of Participatory Budgeting: Buenos Aires, Argentina*, UN-Habitat, Nairobi.

Cullingworth, B. and Nadin, V. (2001) *Town and Country Planning in Britain*, Routledge, London.

Cullingworth, J. B. and Caves, R. W. (2003) *Planning in the USA: Policies, Issues and Processes*, Routledge, London.

Cunningham, F. (2002) *Theories of Democracy: A Critical Introduction*, Routledge, London.

Davidoff, P. (1965) Advocacy and pluralism in planning, *Journal of the American Institute of Planners*, 31, 331–8.

Davies, H. W. E., Edwards, D., Hooper, A. and Punter, J. (1989) *Development Control in Western Europe*, HMSO, London.

Davoudi, S. (2003) Polycentricity in European spatial planning: From an analytical tool to a normative agenda, *European Planning Studies*, 11, 979–99

Davoudi, S. and Healey, P. (1990) *Using Planning Consultants: The Experience of the Tyne and Wear Development Corporation*, Project Paper No 2, University of Newcastle (Department of Town and Country Planning), Newcastle.

Dean, M. (1999) *Governmentality: Power and Rule in Modern Societies*, Sage, London.

Dewey, J. (1927/1991) *The Public and its Problems*, Swallow Press/Ohio University Press, Athens, OH.

Diaz Orueta, F. and Fainstein, S. (2008) The new mega-projects: Genesis and impacts, *International Journal of Urban and Regional Research*, 32, 759–67.

du Gay, P. (2000) *In Praise of Bureaucracy*, Sage, London.

Duany, A., Plater-Zyberk, E. and Speck, J. (2000) *Suburban Nation: The Rise of Sprawl and the Decline of the American Dream*, North Point Press, New York.

Dühr, S. (2007) *The Visual Language of Spatial Planning: Exploring Cartographic Representations for Spatial Planning in Europe*, Routledge, London.

Edwards, I. (1994) Cato Manor: Cruel past, pivotal future, *Review of African Political Economy*, 61, 415–27.

Edwards, M. (1992) A microcosm: Redevelopment proposals at King's Cross, in Thornley, A. (ed.) *The Crisis of London*, Routledge, London, pp. 163–84.

Edwards, M. (2009) King's Cross: Renaissance for whom?, in Punter, J. (ed.) *Urban Design, Urban Renaissance and British Cities*, Routledge, London.Ellis, H. (2002) Planning and public empowerment: Third party rights in development control, *Planning Theory and Practice*, 1, 203–18.

Ellis, H. (2002) Planning and public empowerment: Third Party Rights in Development Control, *Planning Theory and Practice*, 1, 2, 203–18.

Elson, M. J. (1986) *Green Belts: Conflict Mediation in the Urban Fringe*, Heinemann, London.

Esteban, J. (2004) The planning project: Bringing value to the periphery, recovering the centre, in Marshall, T. (ed.) *Transforming Barcelona*, Routledge, London, pp. 111–50.

Evans, N. (2001) Community planning in Japan: The case of Mano and its experience of the Hanshin earthquake, unpublished PhD, School of East Asian Studies, University of Sheffield, Sheffield.

Fainstein, S. (1997) The egalitarian city: The restructuring of Amsterdam, *International Planning Studies*, 2, 295–314.

Fainstein, S. (2001a) *The City Builders: Property Development in New York and London 1980–2000,* University of Kansas Press, Kansas.

Fainstein, S. (2001b) Competitiveness, cohesion and governance: Their implications for social justice, *International Journal of Urban and Regional Research,* **25,** 884–8.

Fainstein, S. (2005) Cities and diversity: Should we plan for it? Can we plan for it? *Urban Affairs Review,* **41,** 3–19.

Fainstein, S. and Fainstein, N. (eds) (1986) *Restructuring the City: The Political Economy of Urban Redevelopment,* Longman, New York.

Faludi, A. (2003) Special issue on the application of the European Spatial Development Perspective (introduction and conclusion by A. Faludi), *Town Planning Review,* **74,** 1–12, 121–40.

Faludi, A. and van der Valk, A. (1994) *Rule and Order in Dutch Planning Doctrine in the Twentieth Century,* Kluwer Academic Publishers, Dordrecht.

Faludi, A. and Waterhout, B. (eds) (2002) *The Making of the European Spatial Development Perspective,* Routledge, London.

Feagin, J. (1988) *Free Enterprise City,* Rutgers University Press, New Brunswick.

Fischer, F. (2000) *Citizens, Experts and the Environment: The Politics of Local Knowledge,* Duke University Press, Durham, NC.

Fischer, F. (2003) *Reframing Public Policy: Discursive Politics and Deliberative Practices,* Oxford University Press, Oxford.

Fischer, F. and Forester, J. (eds) (1993) *The Argumentative Turn in Policy Analysis and Planning,* UCL Press, London.

Fishman, R. (1977) *Urban Utopias in the Twentieth Century: Ebenezer Howard, Frank Lloyd Wright, Le Corbusier,* Basic Books, New York.

Flyvbjerg, B. (1998) *Rationality and Power,* University of Chicago Press, Chicago.

Flyvbjerg, B. (2001) *Making Social Science Matter: Why Social Inquiry Fails and How It Can Succeed Again,* Cambridge University Press, Cambridge.

Flyvbjerg, B., Bruzelius, N. and Rothengatter, W. (2003) *Megaprojects and Risk: An Anatomy of Ambition,* Cambridge University Press, Cambridge.

Font, A. (2007) The urban region of Barcelona: From the compact city to the metropolitan territories, in Font, A. (ed.) *The explosion of the City,* Ministerio de Vivienda/Colegio Oficial de Arquitectos de Catalunya (COAC), Madrid, pp. 224–66.

Forester, J. (1989) *Planning in the Face of Power,* University of California Press, Berkeley.

Forester, J. (1999) *The Deliberative Practitioner: Encouraging Participatory Planning Processes,* MIT Press, London.

Forester, J. (2007) No longer muddling through: Institutional norms fostering dialogue, getting the facts, and encouraging mediated negotiation, in Verma, N. (ed.) *Institutions and planning,* Elsevier, Oxford, pp. 91–105.

Frieden, B. J. and Sagalyn, L. B. (1991) *Downtown Inc. How America Rebuilds Cities,* MIT Press, Boston, MA.

Friedmann, J. (1973) *Re-tracking America: A Theory of Transactive Planning,* Anchor Press, New York.

Friedmann, J. (1987) *Planning in the Public Domain,* Princeton University Press, Princeton.

Friedmann, J. (2002) *The Prospect of Cities,* University of Minnesota Press, Minneapolis.

Funck, C. (2007) Machizukuri, civil society, and the transformation of Japanese city planning: Case from Kobe, in Sorensen, A. and Funck, C. (eds) *Living Cities in Japan: Citizens' Movements, Machizukuri and Local Environments,* Routledge, London, pp. 137–56.

Galster, G. (1996) *Reality and Research: Social Science and U.S. Urban Policy since 1960,* Urban Institute, Washington, DC.

Gans, H. (1969) Planning for people not buildings, *Environment and Planning A,* 1, 33–46.

Geddes, P. (1915/1968) *Cities in Evolution,* Ernest Benn, London.

Geertz, C. (1983) *Local Knowledge,* Basic Books, New York.

Giddens, A. (1984) *The Constitution of Society,* Polity Press, Cambridge.

Gilbert, A. (1998) *The Latin American City,* 2nd edn, Latin America Bureau, London.

Glenn, H. P. (2007) *Legal Traditions of the World,* 2nd edn, Oxford University Press, Oxford.

Goodman, R. (1972) *After the Planners,* Penguin, Harmondsworth.

Graham, S. and Healey, P. (1999) Relational concepts in time and space: Issues for planning theory and practice, *European Planning Studies,* 7, 623–46.

Graham, S. and Marvin, S. (1996) *Telecommunications and the City: Electronic Spaces, Urban Places,* Routledge, London.

Graham, S. and Marvin, S. (2001) *Splintering Urbanism,* Routledge, London.

Grant, J. (2006) *Planning the Good Community: New Urbanism in Theory and Practice,* Routledge, London.

Grant, J. (2009) Experiential planning: A practitioner's account of Vancouver's success, *Journal of the American Planning Association,* 75, 358–70.

Gualini, E. (2004) *Multi-level Governance and Institutional Change: The Europeanisation of Regional Policy in Italy,* Ashgate, Aldershot.

Gualini, E. (2006) The rescaling of governance in Europe: New spatial and institutional rationales, *European Planning Studies,* 14, 881–904.

Habermas, J. (1984) *The Theory of Communicative Action: Vol 1: Reason and the Rationalisation of Society,* Polity Press, Cambridge.

Hajer, M. (1995) *The Politics of Environmental Discourse,* Oxford University Press, Oxford.

Hajer, M. (2005) Setting the stage: A dramaturgy of policy deliberation, *Administration and Society,* 36, 624–47.

Hajer, M. and Wagenaar, H. (eds) (2003) *Deliberative Policy Analysis: Understanding Governance in the Network Society,* Cambridge University Press, Cambridge.

Hall, P. (1982) *Great Planning Disasters,* University of California Press, Berkeley, CA.

Hall, P. (1988) *Cities of Tomorrow,* Blackwell, Oxford.

Hall, P., Thomas, R., Gracey, H. and Drewett, R. (1973) *The Containment of Urban England,* George, Allen and Unwin, London.

Hamaguchi, E. (1985) A contextual model of the Japanese: Toward a methodological innovation in Japanese Studies, *Journal of Japanese Studies,* 11, 289–321.

Hanley, L. (2007) *Estates: An Intimate History,* Granta Books, London.

Harrison, P., Todes, A. and Watson, V. (2007) *Planning and Transformation: Learning from the Post-Apartheid Experience,* Routledge, London.

Harvey, D. (1973) *Social Justice and the City,* Edward Arnold, London.

Harvey, D. (1989) *The Condition of Postmodernity,* Blackwell, Oxford.

Haughton, G. (1999) Environmental justice and the sustainable city, *Journal of Planning Education and Research,* 18, 233–43.

Hayek, F. A. (1944) *The Road to Serfdom,* Routledge and Kegan Paul, London.

Healey, P. (1985) The professionalisation of planning in Britain: Its form and consequences, *Town Planning Review,* 56, 492–507.

Healey, P. (1988) The British planning system and managing the urban environment, *Town Planning Review,* 59, 397–417.

Healey, P. (1992) A planner's day: Knowledge and action in communicative practice, *Journal of the American Planning Association,* 58, 9–20.

Healey, P. (1997/2006) *Collaborative Planning: Shaping Places in Fragmented Societies,* 2nd edn, Macmillan, London.

Healey, P. (2004a) Creativity and urban governance, *Policy Studies,* 25, 87–102.

Healey, P. (2004b) The treatment of space and place in the new strategic spatial planning in Europe, *International Journal of Urban and Regional Research,* 28, 45–67.

Healey, P. (2007) *Urban Complexity and Spatial Strategies: Towards a Relational Planning for our Times,* Routledge, London.

Healey, P. (2008) Knowledge flows, spatial strategy-making and the roles of academics, *Environment and Planning C: Government and Policy,* 26, 861–81.

Healey, P., Khakee, A., Motte, A. and Needham, B. (eds) (1997) *Making Strategic Spatial Plans: Innovation in Europe,* UCL Press, London.

Hillier, J. (2002) Direct action and agonism in democratic planning practice, in P. Allmendinger and M. Tewdwr-Jones (eds) *Planning Futures: New Directions for Planning Theory,* Routledge, London, pp. 110–35.

Hillier, J. (2007) *Stretching Beyond the Horizon: A Multiplanar Theory of Spatial Planning and Governance,* Ashgate, Aldershot.

Hillier, J. and Healey, P. (eds) (2008) *Critical Readings in Planning Theory: Vol 1 Foundations of the Planning Enterprise; Vol 2 Political Economy, Diversity and Pragmatism; Vol 3 Contemporary Movements in Planning Theory*, Ashgate, Aldershot.

Hirayama, Y. (2000) Collapse and reconstruction: Housing recovery policy in Kobe after the Hanshin great earthquake, *Urban Studies*, 15, 111–28.

Hoch, C. (1994) *What Planners Do*, Planners Press, Chicago.

Hoch, C. (2007) Pragmatic communicative action theory, *Journal of Planning Education and Research*, 26, 272–83.

Hopkins, L. (2001) *Urban Development: The Logic of Making Plans*, Island Press, Washington, DC.

Howard, E. (1989) *Garden Cities of Tomorrow*, Attic Books, Eastbourne.

Ikejiofor, U. C. (2009) *Planning within a Context of Informality: Issues and Trends in Land Delivery in Enugu, Nigeria*, UN-Habitat, Nairobi.

Imrie, R. and Raco, M. (eds) (2003) *Urban Renaissance? New Labour, Community and Urban Policy*, Policy Press, Bristol.

Innes, J. E. and Booher, D. E. (2010) *Beyond Collaboration: Planning and Policy in an Age of Complexity*, Routledge, London.

Ishida, Y. (2007) The concept of *machi-sodate* and urban planning: The case of Tokyu Tama Den'en Toshi, in Sorensen, E. and Funck, C. (eds) *Living Cities in Japan*, Routledge, London, pp. 115–36.

Jabareen, Y. (2006) Spaces of risk: The contribution of planning policies to conflicts in cities: Lessons from Nazareth, *Planning Theory and Practice*, 7, 305–23.

James, W. (1920) *Collected Essays and Reviews*, Longmans, Green, London.

Jessop, B. (1995) Towards a Schumpeterian workfare regime in Britain? Reflections on regulation, governance and the welfare state, *Environment and Planning A*, 27, 1613–26.

Jessop, B. (2002) *The Future of the Capitalist State*, Polity Press, Cambridge.

Johnson, S. R. (2004) The myth and reality of Portland's engaged citizenry and process-oriented governance, in C. P. Ozawa (ed.) *The Portland Edge: Challenges and Successes of Growing Communities*, Island Press, Washington, DC.

Johnson, T. J. (1972) *Professionals and Power*, Macmillan, London.

Jolles, A., Klusman, E. and Teunissan, B. (eds) (2003) *Planning Amsterdam: Scenarios for Urban Development 1928–2003*, NAi, Rotterdam.

Keeble, L. (1952) *Principles and Practice of Town and Country Planning*, Estates Gazette, London.

Keifer, M. J. (2006) Public planning and private initiative: The South Boston Waterfront, in Saunders, W. S. (ed.) *Urban Planning Today*, University of Minnesota Press, Minneapolis.

Kingdon, J. W. (2003) *Agendas, Alternatives, and Public Policies*, Longman, New York.

Kitchen, J. E. (1997) *People, Politics, Policies and Plans*, Paul Chapman, London.

Kitchen, T. (1991) A client-based view of the planning service, in Thomas, H. and Healey, P. (eds) *Dilemmas of Planning Practice: Ethics, Legitimacy and the Validation of Knowledge*, Avebury, Aldershot.

Kitchen, T. (2007) *Skills for Planning Practice*, Palgrave, Basingstoke.

Krumholz, N. and Forester, J. (1990) *Making Equity Planning Work*, Temple University Press, Philadelphia.

Latham, I. and Swenarton, M. (eds) (1999) *Brindleyplace: A Model for Urban Regeneration*, Right Angle Publishing, London.

Latour, B. (1987) *Science in Action*, Harvard University Press, Cambridge, MA.

Le Galès, P. (2002) *European Cities: Social Conflicts and Governance*, Oxford University Press, Oxford.

Leitner, H., Peck, J. and Sheppard, E. S. (eds) (2007) *Contesting Neoliberalism: Urban Frontiers*, Guilford Press, New York.

Leonardsen, D. (2007) Planning of mega projects: Experiences and lessons, *Planning Theory and Practice*, 8, 11–30.

Loftman, P. and Nevin, B. (1994) Prestige project developments: Economic renaissance or economic myth? A case study of Birmingham, *Local Economy*, 8, 307–25.

Logan, J. and Molotch, H. (1987) *Urban Fortunes: The Political Economy of Place*, University of Califiornia Press, Berkeley, CA.

Madanipour, A. (2003) *Public and Private Spaces in the City*, Routledge, London.

Madanipour, A. (2007) *Designing the City of Reason: Foundations and Frameworks*, Routledge, London.

Madanipour, A., Cars, G. and Allen, J. (eds) (1998) *Social Exclusion in European Cities*, Jessica Kingsley/Her Majesty's Stationery Office, London.

Majone, G. (1987) *Evidence, Argument and Persuasion in the Policy Process*, Yale University Press, New Haven, CT.

Majoor, S. (2008) *Disconnected Innovations: New Urbanity in Large-Scale Development Projects*, Uitgeverij Eburon, Delft.

Majoor, S. and Salet, W. (2008) The enlargement of local power in trans-scalar strategies of planning: Recent tendencies in two European cases, *GeoJournal*, 72, 91–103.

Mansuur, A. and van der Plas, G. (2003) *De Noordvleugel*, DRO/Gemeente Amsterdam, Amsterdam.

Maragall, P. (2004) Governing Barcelona, in Marshall, T. (ed.) *Transforming Barcelona*, Routledge, London, pp. 65–89.

Marshall, T. (ed.) (2004) *Transforming Barcelona*, Routledge, London.

Massey, D. (2005) *For Space*, Sage, London.

Mastop, H. and Faludi, A. (1997) Evaluation of strategic plans: The performance principle, *Environment and Planning B: Planning and Design*, 24, 815–32.

Mayer, H. and Provo, J. (2004) The Portland Edge in context, in Ozawa, C. P. (ed.) *The Portland Edge: Challenges and Successes in Growing Communities*, Portland State University, Portland, OR.

McLoughlin, B. (1992) *Shaping Melbourne's Future*, Cambridge University Press, Melbourne.

Meyerson, M. and Banfield, E. (1955) *Politics, Planning and the Public Interest*, Free Press, New York.

Mitlin, D. and Satterthwaite, D. (eds) (2004) *Empowering Squatter Citizens: Local Government, Civil Society and Urban Poverty Reduction*, Earthscan, London.

Moulaert, F., with Delladetsima, P., Delvainquiere, J. C., Demaziere, C., Rodriguez, A., Vicari, S. and Martinez, M. (2000) *Globalisation and Integrated Area Development in European Cities*, Oxford University Press, Oxford.

Murie, A. and Musterd, S. (2004) Social exclusion and opportunity structures in European cities and neighbourhoods, *Urban Studies*, 41, 1441–59.

Murray, H. (2006) Paved with good intentions: Boston's Central Artery Project and a failure of city building, in Saunders, W. S. (ed.) *Urban Planning Today*, University of Minnesota Press, Minneapolis, pp. 63–82.

Musterd, S. and Salet, W. (eds) (2003) *Amsterdam Human Capital*, Amsterdam University Press, Amsterdam.

Nadin, V. (2007) The emergence of the spatial planning approach in England, *Planning Practice and Research*, 22, 43–62.

Newman, P. and Thornley, A. (1996) *Urban Planning in Europe*, Routledge, London.

Newton, K. (1976) *Second City Politics: Democratic Processes and Decision-Making in Birmingham*, Clarendon Press, Oxford.

Nicholson, D. (1991) Planners' skills and planning practice, in Thomas, H. and Healey, P. (eds) *Dilemmas of Planning Practice: Ethics, Legitimacy and the Validation of Knowledge*,) Avebury Technical, Aldershot, pp. 53–62.

Nishida, K. (1921/1987) *An Inquiry into the Good*, Yale University Press, New Haven, MA.

Nnkya, T. J. (1999) Land use planning practice under the public land ownership policy of Tanzania, *Habitat International*, 23, 135–55.

Nussbaum, M. (2001) *Upheavals of Thought: The Intelligence of Emotions*, Cambridge University Press, Cambridge.

O'Connor, T. H. (1993) *Building a New Boston: Politics and Urban Renewal: 1950–1970*, Northeastern University Press, Boston, MA.

Ozawa, C. P. (ed.) (2004) *The Portland Edge: Challenges and Successes in Growing Eommunities,* Island Press, Washington, DC.

Payne, G. (2005) Getting ahead of the game: A twin-track approach to improving existing slums and reducing the need for future slums, *Environment and Urbanisation*, 17, 133–45.

Pell, B. (1991) From the public to the private sector, in Thomas, H. and Healey, P. (eds) *Dilemmas of Planning Practice: Ethics, Legitimacy and the Validation of Knowledge,*) Avebury, Aldershot, pp. 53–62.

Pennington, M. (2002) *Liberating the Land: The Case for Private Land-Use Planning,* Institute for Economic Affairs, London.

Peterson, P. (2008) Civic engagement and urban reform in Brazil, *Planning Theory and Practice,* **9**, 406–10.

Pieterse, E. (2006) Building with ruins and dreams: Some thoughts on realising integrated urban development in South Africa through crisis, *Urban Studies,* **43**, 285–304.

Porter, R. (2000) *Enlightenment: Britain and the Creation of the Modern World,* Penguin Books, London.

Punter, J. (2003) *The Vancouver Achievement,* UBC Press, Vancouver.

Putnam, R. (1993) *Making Democracy Work: Civil Traditions in Modern Italy,* University of Princeton Press, Princeton, NJ.

Ritzdorf, M. (1985) Challenging the exclusionary impact of family definitions in American Municipal Zoning Ordinances, *Journal of Urban Affairs,* **7**, 15–26.

Rose, R. (2009) *Learning from Comparative Public Policy: A Practical Guide,* Routledge, London.

Roy, A. (2005) Urban informality: Towards an epistemology of planning, *Journal of the American Planning Association,* **71**, 147–58.

Rydin, Y. (2003) *Urban and Environmental Planning in the UK,* Palgrave, Basingstoke.

Sager, T. (2009) Planners' role: Torn between dialogical ideals and neoliberal realities, *European Planning Studies,* **17**, 65–84.

Salet, W. and Gualini, E. (eds) (2007) *Framing Strategic Urban Projects: Learning from Current Experiences in European Urban Regions,* Routledge, London.

Salet, W. and Thornley, A. (2007) Institutional influences on the integration of multilevel governance and spatial policy in European city-regions, *Journal of Planning Education and Research,* **27**, 188–98.

Salet, W., Thornley, A. and Kreukels, A. (eds) (2003) *Metropolitan Governance and Spatial Planning: Comparative Studies of European City-Regions,* E&FN Spon, London.

Sandercock, L. (2000) When strangers become neighbours: Managing cities of difference, *Planning Theory and Practice,* **1**, 13–30.

Sandercock, L. (2003) *Mongrel Cities: Cosmopolis 11,* Continuum, London.

Sandercock, L. (2005) An anatomy of civic ambition in Vancouver, *Harvard Design Magazine,* **22**, 36–43.

Sanyal, B. (ed.) (2005) *Comparative Planning Cultures,* Routledge, London.

Satterthwaite, D. (ed.) (1999) *The Earthscan Reader in Sustainable Cities,* Earthscan, London.

Schlosberg, D. (1999) *Environmental Justice and the New Pluralism,* Oxford University Press, Oxford.

Schon, D. (1983) *The Reflective Practitioner*, Basic Books, New York.

Secchi, B. (1986) Una nuova forma di piano, *Urbanistica*, **82**, 6–13.

Seidman, S. (1998) *Contested Knowledge: Social Theory in the Post-Modern Era*, Blackwell, Oxford.

Shipley, R. (2002) Visioning in planning: Is the practice based on sound theory?, *Environment and Planning A*, **34**, 7–22.

Sieverts, T. (2003) *Cities without Cities: An Interpretation of Zwischenstadt*, Spon/Routledge, London.

Simon, D. and Narman, A. (eds) (1999) *Development as Theory and Practice*, Addison Wesley Longman, Harlow.

Smith, C. (2006) *The Plan of Chicago: Daniel Burnham and the Remaking of the American City*, University of Chicago Press, Chicago.

Smith, T. D. (1970) *An Autobiography*, Oriel Press, Newcastle upon Tyne.

Smyth, H. (1994) *Marketing the City: The Role of Flagship Developments in Urban Regeneration*, E&FN Spon, London.

Sorensen, A. (2002) *The Making of Urban Japan*, Routledge, New York.

Sorensen, A. and Funck, C. (eds) (2007) *Making Livable Places: Citizens' Movements, Machizukuri and Living Environments in Japan*, Routledge, London.

Sørensen, E. and Torfing, J. (eds) (2007) *Theories of Democratic Network Governance*, Palgrave Macmillan, Basingstoke.

Sorkin, M. (ed.) (1992) *Variations on a Theme Park*, The Noonday Press, New York.

Stone, C. N. (2005) Looking back to look forward: Reflections on urban regime analysis, *Urban Affairs Review*, **40**, 309–41.

Strobel, R. W. (2003) From 'cosmopolitan fantasies' to 'national traditions': Socialist realism in East Berlin, in Nasr, J. and Volait, M. (eds) *Urbanism Imported or Exported: Native Aspirations and Foreign Plans*, Wiley-Academic, London, pp. 128–54.

Sutcliffe, A. (1981) *Towards the Planned City: Germany, Britain, the United States and France, 1780–1914*, Blackwell, Oxford.

Talen, E. (1999) Sense of community and neighbourhood form: An assessment of the social doctrine of new urbanism, *Urban Studies*, **36**, 1361–79.

Tarrow, S. (1994) *Power in Movement*, Cambridge University Press, Cambridge.

Taylor, M. (2003) *Public Policy in the Community*, Palgrave, Houndmills.

Thornley, A. (1991) *Urban Planning under Thatcherism: The Challenge of the Market*, Routledge, London.

Tomalty, R. (2002) Growth management in the Vancouver region, *Local Environment*, **7**, 431–45.

Tonnies, F. (1988) *Community and Society*, Transaction Books, New Brunswick, NJ.

UN-Habitat (2003) *The Challenge of Slums: Global Report on Human Settlements 2003*, Earthscan, London.

UN-Habitat (2009) *Global Report on Human Settlements 2009: Revisiting Urban Planning*, London, Earthscan.

Urry, J. (1981) *The Anatomy of Civil Society: The Economy, Civil Society and the State,* Macmillan, London.

van Horen, B. (2000) Informal settlement upgrading: Bridging the gap between the *de facto* and the *de jure*, *Journal of Planning Education and Research*, **19**, 389–400.

Vigar, G., Healey, P., Hull, A. and Davoudi, S. (2000) *Planning, Governance and Spatial Strategy in Britain*, Macmillan, London.

Wacquant, L. (1999) Urban marginality in the coming millennium, *Urban Studies*, **36**, 1639–48.

Ward, S. (2002) *Planning in the Twentieth Century: The Advanced Capitalist World*, Wiley, London.

Watanabe, S.-i. J. (2007) *Toshi keikaku* vs machizukuri: Emerging paradigm of civil society in Japan, in Sorensen, A. and Funck, C. (eds) *Living Cities in Japan: Citizens' Movements, Machizukuri and Local Environments*, Routledge, London, pp. 39–55.

Watson, V. (2003) Conflicting rationalities: Implications for planning theory and practice, *Planning Theory and Practice*, **4**, 395–407.

Wenger, E. (1998) *Communities of Practice: Learning, Meaning and Identity*, Cambridge University Press, Cambridge.

Westbrook, R. B. (2005) *Democratic Hope: Pragmatism and the Politics of Truth*, Cornell University Press, Cornell, NY.

Wheeler, S. M. (2002) The new regionalism: Characteristics of an emerging movement, *Journal of the American Planning Association*, **68**, 267–78.

Wheeler, S. M. (2004) *Planning for Sustainability: Creating Livable, Equitable and Ecological Communities*, Routledge, London.

Williams, K., Burton, E. and Jenks, M. (2000) *Achieving Sustainable Urban Form*, E&FN Spon, London.

Wilson, D. and Game, C. (2002) *Local Government in the United Kingdom*, Palgrave Macmillan, London.

Witt, M. (2004) Dialectics of control: The origins and evolution of conflict in Portland's Neighborhood Association Program, in C. P. Ozawa (ed.) *The Portland Edge: Challenges and Successes in Growing Communities*, Island Press, Washington, DC.

Yanow, D. and Schwartz-Shea, P. (eds) (2006) *Interpretation and Method: Empirical Research Methods and the Interpretive Turn*, M. E. Sharpe, New York.

Yiftachel, O. (1994) The dark side of modernism: Planning as control of an ethnic minority, in Watson, S. and Gibson, K. (eds) *Postmodern Cities and Spaces*, Blackwell, Oxford, pp. 216–42.

Yiftachel, O. (1998) Planning and social control: Exploring the dark side, *Journal of Planning Literature*, **12**, 396–406.

Young, I. M. (1990) *Justice and the Politics of Difference*, Princeton University Press, Princeton, NJ.

Index

Page numbers in *italics* denote an illustration/diagram